# THE UNITED STATES
# AND THE CARIBBEAN

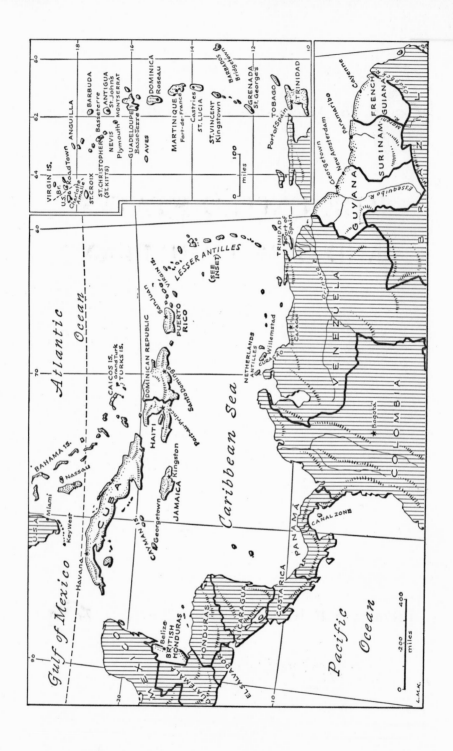

 The American Assembly, *Columbia University*

# THE UNITED STATES
# AND THE CARIBBEAN

Prentice-Hall, Inc., *Englewood Cliffs, N.J.*
A SPECTRUM BOOK

PRENTICE-HALL INTERNATIONAL, INC. (*London*)
PRENTICE-HALL OF AUSTRALIA, PTY. LTD. (*Sydney*)
PRENTICE-HALL OF CANADA, LTD. (*Toronto*)
PRENTICE-HALL OF INDIA PRIVATE LIMITED (*New Delhi*)
PRENTICE-HALL OF JAPAN, INC. (*Tokyo*)

# Preface

"For the decade of the 1970s, the United States must rethink its relationships to the Caribbean area in response to new situations, dynamics and aspirations," concluded the participants in the Thirty-eighth American Assembly, which met at Arden House, Harriman, New York, in late October 1970, to consider social, political, and economic relationships between the United States and the lands of the Caribbean. For the purposes of their discussions—and the contents of this book—the area is defined as, in the main, the islands of the Caribbean Sea and to some extent Guyana, Cayenne, and Surinam in South America, as well as British Honduras in Central America. Stating that the past conception of the Caribbean may have lost its validity and that "the old political notions of the region are being eroded by changes in the world power situation," the participants released a statement of findings and recommendations for United States policy. This statement, in pamphlet form, may be obtained from The American Assembly.

Reflecting the profound changes of the quarter of a century since the Second World War, the chapters which follow were designed by their editor, Tad Szulc, as background reading for the Arden House Assembly as well as for general readership.

Inasmuch as The American Assembly, a national nonpartisan educational organization, takes no stand on the matters it presents for public discussions, the opinions on these pages should be looked upon as belonging to the authors themselves.

Clifford C. Nelson
*President*
The American Assembly

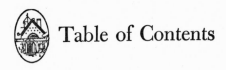 Table of Contents

Tad Szulc, Editor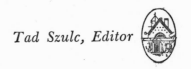

# Introduction

In the quarter of a century between 1945 and 1970—since the end of World War Two—the Caribbean region has undergone a series of fundamental political, social, economic, and cultural transformations.

Old European empires—the British, the Dutch, and the French—have lost the ownership or, at least, the full colonial control of the myriad islands and the mainland possessions comprising the Caribbean. The relationships between the United States, the leading metropolitan power in the Western Hemisphere, and Cuba and Puerto Rico, whom it freed from Spanish rule at the turn of the century, have also been profoundly altered.

With a few exceptions, the character of the Caribbean is totally distinct from what it was a generation earlier. Political independence or autonomy prevail throughout the region. Experimentation with political and social systems is in exciting motion almost everywhere.

The change has also brought conflict, tensions and crises of national, cultural and racial identity. The man of the Caribbean increasingly asks, in many voices and tongues, "Who am I . . . What am I?"

For all these reasons, the Caribbean can no longer be regarded as a tropical playground paradise or simply a source of raw materials or manpower for the markets of Europe and America. It has acquired a significance that cannot be ignored in serious policy considerations on

TAD SZULC, *now foreign affairs correspondent for* The New York Times, *was for five years chief South American correspondent for that paper. Winner of several awards in journalism, including the Maria Moors Cabot Gold Medal for Hemispheric Reporting, Mr. Szulc has written a number of books on Latin America and the Caribbean, including* Winds of Revolution, Cuban Invasion, *and* Dominican Diary.

the part of the United States, even if the old mental and political habits in dealing with the Caribbean still seem to linger on.

The Caribbean represents in the decade of the 1970s a major policy reality that is political as well as strategic in a broad sense and economic as well as social.

The purpose of this volume published by The American Assembly is, therefore, to study and attempt to assess the new Caribbean reality and the issues and problems facing this multicultural, multilingual, and multiracial world. Flowing from it, evidently, is an effort to explore the relations between the Caribbean and the United States and examine their present status and their likely development in the future.

To the extent that the Caribbean may be defined with some degree of precision, not only geography but also special regional affinities have been considered in preparing this book.

The essays herein contained thus deal with the former Spanish colonies prior to the twentieth century represented by Puerto Rico and Cuba; the Commonwealth Caribbean formed by what once was known as the British West Indies along with Guyana on the South American mainland and British Honduras in Central America; the Dominican Republic and Haiti occupying the island of Hispaniola with their distinctive Spanish and French heritage; and the insular and mainland territories linked to France and the Netherlands.

The opening sections in this volume address themselves to the broad issues of the Caribbean—political and social. The closing chapter is the summation of the new Caribbean realities.

Outstanding specialists on Caribbean problems have contributed the essays included in this book. They have brought their backgrounds and their experience as scholars, diplomats, and journalists to the task of examining the new Caribbean. No attempt was made, however, to seek a perfect consensus in their perception and appreciation of the Caribbean situation. Each author has presented his assessments and conclusions according to his own understanding of the area he undertook to study. I believe, however, that a common theme does emerge from these eight essays: a sense of urgency in searching for solutions to the problems of the Caribbean and its relationship to North America.

Two Caribbean scholars are among the authors represented here. They are Anthony Maingot and Gérard Latortue. Gordon K. Lewis is a British scholar. Among the North American writers, Ben Stephansky is a career diplomat. Kalman Silvert is a leading American authority on Latin America and the Caribbean. Juan de Onis, Frank McDonald, and George Volsky are active journalists.

It is with pride and pleasure that I present their collective view of the world of the Caribbean.

# CARIBBEAN ISSUES

*Gordon K. Lewis*

# The Politics of the Caribbean

## The Historical Setting

The contemporary politics of any society are shaped, ineluctably, by the general impress of its historical past. Of no region is this more true than the Caribbean, where the major constituent elements of practically every island politics, granted individual idiosyncrasies, have been shaped by the seminal forces of the past—slavery, slavery emancipation, class structures arising out of the plantation system, color differentiations based on the tremendous ethnic variety of the island populations. Slavery, thus, is dead, abolished throughout the region at different dates between 1834 and 1886; but its memory still permeates much of the Caribbean communal psychology, and the greatest indictment any movement of political protest in the islands can bring against any established regime is to assert that it seeks to reimpose "slavery" on the masses, or at the least that establishment policies constitute a new form of "slavery." The slavery emancipation movement also plays its contemporary role: so, contemporary Haitian politics are dominated by the memory of the great black war of liberation against the French after 1803, just as the slogan "Massa Day Done," indicating the overthrow of the white master class in the English-speaking Caribbean after 1834, becomes the war cry of a nationalist-independence movement in Trinidad after 1956. Likewise, both slavery and post-slavery Caribbean societies bequeathed a legacy of complicated and subtle class-color relationships to their descendants, so that today there exists in all of the island societies a multilayered pig-

GORDON K. LEWIS, *a British subject, is currently professor of political science at the University of Puerto Rico. Dr. Lewis has written a number of works on Caribbean topics, including a book (at press) on* The Virgin Islands.

5

mentocracy the various factions of which produce their own peculiar political expressions.

Finally, all of these societies possess a pantheon of political heroes that bestraddle the gulf between past and present. Thus, to take examples only from the Hispanic Caribbean area, Puerto Rican politics still revere the memory of the great figures who fought for local autonomy under both the Spanish and the American regimes, while the Cuban Revolution invokes the memory of the great Cuban liberal/ patriot José Martí. And that all this—the omnipresent shadow of the past bearing down upon the present—is endemic throughout the Caribbean is plain enough from the fact that its manifestations are equally evident in contemporary Puerto Rico, the most Americanized of Caribbean societies, and in present-day Cuba, the *avant-garde* of the anti-American crusade in the region.

This, briefly, then, is the historical legacy of the area. The legacy divides itself into three major periods: (1) the slavery period, ending with the various emancipatory acts of the nineteenth century; (2) the post-Emancipation period, ending generally with the Second World War; and (3) the contemporary period of political independence. The three major episodes of the area, this is to say, are thus identified as discovery, emancipation, and independence.

In social terms, the discovery set the original pattern of Caribbean society as a slave-based sugar monoculture producing massive profits for absentee owners and their local agents, all arranged around the semi-militaristic regime of the plantation. Emancipation, in its turn, laid the foundations, with slavery abolished, of a changing Creole society of limited commercial capitalism and widespread peasant proprietorship, also giving rise to the well-known phenomenon of the West Indian brown-black middle class, the *gens de couleur*. Independence, finally, brought all the social classes of the modern period into new relationships set by the changes of political sovereignty.

In economic terms, likewise, each period was characterized by unique features. The plantation period, because of its indiscriminate use of imported slave labor (a recent attempted census of the Atlantic slave trade estimates a total import of some ten million slaves over the full period 1451–1870), produced an economic structure of excessive labor population in relation to available resources. The emancipation period, in part because of its use, after slavery ended, of imported indentured labor from India and China, produced in its turn a low-wage economy with living standards kept low by the pressure of a reservoir of unemployed and underemployed persons. The independence period has inherited these negative features, which are in turn complicated by the effort of the modern Caribbean economies (still essentially single-crop economies exporting their raw materials to the developed industrial nations) to stay alive in an international economy geared against their interests.

In political terms, the three periods were equally distinctive. The slave period, of course, generated the habit of colonial autocracy in all of the colonizing European nations in the area—English, French, Spanish, Dutch. All of them applied, with individual idiosyncrasies, the device of the colonial governorship to their slave colonies, accompanied by an elite administrative class appointed by the imperial center; with the major end of policy being, naturally, the maintenance of "law and order," that is to say, the prevention of the always possible slave revolt.

The post-emancipation period witnessed the gradual liberalization of that autocracy, giving rise, most notably in the British Caribbean, to the model of the Crown Colony system, with governors gradually sharing their power with local councils carefully recruited from the Creole respectability. That gave way, in its turn, especially after 1945, to the general movements toward self-government, autonomy and independence, as the comparatively peaceful dismantling of the European empires in the region meant the transference of rule to their Creole successor-states; the politics of liberal imperialism thus yielding to the politics of assertive nationalism.

That process, of course, has been unequal. Britain has favored the line of independence; France the line of departmental assimilationism; Holland and the United States the line, in varying degree, of gradualist autonomy accompanied by continuing constitutional partnership between metropolitan center and Caribbean capital town. Each particular period confronted its own peculiar problem of government and politics. The early colonization period, the early post-slavery period, the modern independence period—all of them have necessitated the invention of new politico-constitutional forms to meet the special needs of socio-cultural change.

THE FACTOR OF RACE

Certain leading qualities about Caribbean society flow out of this historical legacy. The first, of course, is that it is a racially mixed society. The early European colonist mixed sexually, first, with the Indian aboriginal native and then with the imported black African slave; and to that mixture was added the later ingredients of Indian, Chinese, and Indonesian through the medium of the indenture systems of the nineteenth century. So today it is a society of intense biological mixture. Sir Alan Burns has recalled, as governor of British Honduras, looking on at a Honduran schoolhouse in which German nuns were attempting to teach Mayan children out of an English textbook which they had to explain in Spanish. The degree of ethnic variation varies, of course, from society to society; so, Haiti is predominantly Negro, Puerto Rico light-skinned. But the racial mixture is evident everywhere. It can be seen in the rise within the regional class structure of colored aristocracies, middle and upper middle groups of people with social composure and quiet self-confidence, a fact astonishingly noted by all travelers. It can be seen in the psychology, likewise, of the lower-class Caribbean colored person; since he is part of a numerical majority and since, too, he is part of the political majority supporting black governments, he has little of the depressed minority complex, the psychic anxieties that arise out of being a black minority in a white society that characterize the American Negro. The white groups, in fact, in these societies, live on sufferance, possessing real economic power but living only on the margins, as it were, of political power; that is the case, for example, of the tourist-based group of "Continentals" in the American Virgin Islands, who suffer from the frustration that, however long their residency, they will never be permitted to membership of the social club of the black majority, the "native Virgin Islanders."

This, then, generally is a society of racial mixture and racial tolerance. This is not to say, of course, that it is a perfected racial democracy. There is still a "white bias"; and continuing marriage patterns designed, as the saying goes, to put some cream in the coffee, testify to its continuing deep power in Caribbean modes of thought. The bitter mutual hostility between Haitians and the people of Santo Domingo is in large part racially inspired; and for years the policy of the Trujillo regime in Santo Domingo was one designed to maintain the racial "purity" of the society against Haitian black penetration, leading to the infamous border massacre of Haitian peasants in 1939. The East Indian-Negro Creole rivalry in Guyana amounted in fact to a situation of racial civil war between 1962 and 1964; the nationalist Peoples' National Movement in Trinidad has signally failed so far to recruit in any successful measure in the Indian rural areas; while the political picture in Surinam can only be understood in terms of the general thesis that the main political parties tend to represent the principal racial groups: Negro, East Indian, Indonesian. For years, again, and until only recently, politics in the other Dutch society of Curaçao have been dominated by the close alliance of the Protestant-Jewish power group and the Roman Catholic Church.

All this is true. But before it is all accepted as a basis for a legend of Caribbean racialist politics—the theme of many sensationalist novels on the area—one must recognize that it is assuaged by certain factors. There is the fact that race relations in the region have never taken over the simplistic black-white category of South African-North American race relations. The classificatory system in the Caribbean, on the contrary, has been more subtle, more benign, based essentially on the concept of "shade." It is the degree of skin-color, not the presence of "Negro blood," that has traditionally been the criterion of social acceptance; so, the prejudice that arises from the system, although real, is at least more sophisticated than the negrophobia secreted in the North American variant of race relations. There is the fact that prejudice in Caribbean society is likewise softened by social occupancy; in the West Indian phrase, "money whitens." Both of these factors mean, in the end-result, a complex class-color structure permitting a social mobility of the colored person almost quite unknown in American society. Thus, to take the realm of politics and government alone, this is a regional society in which, as the phrase goes, "black rules white." That has been the case, of course, in Haiti ever since the early foundation (1804) of that black republic, so that the presidential politics in Port-au-Prince have oscillated between the brown mulatto candidates and the black candidates. It has been the case, more recently, in the English-speaking Caribbean; so that, today, there are black premiers, of outstanding personal competence, in Jamaica, Trinidad, Guyana, and Barbados. To realize the real character of the multiracial West Indian society of the contemporary period, it is only necessary to recall the dismal prophecy of the English historian, Froude, writing on the colonial West Indies of nearly a century ago— that, as he argued, the advent of black governments in the islands would lead to the mass exodus of the white groups in protest—and then to note that, today, with that condition in fact realized, there has been no such exodus. Or—to put all this in another way—a Negro mayor in Cleveland or Newark is still a rarity in American politics. In Caribbean politics it is the order of the day.

THE FACTOR OF CULTURE

But Caribbean society is not only multiracial. It is also multicultural. Race admixture is one thing; cultural assimilationism is another. From the historical beginnings, this was, still largely is, a society formed by really massive movements of peoples—sometimes forcible, as with slavery; later voluntary, as with the migratory movements of the twentieth century. It meant, generally, the peopling of the region with persons of different cultures and, frequently, physical type. This accounts, in brief, for the amazing sociocultural diversity of the region today. It is there in the multiplicity of languages, not only of the major imported European languages, but also of the indigenous *patois* languages; with the result, of course, that the political balkanization of the region worked by colonialism has been further accentuated by the barriers of language. It is there in the amoebic proliferation of diverse religions—obeah, voudun, the Shouter-pocomania groups, the Jamaican Rastafarians. This characteristic is even shared by the more respectable church religions, as can be seen in the legend relating to the old Dutch Reformed Church in the Virgin Islands—that it is Protestant in its teaching, Presbyterian in its government, Dutch in national origin, biblical in its emphasis, English in its language, and American in its support of equal rights. It is there, finally, in the variety of transplanted general life-styles of the separate Caribbean populations.

Puerto Rico, despite the fact that it is probably the most Americanized of the regional societies, still has an indubitably Hispanic character about it; Haiti is France with Creole overtones; Barbados, the most anglophile of all, is in many ways a little corner in a foreign field that is forever England.

Or—to put all this differently—the Caribbean is a multiform society overwhelmingly immigrant in its character. Like the Americas as a whole, it began as a New World society. What there were of aboriginal peoples rapidly disappeared after the discovery; and every Caribbean people after that, including the Americans of the present period, were imported stranger groups. Neither the master class nor the slave class in the slavery period managed to transplant more than a fraction of their ancestral customs or social forms; and the pattern has persisted into the twentieth century. Dr. Sidney Mintz has observed:

> The Caribbean colonies were not European imperial possessions erected upon massive indigenous bases in areas of declining great literate civilizations, as was true in India and Indonesia; they were not mere ports of trade, like Macao or Shanghai, where ancestral cultural hinterlands could remain surprisingly unaffected in spite of the exercise of considerable European power; they were not "tribal" mosaics, within which European colonizers carried on their exploitation accompanied by some curious vision of the "civilizing" function, as in the Congo, or New Guinea; nor were they areas of intense European settlement, where new forms of European culture provided an acculturational "anchor" for other newcomers, as in the United States or Australia. They were, in fact, the oldest "industrial" colonies of the West outside Europe, manned almost entirely with introduced populations, and fitted to European needs with peculiar intensity and pervasiveness.

Once this is understood about the historical background of the Caribbean it becomes easier to understand the historicocultural bases of contemporary Caribbean politics.

## The Politics of Nationalism

In the first place, the response to the old colonialism, briefly outlined here, is the emergence, as in all the Third World, of a new nationalism. This is so whether the particular Caribbean society is formally independent, like Haiti or Jamaica, or still bound by constitutional arrangements to a metropolitan power, like Curaçao or

Martinique. The Caribbean person is, in his cultural self, schizoid. He is, in the Martiniquan phrase, *peau noir, masque blanc,* the uneasy possessor of a pseudo-European culture in an Afro-Asian environment. The prolongation of metropolitan cultural influence has meant the continuing impress of European influence. Thus, *fidelista* communism in Cuba has not terminated direct communication with Catholic Spain, and Paris still remains the center of world culture for many Haitians, even though they may follow the doctrines of *duvalierisme.* The result of this is, since World War II, the growth in politics, as in other spheres, of an effort to discover a viable Caribbean cultural identity. Most of the region's postwar political parties are fiercely obsessed with that problem, which goes hand in hand with public policies of decolonization.

It is vital to appreciate the novelty of this. For in the American-European societies, of some cultural antiquity, there is little of a problem of cultural identity. Englishmen and Americans do not have to inquire who they are; they entertain a massive self-confidence born of centuries of being, in Kiernan's phrase, the lords of human kind. Colonialism strips the colonial person bare of self-respect; he develops a chronic inferiority complex. It is in the light of this that the search for national identity must be understood; meaning by that term, of course, a shared feeling in the citizen-body of belonging to a nation-state. This, in a way, is the process known as "Creolization," that is, the growth in the Caribbean groups of cutting away from the umbilical cord of the metropolitan power and identifying fully with the local island norms and values. The white groups of the earlier period developed it; and a book like Jean Rhys' *Wide Sargasso Sea* is a moving account of its psychological ingredients. The contemporary problem is to transfer that process to the Caribbean masses as a whole, as, with universal suffrage, they have been incorporated into the active political life of their respective island-nations.

THE STYLE OF POLITICAL LEADERSHIP

This can be best appreciated from a glance at the styles of political leadership in the region. There is an old style, gradually being replaced by a new style. The old style was essentially related to the earlier struggle against the colonial power. The sort of politician who graduated in that school was summed up in the 1932 report (speaking now of the English-speaking Caribbean) of the Dominica conference. That report noted:

Powerless to mould policy, still more powerless to act independently, paralysed by the subconscious fear of impending repression and therefore bereft of constructive thought, the West Indian politician has hitherto been inclined to dissipate his energies in acute and penetrating but embittered and essentially destructive criticism of the government on which, nevertheless, he has waited for the initiation of all policies intended to benefit his people, and which he has expected to benefit his people, and which he has expected to assume the full responsibility for all necessary decisions. His political life has been overshadowed by a government too omnipotent and too omnipresent, and he has had little opportunity for independent growth.

That is still the style wherever a European government still remains: in the associated states of the Leeward and Windward islands, in the French and Dutch Antilles, even to some degree in Puerto Rico. It is, in essence, a negative politics, seeking to frighten the colonial rulers, always attempting to get what it can from them. Merely to read A. W. Singham's book on Eric Gairy, the Grenada leader—*The Hero and the Crowd in a Colonial Polity*—is to realize how much it stands in the way of a positive politics.

With the advent of independence, however (Trinidad and Jamaica in 1962, Guyana and Barbados in 1966), the old is now being replaced with a new style. Colonial agitation is replaced with nation-building as the chief aim of leadership. The typical leader at this point fills a variety of roles: he is political chieftain, cultural commissar, national spokesman all in one. He is, at his best, Burke's definition of the politician, the philosopher in action. Whereas in other societies culture and education, for example, can be left to other institutions, in these newly-found nations they come within the purview of politics. So, there is a mixture of politics, art, culture, and education that defies the more conventional rules.

And this is the measure, in fact, of the new political talent of the region. Prime Minister Eric Williams in Trinidad (like the late Norman Manley in Jamaica) is an Oxford scholar, a brilliant historian, and in fact writes the textbook of his country's independence. Former President Juan D. Bosch in the Dominican Republic, likewise, is a scholar and writer of books. Ex-Governor Luis Muñoz-Marín in Puerto Rico is—in the phrase of one of his admirers— the "poet in the fortress," frequently more interested, it seems, in discussing ideas like federalism as it applies to the Caribbean than in exercising the panoply of political power. Aimé Césaire in Martinique is the Marxist scholar who writes, in the grand manner of Rousseau, the *recherche du temps perdu* of his colonial society. If one puts all of these together into a single prototype, a remarkable personage emerges. He patronizes the steel band; gives lectures at Harvard; discourses on his front porch on Caribbean history to interested crowds; educates the European Communist parties on the dangers of a racialism of the Left in the metropolitan societies which is as insidious as the racialism of the Right. One could even include in this pantheon a figure like "Papa Doc" Duvalier in Haiti; for if that sinister figure has abused his learning to construct one of the most evil of Caribbean personal dictatorships, it is nonetheless true that he is, in his own right, an accomplished cultural anthropologist who has contributed by his writings to a fuller understanding of the Haitian peasant folklore.

THE ISSUE OF NATIONAL UNITY

The stated purpose of all of these leaders, granted individual idiosyncrasies of separate island character and development, is the gospel of national unity; against internal divisive forces, either of social class (as in Jamaica) or of racial group (as in Guyana), and external intervention. Even an avowed Marxist leader like Cheddi Jagan in the Guyanese situation feels compelled to state his ideology in those nationalist terms.

It is worth noting that the successful growth of such a spirit of national identity, based on a national culture, seems to be most vibrant in those Caribbean societies in which, historically, the process of "Creolization" has advanced most rapidly. For if a Creole group—born in the New World, but of Old World ancestral origins—establishes itself early on as a New World people, turning its back decisively on the transatlantic roots, it follows that it will the more easily develop a national identity. That process did in fact take place, in the seventeenth and eighteenth centuries, in the colonial societies of the Hispanic Caribbean—Cuba, Santo Domingo, Puerto Rico. It took place, less markedly, in the British and Dutch Caribbean areas, where the planter groups were less settlers than temporary profiteers, living in conscious exile, anxious to get back home, and mixed to a much lesser degree with the slave populations. It follows that, today, there is more of an integrated, cohesive sense of national society in the Hispanic area than in the non-Hispanic area. It is at least suggestive that in the English-speaking societies the public debate revolves anxiously around the question "Who are we?" whereas this is much less so in the Spanish-speaking societies.

The examples that illustrate this difference are illuminating and demonstrate the variety of political debate in the region as a whole. Thus, the nationalist movement in Trinidad after 1956—Dr. Eric Williams' Peoples' National Movement—has always remained in essence a Negro-Creole party, failing to assimilate the East Indian groups; whereas the *Partido Democratico Popular* in Puerto Rico, starting with the great campaigns of its charismatic leader, Muñoz Marín, in 1938 and 1940, was from the beginning a national-reformist movement recruiting its strength from all classes, although of course based preeminently on the *campesinos,* the Puerto Rican highland-peasant class. So, consequently, the leading political topic in Puerto Rico is that of political status, its politico-constitutional relationship with the United States; whereas the leading issue in Trinidadian politics still remains the problem of cementing the hostile barrier between Negro and East Indian. Similarly, the leading issue in the French colonial societies of Martinique and Guadeloupe is the running war between the local mass movements and the alien *metropolitains,* the planters and the French administrative governing group who remain in the classic colonial situation. By contrast, the political rhetoric of the Cuban Revolution can concentrate on the ideology of the anti-colonial struggle against "American imperialism" because there exists no such internal, divisive barrier in Cuban society. The Negro element in Cuba, in another way of putting this, has always been an honored constituent group in the Afro-Cuban society. It would be difficult to say that about the place of the Amerindian aboriginal groups in Guyana or British Honduras, whose status has been somewhat akin to the depressed status of the Indian tribal remnants in North American society.

There is, all this is to say, a dual politics in the region as a whole. There is, on the one hand, the politics of the "melting pot," that is, of those island societies, mostly Caribbean-Hispanic, where some sort of effective amalgamation of immigrant peoples has taken place, in something approximate to what has taken place, historically, in the North American democracy. There is, on the other hand, the politics of the "plural society," to employ the phrase used by recent West Indian scholarship, referring to the Anglophile Caribbean island societies; the phrase denoting, in the words of its original usage, a mixed society in which the various ethnic member-groups mix but do not combine. One's view of the region as a whole depends pretty much, then, on what model, out of these two, one prefers to adopt. The first model, clearly, is optimistic: it looks forward to a continuing process of racial admixture, so that within a few generations those Caribbean elements that are not yet mixed will in fact become effectively mixed, with perhaps the exception of a few Syrian and Lebanese mercantile families, the final point of that process being a genuinely Caribbean *mestizo* society much, indeed, as present-day Cuba is already.

The second model, equally clearly, is pessimistic. It emphasizes the mutual dislike, say, of East Indian and Negro, which is so deep-grained as almost to seem a law of nature. It sees the colonial power as a protective umbrella which keeps the near-warring groups together in an uneasy social truce; and it follows, logically, that once the umbrella is withdrawn (that is, once national independence is gained) the situation is ripe for racial civil war. This argument, it is worth noting, comes pretty near to saying that the ex-colonial person, once independent, is incapable of organizing a viable nationhood based on the principle of self-government.

What is the true situation? It is possible that both of these theoretical models suffer from overstatement. The first tends to be utopian. It embraces too uncritically the North American ideal of ethnic assimilationism, leading to a common standardization. The "melting pot" thesis argues for too much; it desires the subjugation of all minority characteristics into the common mold of the "all-American" citizen-person. Yet it may well be that a democratic society can be compatible with the retention of a rich variety of subcultural life-styles; how much, for instance, has American civilization lost by not utilizing the vast riches of its multilingual minorities, so that the Spanish of its Mexican and Puerto Rican minorities, for example, instead of being looked upon with disdain, could be recruited into the service of a multi-language society? The richness of Caribbean society is the presence of that cultural multiplicity. It would be tragic to lose it. It is surely not for nothing that of the three great centers of the Carnival of the Americas, where the tremendous theme of the Black Orpheus finding his salvation in the labyrinth of the multiracial crowd reigns over the fiesta-bacchanal—Rio, Havana and Port of Spain—two of them are located in the Caribbean Middle-America district.

The "plural society" thesis, likewise, suffers from overstatement. It assumes too readily that, once politically independent, the various groups of Caribbean society will tear each other apart. But this in fact has not occurred. The Guyanese Negro-East Indian disturbances of the early 1960s are a special case, with evidence that outside intervention helped to exacerbate the differences. The thesis overlooks the things that unite the groups, rather than the things that divide them. They all, for example, accept the unifying structure of civil government and its parliamentary rules, including the East Indian opposition in the new cooperative republic of Guyana. The transition from colonial to nationalist politics has, in fact, been remarkably peaceful. Even where—as in Puerto Rico and the Dominican Republic—there exist political groups that elect to stay outside of what they regard as a colonial or a dictatorial regime, they still adhere to constitutionalist methods of political agitation.

The truth probably lies somewhere in the middle of these two competing theories of Caribbean society. In the meantime, it is worth emphasizing two general points. In the first place, where there are serious divisions they tend to be social rather than racial in character. The serious disturbances in Curaçao and Trinidad in 1969 and 1970 were thus not racial clashes but partial revolts of the socially dispossessed, the "have-nots," against the "haves" of the middle and upper classes. This is a social discontent, directed against ruling social groups, feeding on mass unemployment and social inequity. In the second place, the disparate groups nearly everywhere manage at least to tolerate each other. Where there exists even separate institutions—in family structure, religion, and social life—the mutual acceptance remains. A polyglot society like the Virgin Islands, for instance, illustrates this as much as any; for it is a society in which (speaking now of the decade of the 1960s) government was shared between a Creole-Jewish governor, a black-dominated legislature, and an electorate composed of native blacks, Puerto Ricans and Creole French, not to speak of the large section of domiciled "Continentals"; and all of them generally united in their collective pride as American citizens living in an American tropical dependency.

## The Politics of Democracy

Caribbean politics are thus the politics of nationalism. But they are also the politics of democracy. For the rise of nationalism since 1945 has gone hand in hand with the advent of democratic institutions to the region. Universal suffrage is now widespread, going back as far as 1866, indeed, in the case of the French islands, when popular voting was granted for municipal elections. The Jamaican constitution of 1944 set the pattern for the British islands; while in the case of the American Caribbean the Virgin Islands, for example, were granted the popular suffrage as early as 1936. In part, this was the result of mass popular agitation, as with the riots that swept the islands in the 1935–38 period. In part, it was the result of imperial liberal measures unleashed by the Second World War, so that after 1945 all the European nations in the area took steps, in varying degree, to dismember their empires, cultivating the growth of local participation, creating new nations or autonomous states, or incorporating their Caribbean subordinate colonies into the politico-administrative structure of the metropolitan center.

The end-result, in any case, was the gradual democratization of Caribbean politics. It meant a number of things. It meant the democratization of the executive branch of government, so that the old-style colonial governor was replaced by the popularly elected governor: for Puerto Rico, in 1947, for the Virgin Islands, in 1970. It meant, with universal suffrage, the appearance of modern-type mass political parties (like the Peoples' National Party and the Labor Party in Jamaica). That, in turn, meant the replacement, in the legislatures, of the old-style political leader with the new-style; that is, replacement of the legislative individualist, accountable at best to a small electoral body, with the party member, accountable to the more coherent program of his party. Legislative irresponsibility—the hallmark of the old colonial politics—gave way to party responsibility. So, the contemporary Caribbean political scene is characterized, typically, by large, mass-based political party organizations. Inevitably, of course, they have been shaped in the mold of the respective metropolitan party forms: thus, the Martiniquan leftist parties reflect the influence of the French Communist party, the various labor-union parties of the English-speaking islands reflect the influence of the British Labor party, the Puerto Rican *Populares* of the Muñoz era (now coming to a close) reflect the influence of the Rooseveltian New Deal. Even the leading Cuban revolutionary party (which fuses political party and state machinery into a single whole, Soviet-style) reflects in its ideology much of the socialist-anarchist elements of French political thought before Marx. It is only necessary to look at the new public style of the Cuban Revolution, in which the *maximo líder* acts as the intuitive interpreter of the general will of the people elucidated in the great mass meeting, to appreciate the influence of Rousseau and his idea of the populist democracy on the *fidelista* leadership.

But all this is not colonial mimicry. The Caribbean party leadership may borrow their political style, even their ideology at times, from Washington or London or Paris. But they apply it all with real innovative genius to the special problems of their societies. Two things especially must be noted about the democratic surge in the area. The first is that it has actively incorporated the masses into the regional political life. The second is that, thereby, it has produced a new political elite.

THE POLITICIZATION OF THE MASSES

In the colonial regime the role of the masses was at once passive and negative. They were the unenfranchised majority, the anonymous audience hissing or cheering the actors of the restricted colonial political stage. They would erupt occasionally: the slave revolt in the slave period, the riot in the sugar plantation or the oil belt in the post-emancipation period. In the independence regime the colonial mass becomes the citizen-body. A more mature and educated public opinion makes itself felt, to which the party leaderships more and more address themselves. Each territory, of course, produces its own special expression of this process.

In revolutionary Cuba, it is the mass meeting. In reformist Trinidad, it is the conversion of the major downtown plaza of Port of Spain into the "University of Woodford Square," in which first Dr. Williams and, more latterly, his radical critics, address their large attentive audiences. In the Dominican Republic of the post-Trujillo period (after 1961) it meant the development of a multiparty system. In the former British territories, on the contrary, it meant the growth of a viable two-party system based on the Westminster model. But in all these instances a common phenomenon can be noted: the process of the political education of the Caribbean crowd, hitherto kept out of the national debate by a narrow colonial franchise, as in the Dutch and British Caribbean, or by dictatorial regimes, as in the case of the Trujillo dictatorship in Santo Domingo until 1961 and, continuingly, in the Duvalier tyranny in Haiti.

THE NEW POLITICAL ELITE: POLITICS AND EDUCATION

This factor has already in part been noted in the discussion of the old and new political styles in the area: the replacement of the old anti-colonial demagogue, knowing what he was against much more than what he was for (Alec Waugh's novel, *Island in the Sun*, in its hero-figure David Boyeur, is a fictional description of the type), with the new nationalist leader. What must be added is the vital importance of education in the rise of the new type. Its members, on the whole, are university educated people of the younger generation.

In the non-Hispanic Caribbean (where colonialism discouraged the foundation of local universities, the University of the West Indies, for example, having been established as late as 1948) this meant education abroad in the British, Canadian, or American universities. The graduates of this type of political schooling include, today, Cheddi Jagan in Guyana, Prime Minister Errol Barrow in Barbados, Prime Minister Williams in Trinidad, Stanley Brown in the Netherlands Antilles, Alexander Farrelly in the Virgin Islands. In the Hispanic Caribbean (where the universities, like those of Santo Domingo and Puerto Rico, were older foundations) they include a large segment of the leadership of both the Dominican revolutionary left-wing parties and the Puerto Rican *independentista* groups. The Dominican case added the important element of young, professionally trained army officers, the young colonels like Caamaño and Fernández Domínguez. In the Puerto Rican case, there is the particular consideration that the University of Puerto Rico has for years been the citadel of the *independentista* intellectual class—a fact in large part due to the inability of the mainland Americans to take over this institution because of the language barrier.

Two further aspects of this relationship between politics and education deserve mention. In the first place, it means, increasingly, the displacement of an amateur politics by professional politics. The supreme example of the older type—speaking of the former British area—is, of course, the grand old Jamaican warrior Sir Alexander Bustamante, who rose to political power as a flamboyant orator in the 1937–38 riots. A representative example of the new type is Bustamante's successor in the leadership of the Jamaica Labor Party, the present Prime Minister Hugh Shearer, who came up through the ranks of the organization as a professional union organizer, not unlike, indeed, his opposition rival Michael Manley. Senator Ottley in the American Virgin Islands is another example. The letters of credit in the political career have thus become more exacting. The pen, in a way, has replaced the sword. Thus, the leadership of the new critics of the Trinidadian PNM regime, who combine "black power" slogans with intellectual analysis of West Indian economic and social structure, has come out of the graduating classes of the University of the West Indies. What is taking place, altogether, is the emergence of a new modernizing oligarchy, eager to place its mastery of the social sciences into the service of a reinvigorated Caribbean society. Only Haiti and, to some degree, the French West Indian territories, being special cases, seem to resist this general law of post-colonial developmental politics.

The second aspect to be noted about all this is its comparative novelty, historically speaking. Like all colonial societies based on slavery, the Caribbean society from the beginning was anti-intellectual. Everything, in Père Labat's bitter phrase, was imported into the West Indies except books. With the exception of Santo Domingo, the universities in the region are recent growths, and there is still no institution of higher learning in either the Dutch or the French-speaking areas. The colonial student, then, has had to seek education abroad, with all of the psychological alienation from his home society implied in that process. The alienation profoundly ravaged the West Indian personality; and it is no accident that two of the major prophets of the revolution of the Third World should have originated from the region—Garvey from Jamaica and Fanon from Martinique. Caribbean politics and government, like Caribbean culture and society, are only now beginning to emancipate themselves from this legacy of anti-intellectual anarchy.

All this, of course, is to view the area as a regional whole. Yet there is little uniformity in the way in which all of these various factors express themselves in the politics of the separate Caribbean units. That is natural, once it is appreciated that each European power imposed different standards of development upon its subordinate colonial groups. Constitutional advance in the colony depended, quite arbitrarily, upon the accidents of the metropolitan politics—a liberal Republic in Madrid, a revolutionary Assembly in Paris, a New Deal administration in Washington. It is only possible to appreciate the detail of the regional politics by analyzing it on the territorial rather than the regional level.

## The English-Speaking Caribbean

It is always difficult to export political forms. Yet the remarkable thing about the former British West Indies is the successful exportation of British political institutions to the constitutional regimes of, first, the four independent nations—Jamaica, Trinidad, Guyana, and Barbados—and, second, the smaller "associated states" of the Leeward and Windward Islands. There is, initially, political stability. Political power is transferred, through the mechanism of periodical elections democratically engineered, from party to party. Cabinets rule under the surveillance of parliamentary bodies. It is even possible, as in the Bahamian election of 1967, for a black political group to wrest control from a long-established local white business oligarchy, the notorious "Bay Street boys" of Nassau, and establish a Negro government for the first time in the history of that colony, without serious disturbance—a striking testimony to the success of British imperialism (whatever its shortcomings) in teaching its West Indian subject-peoples the habit of constitutional government based on consent.

The purpose of constitutional government, then—the transfer of power, effected peacefully—is assured. Even the Marxist parties, like the Jaganite Peoples' Progressive Party in Guyana, accept the principle; and it is worth noting that its earlier electoral victories disprove one of the American Cold War myths—that no Marxist party can win in a free election system. The crucial problems lie, so far, elsewhere. For although the Westminster model has been absorbed, it confronts in the Caribbean strains and stresses it has never known at home. There is the division of the Guyanese and Trinidadian electorates into racial blocs. They are not ready, it is true, to tear each other apart. At the same time there exists, at best, an uneasy social and political truce between them; and neither side has that mutual trust, the assurance that the other will not use political power to destroy its opponent, which is the *sine qua non* of the British parliamentary politics. At the same time, that situation is made more complicated in Trinidad by the fear that the long reign of the PNM (since 1956) presages the intrusion into the island politics of the Latin American element of *continuismo*. That may be an exaggerated fear. But it is true that the PNM regime has shown itself willing to import the worst of American models—the Subversive Activities Commission, for example—to maintain its hold on power; while the crisis of early 1970— in which the government was almost toppled by a mixture of "black power" demonstrations and a partial army revolt—allowed the regime the excuse to use other equally dubious methods such as preventive detention, without charges, of political opponents. Civil liberties, notoriously, is a delicate plant. It is threatened constantly in newly independent societies tasting self-government for the first time.

In the other islands—Jamaica and Barbados, for example—there is the separate pressure of social class divisions. Jamaican society, especially, is divided horizontally between affluent and poor, with a great deal of class enmity intruding. Politics, there, has performed a safety-valve function, with Labor Party partisan competing fiercely with PNP partisan; and it is not unknown for the rival party machines to give weapons to their strong-arm elements as a method of intimidation. In such a situation the depths of political fury have to be seen to be believed; politics becomes a sort of social therapy, in which political co-religionists work off their frustrations against their historic rivals. It is not unlike the Guelph-Ghibelline rivalries of the old Italian city-states. It is much the same in Barbados, except that a deeper sense of Barbadian national identity, felt by all groups, helps to assuage class tensions. The Guyanese-Trinidadian problem is to prevent the breakup of constitutional government under the pressures of race; the Jamaican problem, especially, is to prevent its breakup under the pressures of class.

The problems of the smaller islands are somewhat different. There is a tendency for two-party democracy to yield to mono-party rule, especially in Antigua and St. Kitts. The ruling Labor Party governments, solidly based on island-wide union support, tend to override their opponents with intimidatory methods; that has been the case with the Bradshaw regime in St. Kitts. There is the further problem of small island secessionism where there exist small-island wards of the capital town, as with the Grenadines dependent on St. Vincent. The Anguilla episode of 1968 dramatized the problem; the smaller dependent islands felt neglected, with the major government expenditures going to the larger island-territory, and in that particular case the issue threw up, in the figure of Ronald Webster, the sort of political leader long since disappeared from the modern industrial societies —god-fearing, intensely close to his folk-people, almost wholly innocent of the world outside. Nor must it be forgotten that the pressure of small geographical size accentuates the political temper in these tiny Lilliputs. A disappointed politician or a victimized civil servant can, even in Jamaica, find refuge in private business or other institutional occupation. That is almost impossible in the smaller islands. That explains why there is a running war between politicians and civil servants in most of them. It is as good an example as any of the absurd misapplications of the Westminster rules; the doctrine of civil-service anonymity, possible in London, is utterly impossible in these small-island townships where practically everybody is known personally to everybody else, and certainly where all professional persons, including civil servants, are inevitably public figures.

## The French Caribbean

### THE FRENCH ANTILLES AND FRENCH GUIANA

The leading feature of French Antillean politics is that it is still an old-style colonial politics. The root cause of that fact—which makes the territories almost a classic colonial survival—is the 1946 administrative revolution which incorporated the three units as departments into the structure of metropolitan France, based on full political equality between the French citizen and the Antillean person. It is perhaps ironic that a change, so progressive on the face of it, should have turned out to be a running sore between the French

bureaucracy and an emergent French Antillean political consciousness. First applauded by an Antillean leader as radical as Aimé
Césaire, it is now the overriding issue that divides the local political
parties. As in Puerto Rico, but for different reasons, French Antillean
politics is a politics of status.

It is easy to see what has gone wrong. The 1946 change has in effect
worked a debilitating assimilation of everything Antillian into the
centralized Parisian *bureaux*. The prefects, following the pattern of
their equivalent at home, are the creatures of Paris, nominated in
accordance with the patronage system of French coalition governments; thus the prefecture of Guadeloupe was for a long time the fief
of the French Socialist Party. The appointment of a locally-born prefect is possible, indeed, as was shown in 1963. But the fact remains
that, for many of its critics, the overseas prefecture has become a copy
of the previous colonial governorship. Nor does direct representation
of the territories in the French Parliament—three deputies and two
senators apiece—alleviate the situation. For they serve in Paris, not
Fort-de-France or Point-á-Pitre; the prefects and the General Councils in the islands have special administrative powers that legislative
action cannot touch; while the deputies are at best birds of passage,
as against the permanent power of the national civil-service machine.
Those Puerto Ricans who clamor for a Puerto Rican Congressional
delegation might learn a lot from looking at the French Caribbean
system and its calamitous failure to satisfy Antillean aspirations.

The end-result is the old colonial politics. The local Communist
parties, along with Césaire's Progressive Party and various anti-
colonial youth organizations, fight for a larger autonomous status;
the local Socialist Party and the Gaullist group fight to retain the present status. Paris and the prefects respond, on the whole, with increasingly repressive acts—the police measures that followed the Martiniquan riots of 1959, and the 1963 conspiracy trial of the anti-
colonial youth leadership. The *canard* is put out that autonomy means
independence, a veritable fear tactic, not unlike the legend put out
by the planter class of the nineteenth century that slavery emancipation would mean a Haitian-type war of racial slaughter in the islands.
Yet it is difficult not to feel that the pro-autonomy forces are correct
in their analysis. Long-distance government from a faraway metropolitan capital is increasingly anachronistic in the area as a whole.
Nor is this just a matter of ideology; for, as Césaire pointed out in
his now famous letter of 1956, announcing his resignation from the
French Communist Party, there is as much a colonialism of the Left
in European politics as there is a colonialism of the Right.

Two other factors complicate this picture. These are societies
crucially divided within themselves. They are divided, first, by the
mutual disdain and hostility felt between the *beké* class of endog-

amous white property-owning persons and the groups of middle-class mulattoes, peasants, and urban workers—with the *beké* being joined in his social and political reactionary stance by the small group of French administrators, the *metropolitains,* who can scarcely conceal their Parisian contempt for all things colonial. They are divided, in the second place, by the schizoid character of Antillean culture. Martiniquans and Guadeloupans have a profound awareness of their Antillean personality. But its cultivation—to the degree, for example, that it could generate the rich flow of art, literature, and the dance that has come out of Haiti—is held back by their equal adoration of French culture. The tumultuous welcome given to General de Gaulle in his visit to the islands was a measure of how deep the malady of cultural dependence can strike. That is why, save for a few student groups, usually located in Paris, no movement for outright independence has grown up. The sentimental attachment to France, the morbid fear of being cut loose, thus stand in the way of a rational politics envisaging an independent Antilles seeking its own salvation in a viable system of regional security and cooperation.

## HAITI

Because of its different historical evolution—the first black republic in successful revolt against the Caribbean white plantocracy—Haiti has always been a special case. A hermetic peasant society sealed off for a century and a half from external influences, and even more so today than ever, there is no modern sharp break with the historical past that propels change in almost all the rest of the area. Past and present are interwoven with each other. So, Haitian views about the past are shaped by present political allegiances. Thus, in the eyes of the Duvalier supporter, Pétion and Boyer, the mulatto presidents, ruined Haiti. For the elite politicians who preceded the Duvalier regime, Haitian discontents are to be traced back to the often semiliterate black presidents who ruled the country intermittently from 1843 until the American invasion of 1915.

It is important to note the background of the "revolution of 1946" that set the groundwork for the arrival of Duvalier into the presidency in 1957. The theme of the revolution had been the salvation of the black man against the city mulatto elite; and it bred, for a few brief years, some of the rare political parties in Haitian history. The theme died in the scandals of the Magloire presidency (1950–57), in which the black Colonel-President reverted to the traditional style of using the office to accumulate his private fortune, aided in the traditional Haitian manner by the strategic groups of the elite, the army, the Francophile Church and, not least importantly, the United States. The Duvalier success in 1957 grew out of the mass disillusionment with that record, its failure especially to solve the grim problem of the near-starvation life-style of the Haitian peasant masses.

The Duvalier tyranny, as it has grown out of this, is at once traditional and revolutionary. It is traditional in the sense that it has come to power on splendid promises and then betrayed them, thereby reinforcing the peasant's image of the politician as the city gentleman-adventurer who betrays him. It is traditional in that, in its public policy, it has done nothing to reform the feudal class structure of Haitian society; except in so far as Duvalier—like Trujillo before him across the border—has employed his tyranny to bring to their knees the *haute bourgeoisie* whom he has always hated. But the old graft-making relationship between government and business still remains, and the Syrian-Lebanese merchant group, for example, still survives successfully through its willingness to contribute its "pay off" to the regime.

Yet, underneath all this, there are more sinister forces and elements that make the regime revolutionary, but of course, not in a Marxist sense. The device of systematized terror has been added to the old strategy of corruption. The old ritual, whereby a deposed president was allowed, by a sort of gentleman's agreement, to decamp to a foreign port along with his private fortune, has been replaced by a system in which conspirators against the regime quietly disappear into the torture chambers of the presidential palace. Whole families are used as hostages; it is the fear of retaliation against relatives which has aborted so many plots against the palace. Every institution potentially dangerous has been cleverly neutralized—the church, the army, the university. Rapid promotion of individuals in the public service, utterly unrelated to competence, ensures that no vested interest has a chance to solidify itself. A praetorian guard, in the shape of the *ton-ton macoutes,* performs at once and the same time the role of a protective shield for the dictator and a vulgarized democratization of the social structure, as hordes of unemployed youth, in exchange for a uniform and the license to use a gun, are immunized against becoming anti-governmental elements. Apart, perhaps, from the Haitianization of the Catholic Church—in which the French princes of the church have been replaced by an indigenous hierarchy —it is, altogether, difficult to think of anything positive that the regime of "Papa Doc" has achieved.

It is pertinent to ask whether this is a totalitarian system. Perhaps not. There is no omnipresent ideology, as in *fidelista* Cuba, no attempt to encompass all life into a total frame. There is no effort to transform existing social structure, only a determination to stay in power. It is true that there are diverse ideological elements in the literary background of Duvalier, himself an accomplished student of Haitian religion and folklore—nationalism, for example, and the theory of governments who participate directly in matters affecting their interests. They are not bound by international agreements except by express consent, and amendments to all this require a special procedure approved by the Caribbean leaderships. On the other hand, this is at best a limited autonomy, for it still retains a large power of royal appointment to the posts of Governor, Lieutenant-Governor and Attorney-General. There is much room left, especially in defense matters, for unilateral interference by The Hague ministers. The De Wit affair of 1957—in which the Antilles governor refused to approve a deportation order made out by the local cabinet against a recalcitrant newspaper editor—showed how even essentially internal matters can be invaded by the metropolitan appointees.

There has grown up since 1960 an increasingly vocal discontent with the Statute arrangements, especially by the new brand of politicians who were students returning from Dutch universities. They dislike the limited international role afforded the Caribbean members. There is a fundamental disagreement on matters, for example, like attitudes to South African *apartheid,* which raises the question whether there can in reality exist any real accord between a white European people that has kinship relations with the Afrikaaners and a black Caribbean people. There is, beyond it, the larger question as to whether Surinam or the Antilles can ever hope to promote Caribbean solidarity in any way while being a member of a union whose main partner is a non-American state.

Why, then, does not this stimulate an independence movement? The answer is threefold. Surinam, with a simmering border dispute with Guyana on its hands, feels that it needs the metropolitan power as protector and friend in case of real trouble. Aruba and Curaçao, heavily dependent on their rich oil refinery economy, are perennially at the mercy of the big multinational companies that ship in their oil from the Venezuela fields; any setback there would place an added value on the economic benefits that flow from the Kingdom membership. The racial-religious minorities like the Javanese and the Hindustanis possess the typical minority phobia, fearful of majority abuse in case the protective arm of the metropolitan power should be removed. All these reasons, however valid, illustrate the continuing grip of the colonial mentality. The politics of the Netherlands Caribbean will increasingly revolve around the emergence of answers to these overriding considerations.

## The American Caribbean

### THE VIRGIN ISLANDS

The special ingredients that the American Virgin Islands bring to the general portrait of the regional politics are two. First, since, like

*négritude.* But their use has been spasmodic, not persistently over
ing. All in all, it is a regime of traditional despotism, driven by
President's paranoid appetite for power. The fact that it is black
incidental, for absolute power corrupts absolutely, black or white.
is the one national system in the Caribbean area that justifies, p
haps, the political theory of tyrannicide.

## The Dutch Caribbean

The politics of the Netherlands Antilles and Surinam revolv
around their constitutional status as a federative state comprisin
Curaçao, Aruba, Bonaire, and the three tiny Windward Islands of S
Martin, Saba and St. Eustatius, and as an intercontinental state ii
which both Surinam and the Antilles are partners with the metropoli
tan Netherlands through the instrumentality of the Dutch Kingdom
Statute of 1954. It is, then, a federal politics; and its characteristic
problems are those of federal states everywhere, where dual sovereignty
creates twilight areas of dispute between the two jurisdictions.

The federal politics of the Antillian group means a continuing politics of maneuver to set up coalition governments. The two major blocs
in the leading Curaçao territory—for years the National Peoples
Party under Moises Frumencio Da Costa Gomez and the Democratic
Party under Efrain Jonckheer—must court the votes of the Aruban
and Windward group representatives in the federal legislative council. This means, inevitably, a maximum of compromise and a minimum of ideology, despite the fact that the Gomez faction generally has
stood for the black, lower-class elements, while the Jonckheer party
has been generally identified with the Protestant-Jewish power group
that for so long has regarded itself as the natural ruling class of
Curaçaoan society. All this has been complicated, in turn, by the Curaçaoan conviction that, as the leading island of the group, she is un
necessarily restricted by the federal bond (not unlike the position of
Jamaica in the British West Indies Federation). The end-result o
this has been to produce a highly personalist politics; the two leadin
Aruban parties, thus, were formed by two dominant personalities i
Aruban life, Juan Enrique Irausquin and Henry Eman. The socia
racial disturbances in Curaçao in 1969, engineered in part by the ne
Workers' Front, may be seen as the expression of mass discontent wit
this style of opportunistic politics.

On a higher political level, the Antillian territories, along wi
Surinam, are meshed together in their special constitutional relatio
ship with The Hague, as joint partners in the Dutch Kingdom. C
the face of it it is a remarkably liberal arrangement. The two Car
bean partners are directly represented in the metropolitan cabir
and parliament by plenipotentiary ministers nominated by their o

the Bahamas and Bermuda, they are a classic example of a tourist economy catering to the visitors of the North American affluent societies, they generate a special politics of tourism. Support of the tourist industry becomes a veritable article of faith. Just as in the sugar islands, before sugar became a dying economy, it was enough to charge that a politician's views on sugar would endanger the industry to seriously embarrass, if not destroy him, so in the tourist islands tourism plays a similar role. A large proportion of political and governmental energy thus goes into promotional activities. Equally, the black populations who serve the industry are from time to time subjected to anxious courtesy campaigns to be "nice" to the tourist, lest discourteous attitudes kill the goose that lays the golden eggs. A single-source economy produces a single-theme politics.

Secondly, tourism and its allied services are in large part manned by the thousands of alien workers who crowd into this full-employment economy from the neighboring Leeward and Windward islands. Many of them are non-bonded illegal entrants, exploited alike by government and employer, and deported by the United States Immigration and Naturalization Service when the economy no longer needs them. They do the dirty work of the economy. In return, their housing conditions constitute some of the worst under the American flag; they cannot vote; they are denied the use of health and social services; and their children have been denied entry to the school system. All in all, this system constitutes a revival of the old, evil Caribbean indenture system of the previous century. There are signs that as the alien labor force begins to stir itself into collective action against their general status of second-class citizens, they will add a new, volatile force to the territorial politics.

PUERTO RICO

The one major clue to Puerto Rican politics is that being, like the Virgins, an unincorporated territory, it has been governed, and is still governed, not by the declarative commands of the United States Constitution, but by the whims of Congressional government. There has been, since 1947, an expansion of internal self-government. But all the areas of Puerto Rican life that possess a federal property about them are still controlled by the Congressional committee system— defense, maritime transportation, civil aviation, postal communications, customs, immigration. The theory of the 1952 Constitution, adopted by the reigning *Populares* group, is that Washington and San Juan are equal partners in a Commonwealth relationship. The grim truth is, however, that the island-territory is ruled by an "oligarchy of strangers," the members of the relevant Congressional committees, and that San Juan has nothing but the weak device of a voteless Resident Commissioner at the federal center to help it in its perennial struggles with the federal agencies. The struggle in 1970 over Culebra island—in which a small population is harassed daily by the bombing practices of the Caribbean Sea Frontier Command of the United States Navy—dramatizes the inequality of power and influence secreted in the relationship.

Politics, then, is a politics of status, divided between the partisans of the three historic status concepts—autonomy (the Commonwealth thesis), statehood, and independence. 1968 was a turning point in the struggle. For the defeat of Muñoz and his *Populares* in that election, ending the long reign of 28 years, had the effect of polarizing the political situation. Political analysts expect future elections to be a direct confrontation between the Statehood Party of Governor Luis Ferré and the independence groups. And a further element of polarization is taking place. On the one hand, the radical Left of the independence ideology, especially the student groups at the University, have become radicalized by the double influence of Cuba and the black movement in the United States. On the other hand, the Republican-Statehood Right has become radicalized, more particularly, by the infiltration of the colony of Cuban exiles in San Juan, whose political temper is raucously reactionary. At the same time, a gradual metamorphosis of strategy is taking place. The leading independence group, the *Partido Independentista Puertorriqueño,* has added socialism and non-violent passive resistance to its program; while the leading militant faction of the student body has learned the art of the aggressive demonstration. That this is an anti-colonial struggle is evident from the way in which ROTC on the campus has become the main target of that militancy. Whereas on the stateside campus ROTC is seen as the symbol of the industrial-military complex, in Puerto Rico it is seen as the symbol of colonialism and of the fact that Puerto Rican youths are subject to obligatory military service although Puerto Rico has no voice in the Congressional legislative process that imposes that obligation. It is a humiliating indignity, be it noted, felt by Puerto Ricans of all political persuasions.

While some 25 years ago Puerto Rico was at the top of the constitutional ladder in the region, today she is pretty near the bottom. Her leadership role, for the radical elements, has been taken over by Cuba. Even the Caribbean liberal-reformist elements now recognize the non-exportability of the Puerto Rican model of economic development inasmuch as it is based on the freedom of movement of persons and goods into the protected American market that cannot be duplicated for other Caribbean economies. There are not wanting critics, indeed, who see Puerto Rico as a privileged sanctuary, passing by the ideal of independence for the economic benefits transmitted by the American connection. The theory of the pro-American groups in San Juan is that the society forms a bridgehead between the North American and

South American cultures. But it is difficult to believe this theory in the light of the massive inundation of the Puerto Rican culture forms by the Americanizing process. More and more it looks, to use a phrase of Herbert Spencer's, like a beautiful theory murdered by a gang of brutal facts.

## The Hispanic Caribbean

Puerto Rico, perhaps, is a politics of American form and Hispanic spirit. But one must go to Cuba and Santo Domingo for the genuine Hispano-Caribbean politics. The crucial point to make about both of them is that they won early the battle of nationhood, but have engaged in the battle of democracy very late. If nationhood means a sense in all classes of belonging to a separate and defined national way of life, that was guaranteed for Cuba by the early development, in the eighteenth and nineteenth centuries, of a large free colored group, and equally guaranteed for Santo Domingo by the growth, during the same period, of a wealthy and politically powerful class of mulatto planters. Both groups lived in societies they felt, by natural law, to be theirs.

Democracy, on the contrary, was a weaker plant. Both societies inherited the spirit of Spanish political authoritarianism. The habits of corruption and privilege bred, only too easily, the habit of dictatorship—Gómez and Batista in Cuba, Trujillo in Santo Domingo. Electoral processes, theoretically free, became the method whereby the local ruling groups tightened their hold over worker and peasant. This internal degradation of the democratic dogma, in turn, was intensified by the way in which both societies, theoretically independent, became for long periods of time client states of American imperialism—Cuba by means of the rule of the American sugar corporations, Santo Domingo through the occupation of the country by the United States Marines. It is, indeed, one of the least creditable aspects of American intervention in the region that so many Caribbean despots learned their art as trainees of the Marine Corps.

SANTO DOMINGO

It is a measure of the inability of Dominican politics to develop a viable system of democratic life and institutions that a decade after the end of the *era de Trujillo*, the chief executive, President Joaquin Balaguer, should be an ex-associate of the assassinated dictator. The 1962 election, in which Juan Bosch was the victor, created the first really freely-elected government the country had ever had. It lasted a brief seven months, to be overthrown by the military in alliance with the church and business. That was followed by the civil war of 1965, ended by the American intervention. The aftermath of all that is the situation in the early 1970s where the leading mass party, Bosch's *Partido Revolucionario Dominicano,* defiantly stays outside the electoral system on the grounds, justified by events, that democracy cannot function within an environment of forces determined to kill it.

The anti-democratic elements are indeed formidable. There is the spirit of massive corruption left behind by three decades of *trujillista* tyranny, a spirit that has permeated all institutions of Dominican life, and has remained powerful even when the dictatorship itself had disappeared. There is the rancorous hatred left behind by the 1965 civil war—a point Americans can appreciate in the light of the fact that the scars of their own Civil War, a century later, are still evident and alive in many sectors of the national life. There is the bitter anti-Americanism left behind by the intervention. When, indeed, as has been said, the second most powerful man in the country at that time was the American ambassador, it becomes difficult to believe in the theory of self-government. There is, finally, a general climate of opinion in Dominican society which is profoundly alienated, even cynical, a feeling of powerlessness. It is a feeling that pervades all the groups that were involved in the 1965 revolution—the younger army officers, the students, the professionals, not least of all the urban proletariat, composed of the peasants who have crowded into the *barrios altos* of the city in search of jobs that do not exist. There is, indeed, a deep social cleavage between the masses and the small middle-upper class; their relationship, in the phrase of one observer, resembles the relationship between a metropolitan power and its colonies rather than the normal flow of communications among different parts of a modern city.

The only politics that means anything to most of these elements is the politics of revolution. They reject the principle stated by José Figueres, the *doyen* of the democratic Left forces in the region, that "We are convinced that it is better to have a bad government rather than a good revolution, so long as the electoral path remains open." The vital condition of the open electoral path seems to them to be unattainable in their position. This analysis is behind the thesis, recently publicized by Bosch, in favor of a "dictatorship supported by the people." The future of Dominican politics depends upon whether conditions continue to favor the Bosch thesis or whether, changing profoundly, they give new validity to the Figueres view.

CUBA

Cuba, of course, is the revolutionary politics in action, guided by a Marxist-Leninist party seeking not merely to control human behavior but to reshape social structure. The outcome of the mountain guerilla campaign of Fidel Castro and his handful of soldiers still carries much of the heroic stamp about it. So many of its foreign friends, indeed, have seen it in this light, as a sort of romantic Heming-wayesque adventure, that they have failed to appreciate its profoundly serious purpose, that of transforming the Cuban colonial society into a Caribbean socialist society.

The revolution seeks to harness the collective energy of the Cuban people for monumental programs—public health for everybody, the tremendous literacy campaign, political education. Its institutional methods reject, therefore, the Anglo-Saxon concept of parliamentary politics. Power is concentrated in the Communist party, within the party in the Central Committee, and within the Central Committee in the person of the *maximo lider*. The uniqueness of this can be seen if it is compared with the Puerto Rican political style. In San Juan, it is an electoral politics, in which whole areas of Puerto Rico do not see a politician except in election periods. In Havana, it is a daily exercise—politics is seen as active participation of the masses, through the local cell system, in the reconstructive tasks of the revolution. Nor is this simply a communist style. In its single-party structure, it is like the style of the ruling Mexican party in which the real discussion of competing viewpoints takes place within, and not outside, the ruling party bureaucracy.

There are at once positive and negative aspects in it. It is positive in harnessing the creative talent and genius of the ordinary folk-people into programs with which they can identify with massive enthusiasm, a task as yet not even begun elsewhere in the Caribbean societies. It is positive in its recognition of the priority of re-energizing the agricultural sector (after a false start in forced industrialization), thus giving new social status to cane-cutting, hitherto stamped with the stigma of slavery work. As Castro put it in his August 1966 speech, the revolution is the abolition of the exploitation of human labor, but not the abolition of human work. It is positive, finally, in its effort to terminate the historic domination of the countryside by the city, endemic in all the Caribbean. This, to some degree, is an attack upon the social corruption of city life. "Capitals," in Règis Debray's acid phrase, "especially in those big Yankee branch offices in the Caribbean, are livable purgatories compared to the urban agglomeration of Asia and even of Europe." One result of that last reality is the changing social background of the Cuban political leadership. It is a refreshing change compared with the fact that Puerto Rican politics continue to be dominated by the professional legal class, with all the limitations of the legal mind.

The negative aspect touches upon the problem of intellectual freedom within the centralized bureaucracy of the national party leadership. With party and state bureaucracies blended together, it is easy for disagreement with party ideology to be identified as treason to the state. The 1963 affair, in which the Aníbal Escalante microfaction

was expelled from the party for activities only vaguely defined as "counter-revolutionary," provides disquieting evidence that this process may already be taking place within the Cuban ruling echelons. If this process entrenches itself as doctrinal orthodoxy and generates the concept of heresy, it will limit the Caribbean appeal of the Revolution. Most of the younger Caribbean radical forces have been educated in the respective metropolitan universities; and whatever the shortcomings of the metropolitan imperialistic structures, they have learned there the habit of intellectual freedom. They will not be willing to exchange that freedom for a new orthodoxy. That fact, as much as any other, helps explain why Havana has not had more success in exporting its ideology to other Caribbean societies.

### The Politics of Regionalism

Since 1945 regional unity and cooperation have been at the heart of Caribbean discussion. There are two main reasons for this. The first is political: the political balkanization of the region has made it excessively vulnerable to outside intervention by the big powers. The Guyana-Venezuela and British Honduras-Guatemala boundary disputes alone show how vital it is for the Caribbean countries to build up some sort of collective security system that will at least give them the power of a united front in the face of such explosive situations. The second reason is economic: the historically deep-rooted links between producing units in the region and metropolitan firms has produced a serious fragmentation of the regional economy, with "vertical" links between the individual colony and the metropolis being stronger than "horizontal" links between the individual island-economies, leading, of course, to self-defeating and counter-productive rivalries among the dependent economies to attract foreign capital and secure favors from metropolitan governments.

This historical legacy, generating in turn the powerful psychology of insular prides and prejudices, still frustrates the growth of either a regional security system or a common economic community. The best-known example of this condition is the collapse of the West Indies Federation (1958–62). In part, the failure sprang from the fact that the federal venture was an artificial growth, imposed by Britain upon an apathetic people (like the Nigerian and Central African federations) for its own imperial administrative convenience. In part, it was due to the absence of any real sentiment of federal nationhood in the West Indians themselves; and there was no anti-colonial military struggle, as with the American colonies after 1776, to help stimulate such a sentiment. There was too much of an imbalance, both of population and resources, between the largest unit, Jamaica, and the other federal members; in turn, the leading political figures decided, disastrously, to stay at home rather than risk their chances at the federal center.

What, then, for the future? Clearly, regional cooperation will most fruitfully grow, not out of such ventures in political federalism, breaking on the rocks of political jealousies, but out of functional federalism; that is, the art of cooperating together along limited, functional lines. That may be done in the area of regional private associations—the Caribbean Mental Health Association, for example. It may express itself through surviving federal institutions, like the University of the West Indies. Or it may take the form of intergovernmental cooperation in the growth of common services, as in the recently-formed Caribbean Free Trade Association (CARIFTA), in which an effort is being made, tentatively, to create genuinely national economies and to encourage regional coordination of agriculture, manufacturing, and mining development as well as to maximize the potential gains to be made from wider markets created by economic integration. This is a less dramatic, but probably more rewarding line of development. As with the historic growth of the European Common Market, it recognizes that the establishment of federal economic structures must precede the establishment of federal political structures. Concrete common interests, concretely met, not vague sentiments of federal idealism, become the order of the day.

## The Politics of Black Power

The intrusion, finally, of Black Power slogans into the region raises the question, of profound importance, of the relevancy of those slogans to the peculiar Caribbean condition. The fact that they have appeared in diverse territories, through the medium usually of a virile underground newssheet press, indicates that they respond to a climate of opinion endemic to the region as a whole.

The ideology, to begin with, is irrelevant; and for two reasons. First, if it means black political power, that, of course, has already been achieved. The massive structure of Henri Christophe's *Citadelle* is there in northern Haiti to remind the historically-minded that a black court, along with a black aristocracy of titles, ruled in the black republic at a time when Jane Austen was still writing her Victorian novels; and today black cabinets, democratically elected, exist throughout the region. Secondly, if the concept means the advance of peoples of African descent then, of course, it ignores the existence, in Trinidad and the Guianas, of substantial Asian populations for whom this concept can only mean a dangerous disruption of that Afro-Indian-Asian solidarity which is surely the ideal in those plural societies.

The positive and relevant aspects of the concept are there, too, however. The "black is beautiful" theme is apposite in societies where the "white bias" still hangs on. Equally, its economic content is deeply relevant, perhaps, indeed, its most important component in the Caribbean environment. For throughout the Caribbean it is safe to say, with certain qualifications, of course, that the political face is black and the economic face is white. For the Caribbean economy exhibits, in exaggerated form, all the major properties of the colonial regime—foreign ownership and control in the major sectors of oil, sugar, banking, insurance, mining and manufacturing; external decision-making with respect to investment and allocation of resources by the head offices of the big multinational corporations; structural unemployment and underemployment, combined with high salary-wage levels in privileged sectors; separation between local extraction of raw materials and overseas manufacture of the finished product; lack of indigenous technology; and the concentration by overseas wealth in capital-oriented industries that do little to absorb the labor surplus inherited from the old plantation economy.

All this, more than anything else, has become the target of the Black Power groups, whether university academician or street activist. Government thus becomes an alliance of the expatriate business force and the local elites, the West Indian brown middle class that has always had such a bad reputation with the masses. Looked at in this way, the historically-determined task of black militancy in the area is to follow the seizure of political independence with the seizure of economic independence. That, in one way, has been the achievement of the Cuban Revolution; and that is the meaning of Stokely Carmichael's observation that Fidel Castro is the "blackest man" in the Caribbean.

### The American Presence

The United States possesses, both by geographical propinquity and historical tradition, a legitimate interest in the Caribbean area. What she does not possess is the illegitimate claim, as under the Lyndon Johnson doctrine of preventive intervention, to become the policeman of the area. The American future in the region, then, depends upon whether Washington prefers to assert the legitimate or the illegitimate role.

No one is entitled to optimism on this score. The Cuban and Dominican interventions have seriously compromised the goodwill for the United States built up over the last thirty years since the liquidation of the old Caribbean protectorates and the initiation of the "Good Neighbor" policy. It would be possible to argue that there has been more American than Cuban intervention in the area—the Central Intelligence Agency intrigues, for example, against Jaganism in Guyana. One outcome of this has been that, regrettably, too much of domestic politics in the countries of the area become bifurcated into pro-American and anti-American factions, weakening serious attention to the real internal problems. The American presence thus becomes, to use a distinction made by Senator Mike Mansfield, an American preponderance.

Clearly enough, the basic issue for the American policymakers is whether they seek to lead the Caribbean revolution into democratic directions or, by seeking to frustrate that revolution, to play the role— as the Cuban revolutionary imagery sees it—of the Roman imperial enemy of the Third World. There is still time, perhaps, to make that choice. For, surprisingly, there still remains a vast reservoir of goodwill toward the United States on the part of the ordinary peoples of the Caribbean. But time, obviously, is rapidly running out.

Anthony P. Maingot

# Social Life of the Caribbean

## Social Relationships

A Trinidadian writer of East Indian descent, travelling and studying the Caribbean in 1961, thus described an anti-white, pro-African manifestation in Port-of-Spain:

> I thought then that it was a purely local eruption, created by the pressures of local politics. But soon, on the journey, I came to see that such eruptions were widespread, and represented feeling coming to the surface in Negro communities throughout the Caribbean: confused feelings, without direction; the Negro's rejection of the guilt he has borne for so long; the last, delayed Spartacan revolt, more radical than Toussaint L'Overture's; the closing of accounts this side of the middle passage.

The author, V. S. Naipaul, was on a mission for Trinidad's Prime Minister Eric Williams, later, paradoxically, to become the target of a Black Power movement in 1970.

Had Naipaul not limited himself to the Dutch, English and French territories and travelled to the islands of the Hispanic Caribbean, he might have witnessed equal manifestations of social discontents although the themes and styles would have been very different inasmuch as the articulation of problems and projection of solutions there vary greatly.

In the former colonies of the British, Dutch and French Caribbean, intimate social relationships are invariably conditioned by criteria of race and color, while broader, more public social concerns consistently

ANTHONY P. MAINGOT *is director of the Antilles Research Program at Yale University as well as assistant professor of history and sociology there. A citizen of Trinidad, Dr. Maingot holds a Ph.D. from the University of Florida at Gainesville.*

reflect a deep-seated apprehension about the "black masses" with which there is little contact and even less knowledge.

On the other hand, in Cuba, Puerto Rico, and the Dominican Republic—the Hispanic Caribbean—racial questions, though of some importance, are subordinate to local political issues and the ever present concern with the possible reaction of the United States. Haiti combines elements of both.

To be sure, behind these general concerns and differences lie the truly structural problems shared by these societies regardless of their particular cultural orientation. Where race is highly correlated with class, as in the case of the first group, class interests are subsumed under racial and color concerns. Class conflicts are consequently defined in racial terms. Similarly, where the dominant nation in the area, the United States, has invariably favored and aided the establishment, as in the case of the Hispanic group, the apprehensions or hopes, as the case may be, of the success of anti-establishment movements wear the mantle of concern over possible United States action and intervention.

Despite these differences there is today one common aspect general to the area. A decade after Naipaul's experience, conversations in middle-class parlors of both variants reflect a general malaise and exude a very similar sense of crisis and foreboding. It appears clear to them, if not to others, that established societies in the Caribbean are in serious trouble.

Differences in the nature of the leadership, both established and revolutionary, and in the appeals and style of politics are important. They reflect deeper social structural differences; and these differences are quite pronounced between the two areas. As a consequence any attempt to cast the whole Caribbean in one mold, attributing similar historical patterns to all, is fundamentally erroneous. It would be equally shortsighted, however, to be carried away by these differences into discussions of "crises of identity" and other cultural and psychological explanations ignoring the truly structural causes of the condition.

In the case studies in this essay, primacy is given to the question of social structure; the way the society is stratified, the role and function of each stratum—here called class. This is not intended to minimize the importance of cultural and psychological approaches, but to subordinate explicitly the latter to the analysis of society. Methodologically, this seems to make sense, for without an analysis of the social milieu, psychological and cultural categories have little meaning or utility. Further, common sense tells us that since it is the established social orders which are being challenged throughout the area, analysis should focus on those societies as they are and how they have evolved.

Necessarily the discussion begins with Cuba. Largest, richest and, to date, the only Caribbean society which has fundamentally restructured itself, its social and economic history shows strong parallels to those of the rest of the area. At the same time Cuba demonstrates just how different are the cultural histories in the Caribbean. Therefore, the case study method is at the same time illustrative of broader trends and facts.

## Pre-Revolutionary Cuba

In studying a society as complex as Cuba it is best to devise a means of looking at historical developments in terms of one central question. In this case the question logically has to refer to the major social movements and reactions to existing social conditions. In Cuba there have been two major reactions in the twentieth century. The first, and, therefore, a major watershed in this case study, was the frustrated social movement of 1933–1934. The second succeeded in 1959 with Fidel Castro's revolution.

By the 1930s, the Cuban society had crystallized and Cuban culture was a tangible identifiable entity. Between the initial Spanish settlement of the island in the early sixteenth century and the British occupation of Havana for a few months in 1762, Cuba was little more than a transshipping port for the Spanish *flota* heading for the mainland. Fewer than six thousand blacks were introduced all through that period, despite the fact that the native Indian population had quickly disappeared from the scene. Cattle ranching, the main enterprise, required little labor. But Cuba could not remain out of the sugar world for long. Both the technical innovations introduced by the English and the sweeping reforms which the Bourbon monarch introduced opened up Cuba to the outside world, a world teeming with the changes wrought by England's successful industrial revolution.

Sugar cultivation had begun towards the end of the sixteenth century, and tobacco was introduced some half century later with important consequences for the society. These crops had increased the number of independent farmers at the expense of the large cattle latifundia. The agrarian sector was largely small scale, farming with very few slaves. Beginning in the third quarter of the eighteenth century, however, a growth trend began because of the enormous international demand for sugar.

Ramiro Guerra y Sánchez, foremost student of this development notes the difference between pre-sugar plantation Cuba and plantation Haiti and Barbados in the last decades of the eighteenth century.

|  | Size/Sq. Mi. | White | Free Colored | Slaves |
| --- | --- | --- | --- | --- |
| Barbados | 166 | 16,167 |  | 62,115 |
| Cuba | 44,000 | 96,440 | 31,847 | 44,333 |
| Haiti | 11,000 | 38,000 |  | 452,000 |

Despite the relative smallness of Cuba's total population it is worth noting that in the few years after 1762 the slave population had grown enormously and the number of sugar mills had doubled. Between 1764 and the emancipation of slavery in 1886, over one million African slaves were introduced into Cuba. The opening up of the North American market, the decline of the sugar producing British colonies, especially Barbados and Jamaica, liberalized Spanish metropolitan policies, and fundamentally, the destruction of the world's largest producer of sugar, Haiti, had created the ideal international conditions for Cuba. Yet, contrary to the pattern of land concentration which had taken place in Jamaica, Barbados, and, to a lesser extent, Trinidad, Cuba at this time increased rather than diminished the number of independent growers.

The expansion of the sugar industry was due to the large increase in growers. In 1827 there were one thousand mills, in 1846 a few hundred more and in 1860 a total of two thousand. Most sugar estates were between fifteen hundred and two thousand acres in size. Capital was still largely Cuban and land was plentiful and easily available. The municipalities were still giving out *mercedes,* land grants, to those who would work them. Original cattle latifundias were eventually subdivided. The *hacienda comunera,* held by several independent farmers, became the predominant land tenure system.

To argue whether slavery in Cuba had been less cruel than in the British West Indies is academic. Regardless of semantics, slavery is never "less cruel." On the other hand, to ask whether there were different social and cultural consequences flowing from master-slave relationships in each area is important. In a position yet to be refuted, Frank Tannenbaum has argued that Spanish law, Roman Catholicism and previous cultural contacts had created certain propitious conditions for the treatment of slaves as humans and not merely chattel. Hispanic America developed, therefore, less harsh relationships between the races than did the non-Hispanic Caribbean. But what Tannenbaum did not consider was how the different economic base of the non-Hispanic Caribbean allowed those cultural factors to function in a meaningful way. Fernando Ortiz's study (*Cuban Counterpoint: Sugar and Tobacco*) of the differential influences of the sugar and tobacco industries does point out, for instance, how, as a result of its development with indigenous capital and labor, the social atmosphere on the paternalistic tobacco plantation contributed to the growth of Cuban culture. By avoiding the cultural sterilization of the large capitalist plantation of which it had few in the nineteenth century, Cuba managed to develop a culture which was a rich mixture of Spanish and African cultural traits.

Widespread race mixing at the lower levels of society had created a dynamic mulatto group which developed a deep loyalty to the country.

Antonio Maceo was only the most outstanding of those mulatto and Negro Cubans who were fundamental to Cuba's wars for independence in 1868–1878 and 1895–1898. Racial prejudice, however, had by no means been absent from this process. The mere existence of a mulatto class reflected the attitudes towards race mixing. That this attitude (similar to that in Trinidad) differed from the English variant is true. Even so, it was that prejudice which prevented Cubans from realizing fully what their real racial and cultural legacy was, until the late 1920s.

This Cuban culture was enormously strengthened by the great suffering and deprivation endured during the Wars for Independence. Only in Venezuela had the wars been so widespread, so bloody and so destructive of property. Much of the Cuban disdain for the island neighbor, Puerto Rico, stems from the odious comparison Cubans traditionally make between their own heroic and Puerto Rico's allegedly timid efforts at independence. Much of their resentment against the United States results from a belief that even Teddy Roosevelt's adventurous "Rough Riders" have been given more credit for independence than the thousands of Cubans who sacrificed life and property in the struggle.

The Cuban's heroic efforts did not come cheaply. Farmers were driven from their lands by the rebels' scorched earth strategy, but most especially by the Spanish war policies. The system of *reconcentraciones* depopulated whole rural areas moving the citizenry to the better guarded urban centers. The agrarian structure, the land holding patterns, especially the *haciendas comuneras* (community farms), and the ethos of the independent farm suffered. Many of these small farmers never returned to their ill-defined properties. Before 1894, the number of independent farms reached an estimated 90,960. By 1899 the number had been reduced to 60,711.

Other events worked against the small independent farmer. For example, the American military government abolished the *hacienda comunera* system in the name of efficiency and true *laissez-faire*. The government was kept out of the adjudication of private claims, leaving the matter up to individual initiatives before special tribunals. Within three decades the number of independent farms was reduced 50 percent to 38,105.

Vagueness and confusion in the recording of land titles and the greed of individuals were minor parts of this dramatic shift in Cuban social structure away from the independent small farming class. The major forces at work were more impersonal and overwhelming.

The process was similar to that which was taking place in Mexico, that which had already taken place in Barbados, and, with less dire consequences, in Trinidad. This process was the growth of the modern sugar estate at the expense of the small producer.

Any cost-accounting approach to modern sugar production has to start with one irreversible and overriding technical principle. Once the *zafra* (harvest), the cutting, grinding and processing of sugar, begins, once the great machines are set in motion, all other aspects of man in society become subordinate instrumentalities which have thereafter only one function—to keep the cane rolling in and the refined sugar and molasses pouring out. This change of life lasting anywhere from three to five months, depending on crop and market conditions, held equally true for Cuba's 1970 season as it did for the seasons at the beginning of the century.

Modernization, with efficiency and profits as its goals, meant a series of transformations in the Cuban world of sugar. It meant technical know-how and ample capital which the new North American protector had in abundance. It meant land to grow their own cane so as to reduce dependence on "unpredictable" Cuban farmers (*colonos*). This land Cuba had in abundance. And usually it was of high quality.

Modernization also meant large supplies of labor at low cost and preferably residential, at least during the all-important *zafra*. Despite the social stigma attached to cane cutting because of slavery, as the estates grew, this supply became more plentiful due to the parallel process of small farm failures. This, for example, was a popular quatrain which expressed the Cuban's attitudes toward cane cutting:

> I do not cut cane
> Let the wind cut it
> Let Lola cut it
> With her wiggle

But when Cubans were insufficient to supply the heavy seasonal demands for labor, there were Haiti and Jamaica, much closer, after all, than the west coast of Africa had been to the nineteenth century planters.

Cuba's "Negro question" is discussed further on; it remains here to be said that in Cuba the large sugar interests had all of the advantages derived from indentured labor by their counterparts in Trinidad and none of the liabilities. The short distance between islands meant little or no transportation costs and there were no official regulations to be met or crusading Christian groups to mollify.

The planters in Cuba had free rein with their labor. It is apparent that in independent Cuba, on the large sugar plantation, and with Haitian labor, the Tannenbaum thesis does not hold.

By 1933, the sugar mills owned, leased or controlled 250,000 *caballerías* (1 *caballería* is 33⅓ acres) with 30 percent of the total area of the island. Of these, 175,000 were directly owned by North

American capital. An additional 43,000 *caballerías* were still farmed by independent *colonos*. The share of the sugar cultivation still in independent *colono* hands had varied with the fortunes of the industry. At the early part of the century (1904–1905) these independent *colonos* had 36.5 percent of the land under actual cultivation compared to 30.3 percent worked by *colonos* on lands leased from the mills.

The hectic and highly speculative rush to invest in sugar of the post World War One years, the so-called "Dance of the Millions," increased the acreage dedicated to sugar on all fronts. In late 1920 the bubble burst and again the independent *colono* was the main victim. In 1931 they owned only 9.3 percent of the total land in sugar and a 1933 survey reported only one mill grinding all independent *colono* cane while 35 mills received no cane from independent farmers at all.

By 1932, therefore, the structure of society in the sector of Cuba dedicated to sugar production—a sector which by 1933 contained well over one third of the island's working force—had crystallized.

The boundaries of that world were those of the plantation and its epicenter, the *batey,* the mill yard or site which contained the factory (*ingenio* or *central*) and outlying buildings, including dwelling quarters (*barracones*), shops, warehouses, also railway track sidings and switches. Professor Leland Hamilton Jenks correctly defined the typical *batey* as "a modern industrial village characterized by the specialization of an urban environment."

It was in the *batey* that two of Cuba's sectors, the urban-industrial and the rural-agricultural, were united to produce some 70% of the nation's income. Technical skills covered the range from chemical engineers, mechanical engineers, transportation experts, to administrators, bookkeepers and security men. Part of the *batey* worked throughout the year, the administrators, the experts, the guards. They prepared for the *zafra* the year out. In short, it was here that the work and life style of hundreds of thousands of Cubans was determined. Yet, only a small number of these actually lived on the *batey,* most, the field hands and their supervisors (*mayorales*), lived in outlying *colonia bateys* where living conditions contrasted starkly to those of the *batey's* managers and technicians. Work for them came only during harvest time, followed by the long months called *tiempo muerto* (dead time). But regardless of where they resided they were guided by the recurring pattern of the sugar cycles—three to five months labor and the rest of the year *tiempo muerto*—and the needs of the *central* or *ingenio* (mill).

Contractually attached to the mill as suppliers, the independent *colonos* cultivated an average of less than 70 acres apiece. That contractual relationship contained few of the two-way provisions for obligations and privileges found in most ordinary landlord-tenant leases, making their relationship to the mill one of complete dependence. Although the relationship changed somewhat after 1934, this dependence continued not only in technical matters such as the selection of cane varieties, when to plant, when to cut, deliver, etc., but also in such vital matters as sources of credit, growing food crops and general utilization of fallow lands. In 1933 the *colono* indebtedness to the mills was calculated by the Cuban Commission of the Foreign Policy Association to be the equivalent of four years of their gross income. Materially much better off than most, the individual *colono* lived a season to season existence which was thoroughly demoralizing. The hopelessness the *colonos* felt at not participating in the vital decisions of the industry was not exclusively theirs; they shared that feeling with the majority of Cubans, rural and urban. It was among the *colonos*, however, that this dependence had its most telling effects, for, as Guerra y Sánchez notes, theirs had been a history and tradition of social, political and economic independence, the healthiest sector of Cuban society.

One need not drag in the old theory of "cultural lag" to understand that the main cause of this general malaise was that economic changes had far outstripped the colonial, traditional society in which Cubans were still living.

If the link between the world of sugar and the urban sector was the *batey*, it was the educational system of the urban center which theoretically had the burden of keeping that link in Cuban hands. Since the modern sugar mill required skilled laboratory technicians, industrial chemists and other types of engineers as well as trained managers, someone had to fulfill those needs. Yet a look at the 1930 graduates from Cuba's only university shows only twelve agricultural sugar engineers, one chemical expert, two chemico-agricultural experts.

On the other hand there were 891 graduates of the law school, 794 in medicine, 427 in pharmacy and 272 dental surgeons. Civil engineering, a profession with ready openings in the governmental bureaucracy, did graduate 75. As late as 1953, the census shows that while there were 6,201 physicians there were only 294 agronomic engineers; while there were 6,560 lawyers there were only 309 mechanical, industrial and mining engineers. This is not to deny that many Cubans had a good apprenticeship right on the *batey*, but this was not the way to control ownership and autonomous decision-making. In fact, it was a perpetuator of technical dependence.

The vital parts of Cuba's largest industry were thus financially and technically virtually in foreign hands. This in turn structured the social atmosphere of the *batey* and plantation. Recruited mostly from Louisiana sugar circles at first, the *batey* personnel of the American-owned sugar estate recreated something of the environment of the

Deep South—charm, gentility and efficiency, certainly. But also rigid racial and class attitudes and continual inability to get the correct perspective of their role as invited guests in Cuba.

"I don't think these people will ever learn English," was the comment of a top sugar expert as remembered by his son. The expression reflects the isolated world of the modern *batey,* an American world, yet the very heart of the Cuban system. The problem of Cuba in the twentieth century was not any crisis of identity, it was the typically Caribbean problem of alienation from the sources of production and the decisions surrounding those. Frustration stemmed not merely from this foreign domination, but also from the despair of knowing that the existing social structure and its institutions, such as the educational system, were contributing to, rather than changing, that dependence.

Urban Cuba faced a similar crisis but the roots of this, though related, were somewhat different. They were related because it was the success of Cuba as a sugar and, to a much lesser degree, tobacco grower which attracted the numerous foreigners who began to change the island's population, to wit:

|                  | 1919      | 1931      | % Increase |
|------------------|-----------|-----------|------------|
| Total Population | 2,889,004 | 3,962,344 | 37.2       |
| Colored Cubans   | 773,905   | 925,297   | 26.1       |
| Haitians         | 21,015    | 79,838    | 279.9      |
| Jamaicans        | 18,122    | 40,471    | 123.3      |
| Spaniards        | 404,074   | 613,970   | 51.9       |
| Chinese          | 10,300    | 24,480    | 137.7      |

The Haitians and Jamaicans went to the rural areas to fill the demands of the large estates, especially of Oriente and Camaguey. Haitians were invariably cane cutters, Jamaicans spreading more widely among the menial occupations. Chinese, via the Philippines, were also brought in for this purpose. Later they formed the majority of the colorful *pregoneros,* street vendors. Spaniards, however, stayed in Havana and other towns. Some, of course, took up farming as did Fidel Castro's father, for example. From Galicia they came in large numbers without much more than a fierce determination to "make it." The *gallego* in Cuba was stereotyped to be an uncouth, money-grubbing, small merchant and rentier. In the same occupations, the immigrant from Asturias never suffered from the same adverse image. Together they became the backbone of Cuba's *petite bourgeoisie,* soon dominating much of the urban retail trade. From these Spanish groups sprang institutions which dominated middle class life in urban Cuba before 1930. Not that native Cubans participated fully in the Spanish immigrant society; in fact, it was the exclusivist policies of the social associations (*casinos* or *centros*) of each Spanish regional group (viz.

the Centro Gallego, the Centro Asturiano) which created much hostility among the less organized Cuban middle class. Each center had a comprehensive cradle-to-grave program which had no parallel in *criollo* society. Cuban professionals on the other hand became very dependent on the fees (medical, legal, etc.) derived from these well-financed associations. They derived no other benefits.

With sugar production and marketing largely in American hands, urban commerce in Spanish, and small scale retailing such as street vendors, laundries, and so on in Chinese hands, urban Cubans had only one sector they dominated. This was government. And even here it should be recognized that between the provisions of the Platt Amendment and the realities of a dependent economic system the autonomy of even the political sector was questionable. It was around the battles for political office and the many *botellas* (sinecures) which it gave that the real energies of urban Cuba were expended.

The Cuban's response to the social structure which had solidified by the 1920s was a complex one. In part his alienation was reflected in his own brand of cynical, ridiculing humor Cubans call *hoteo* or *bachata,* which, among other things, included a tolerance of imperfection, even dishonesty, in others. The numbers of Cubanisms expressing admiration for the sharpie, the astute operator, are multifold. In part, it was reflected in an abandoned gaiety which made Havana such an attraction to foreigners and Cuban alike. *"Que el relajo sea con orden"* (dissoluteness, but with order) was a popular Cuban saying stressing the accepted permissiveness of urban society. It was the picaresque society of the Spanish *zarzuela* taken to heart. But it was also reflected in a nearly suicidal political style, an all-or-nothing quality in moments of final despair. It was here that the thin line between the heroic and the paranoid in Cuban political behavior was drawn.

In 1933, the long struggle against dictator Gerardo Machado exploded into a nationwide social movement. The Cuban middle class and workers began a determined effort to regain control of their nation. The world depression had aggravated the serious setbacks the Cuban economy had been suffering since 1927, and middle class professionals were as seriously affected as were sugar workers. Presently, Machado was overthrown. A mestizo ex-cane cutter from Oriente Province and then sergeant in the army, called Fulgencio Batista, carried out a *coup d'état* and a reformist-nationalist junta was seated. In the rural areas, workers began occupying the sugar mills with more than one "soviet" being set up. The American embassy kept calling for the Marines. The United States, of course, did not need the Marines to bring down the government in a dependent society, as was Cuba.

The movement failed in many of its goals, but many of its reforms had great repercussions in subsequent Cuban history. The 8-hour work day and other pro-labor legislation helped build the labor union movement which became a very important part of Cuban society. But it was the so-called 50 percent law, the Nationalization of Labor Law, which pointedly reflected the temper of the movement. Stipulating that half of all employees of any concern had to be native Cubans, the law also provided for the deportation of unemployed foreigners. Obviously the targets of this law were the Spanish merchants and Haitian field hands, although clearly all foreigners, including North Americans, were on the reformers' minds. Being in irreplaceable technical areas, however, the North Americans suffered much less under this law than the other groups.

The antagonism against Haitian labor, while in some way related to the traditional Cuban fear of "Africanization," was quite distinct from the Cuban "Negro question." With Negroes taking the vanguard of many of the most radical labor movements in 1933 and 1934, this question came to the fore again.

As early as 1907, Cuban Negroes had formed an Independent Party of Color, partly in protest against widespread social discrimination, and partly because they had received few of the political rewards in governmental appointments and otherwise following independence. The law passed in 1910 banning political parties organized along racial lines was to no avail. In 1912 a major racial war broke out, an unequal war since some 3,000 Negroes were killed. Race relations came in for some close scrutiny by Cubans following the racial violence in the town of Trinidad in Camagüey Province in 1934. The custom in many towns was for Negroes and mulattoes to stick to "their" side in public parks. With an atmosphere of change influencing their activities, a group of Negroes decided to "sit in" on the white side of the Trinidad Central Park and at least one Negro died when they were violently repelled. The investigation carried out by the *Comite por los Derechos del Negro*—its existence alone an indication of the presence of a problem—concluded for the Negro in Cuba,

> . . . there are industries where they cannot work; in commerce, in the great foreign enterprises, above all, Negroes are not employed. In certain industries they work where the pay is least: for example, in the graphic arts they may be compositors, but seldom linotypists; in the tobacco industry they are cigarmakers and shippers, but not sorters or trimmers who are the employees that earn the best wages.

It was not surprising, therefore, that there should have existed separatist organizations such as the *Organización Celular Asteria* which preached black pride and demanded that Negroes, Cuban Negroes, that is, be given 50 percent of certain public jobs. When the Cuban intellectual, Juan Marinello, stated in 1930 that "The Negro, a universal theme and motive, on the other hand, has in Cuba a specific significance," he was expressing more than just a political

line from the Communist party to which he belonged and which had
shown great concern over the Negro question. He was expressing the
sentiments of a large group of Cuban thinkers who had begun to
discover the African part of Cuban culture. No one did more to stimulate this trend than the ethnologist, Fernando Ortíz. Beginning in
1906 with *Los Negros Brujos,* Ortíz led others to the rich African
legacy which was Cuban. "In 1928," he later noted, "the drums begin
to beat in Cuban poetry." He might have added prose as well, for, in
1933, Alejo Carpentier published his *Ecué-Yamba-O* and Nicolás
Guillén, the poet, began to write in a vein which was soon identified
as a full-fledged school called Afro-Cuban. In 1937 Guillén's *Revista
de Estudios Afro-Cubanos* made its appearance. Negro musicians such
as Brindis de Salas, José White, and José M. Jiménez, were finally
being recognized for the music which made Cuba famous throughout
Latin America, and Negro poets from the past such as Plácido came
back into style.

Across the Caribbean, the Puerto Rican Luis Palés Matos had already been writing about the Negro and the decadence of the white
world. In Haiti a whole generation of intellectuals were writing about
Africa. In fact, as Gabriel Coulthard notes, in the 1930s the theme of
Africa had become one of the most pervasive themes of Caribbean
poets. The Cubans and Puerto Ricans, however, did not concern themselves with Africa, but with the Negro, the Cuban Negro. This has
remained a characteristic of the Afro-Cuban school.

While specific reforms succeeded, the Cuban revolutionary movement of 1933, as a whole, did not. The malaise which had surfaced
returned to its previous condition forming an undercurrent of some
hope, but mostly disenchantment and despair. Only now it was nurtured by the multiple fonts of radical intellectual thought which
emerged during the struggles and had made the University of Havana
their home base.

It is important to keep this ideological undercurrent in mind because
it played a major role in defining the nature of Cuban society as it
developed after 1934. It defined, but, alas, did not guide society. Other
forces were shaping Cuba between 1934 and 1959.

Perhaps the most important was the growth of urban Cuba, especially Havana, but also the small towns scattered throughout the
island. Those Cubans who joined the labor unions were relatively
well protected; those who could not were worse off than before since,
in the town/city environs, no food could be grown for the family's
needs. A few months' work in seasonal sugar or coffee cultivation was
followed by a bare existence. Unemployment became a structural part
of the economy. In the relatively prosperous war year 1943, out of a
working force of 1,521,000, a total of 665,000 enjoyed full employment only during the *zafra*, while a full 20 percent or 321,000

were permanently unemployed. Rural labor logically constituted the largest number of unemployed, seasonal and structural.

It was rural Cuba which truly began to show the consequences of the kind of economic development which had taken place since the early twentieth century. The patterns of social stratification had solidified and that pattern explains much about the rest of Cuban society.

The major criteria of social class position were type of land tenure, size of land holding, color and style or level of living. The 1946 census is worth citing in this regard:

| Size in Hectares | % of Total Farms |
| --- | --- |
| 0.4–4.9 | 20.1 |
| 5.0–24.9 | 39.4 |
| 25.0–99.9 | 22.0 |
| 100.0–499.99 | 6.5 |
| 500.00–999.99 | 0.9 |
| 1,000 and over | 0.5 |

In 1959, the 28 largest sugar estates owned over 1,400,000 hectares and rented an additional 617,000, thus controlling one fifth of the island's total surface. Cattle holdings showed a similar pattern, and in the 1950s a spectacular growth in rice production was similarly concentrating lands in fewer and fewer hands. In 1958, 5 percent of producers controlled 75 percent of the rice land.

This unequal distribution of land logically affected the land tenure system. In 1945 only 30.5 percent of the total farms were independently owned, 62.5 percent of the rest were divided between renters (28.8 percent), subrenters (4.4 percent), share croppers (20.7 percent) and squatters (8.6 percent). Both size and tenure indicate a highly stratified system with extremes of size and land-man relationships at either end of the scale. Race tended to correlate with farm size and the type of tenure. It should be pointed out, however, that on a nationwide basis and at some levels, the Negro and colored population did not fare very much worse than the white population as indicated by the 1943 census:

| Monthly Income In Pesos | Total Population | White | Colored |
| --- | --- | --- | --- |
| Under 30 | 39.6 | 37.4 | 46.6 |
| 30–59 | 42.5 | 42.8 | 41.4 |
| 60–99 | 12.4 | 13.4 | 9.4 |
| 100–199 | 14.0 | 4.7 | 1.7 |
| 200–299 | 0.8 | 0.9 | 0.4 |
| 300 or more | 0.7 | 0.8 | 0.5 |

Within the general picture of poverty which the figures reflect, it was at the under 30 pesos a month level that the colored sector was considerably more disadvantaged than the white sector. It was at that level that the rural Negro sector was most numerously represented. Some 25 percent of the total population and working force was colored, yet a 1946 survey of 734 farmers demonstrated the following racial breakdown by land tenure type:

|                 | Percentage |          |        |
| --------------- | ---------- | -------- | ------ |
| Tenure Type     | White      | Mulatto  | Negro  |
| Owner           | 25.9       | 27.7     | 6.7    |
| Cash Renter     | 31.0       | 19.1     | 8.9    |
| Share Renter    | 20.9       | 38.3     | 33.3   |
| Wage Worker     | 22.2       | 14.9     | 51.1   |

It is not too difficult to see that the above statistics indicate a clear class division between large, private farms, those who rented, and those who were simple laborers. The agricultural labor sector, some 41 percent of the total, was composed predominantly of laborers, only 27 percent being owners. Blacks were concentrated at the bottom of the structure.

The other criterion of social class position was level of living. This was perhaps the fundamental aspect of pre-revolutionary Cuba. It was here that the grievous differences between urban and rural Cuba were really reflected, and in rural Cuba between the middle and upper classes and lower classes. The *Censo de Población, Viviendas y Electoral, 1953*, showed that three quarters of the rural dwellings were still of the palm built *bohio* type, two thirds with earthen floors, nine tenths with no electricity or running water. In 1958 the *Agrupación Católica Universitaria* published the results of a survey conducted in 1956. The results were terrifying, but hardly surprising to knowledgeable Cubans. Of the one thousand peasant families interviewed in their survey the annual per capita income was $91.25. As is always the case in poverty-ridden populations, 70 percent of that income went for food. But even spending that much, only 11 percent of the families included milk in their diets, 4 percent meat and 2 percent eggs.

Health conditions logically reflected the general poor living and food conditions: 36 percent of the sample had some form of intestinal parasite; 31 percent were paludism cases; 14 percent suffered from tuberculosis; 13 percent had typhus. Nearly 50 percent were illiterate, fully 44 percent had never attended school at all.

How people perceive their problems and the solutions to those problems is an important indicator of the dynamics of society and is fundamental to our understanding of that society. In contrast to the non-Hispanic Caribbean, social problems in Cuba after 1934 were hardly ever stated in racial terms. The figures of the last survey cited revealed that 74 percent of the sample believed that the best way to improve conditions was through employment opportunities and 69 percent thought that the institution most responsible for bringing about that goal was the government. It might be relevant to note here that it was in this sector of Cuba, mostly located in Oriente and Camagüey provinces, that the Cuban rebels who landed in 1956 spent one and a half years.

It is a fact that Cuban governments had been traditionally unresponsive to rural Cuban needs and barely aware that rural poverty was spilling over into urban Cuba. There the unemployed and unprotected by unions formed what Karl Marx called the *lumpenproletariat:* those who exist on the periphery of the working class, eking out a living through prostitution, petty thievery and anything else that came along. Oscar Lewis, in *La Vida,* has described such a sector in Puerto Rico known as La Perla. Similar studies could be done for the Dominican Republic's Las Cañitas, Trinidad's Laventille, or Jamaica's West Kingston. This was, to be sure, quite a different world than that of the traditional lower class sectors of urban Cuba. It was a new disease which only seemed to spread, regardless of the price of sugar.

It was against this Cuba that Eduardo Chibás launched his moral regeneration campaign which by the late 1940's had gathered a massive following. The corruption and moral decadence which exemplified urban Cuba fed by a lopsided rural economy and development were Chibás' main targets; Martí's thought, his ideological font. His Sunday radio programs became something of an institution. Cubans were listening even though they did not know what to do about it. Chibás' suicide in 1951 was an extreme expression of the Cuban reformist style, but his legacy was a group of young reformers upon whom he had had a deep and lasting influence. Fidel Castro was an early and prominent member of that group.

*"Trabajar para el inglés"* (to work for the Englishman) was a lower class saying which meant working for an objective only to have someone else reap the benefits. Cubans before 1959 were giving this saying some serious thought.

## Haiti—Dominican Republic

It is fundamentally necessary to understand that while Cuba was developing the foundation of a prosperous sugar economy based on a system of African slavery which was not abolished by law until the 1880's, its immediate neighbor, Haiti, was developing a totally different type of society. There slavery had been legally abolished by the French Assembly in 1794 and in reality by the black armies of ex-slaves. The physical aspects of the plantation economy with its intricate land divisions, mills, irrigation systems and docks, were literally burned to the ground in the struggles against Napoleon's massive invasion army and later the English forces. What remained is what Haiti has today: a subsistence economy in which the vast majority of the Negro masses, *noirs,* eke out a living, a small commercial class dominated by outsiders (mostly Lebanese and Syrian) and a professional elite still largely mulatto, *gens de couleur* in composition.

The dichotomy between the French oriented *gens de couleur* and the *noirs* has been the motor of Haitian politics and society in general —and a wasting and destructive concern it has been. Alternating in power, each sector has built its own mythology of heroes and written its own interpretation of the island's history. Haitian history, in a sense, stopped in 1805. After that anything else seems to be a matter of opinion. François Duvalier has built his own interpretation of Haiti's past. His claim is that his "Black Revolution" is in the tradition of Negro Presidents Dessalines in the 19th century and Estimé in the twentieth century. But the difference between the two sectors is much more one of class than it is cultural. The French orientation of the mulatto class is today little different from that of the *noir* who has had an education, a trip to France and the wherewithall to keep a standard of living that is urbane and elegant. This last quality is a prized trait of the Haitian who savours entertaining his relatives and acquaintances, and does this as naturally as any of life's necessities. In the arts and *belles lettres,* a rediscovery of Haiti's African past, largely through the works of Dantes Bellegarde and Jean Price-Mars, was something shared by all sectors, at least since the early 1940s, and some say as early as the American occupation of the 1920s.

Despite its small literate population, Haiti has produced more schools of indigenous poetry, painting and ethnology than islands with much more developed and numerous literate populations such as Trinidad, Jamaica, let alone Barbados.

But richness of culture and depth of identity with that culture and with the nation are not enough. No Haitian worries with questions such as "What is a Haitian?" He well knows the answer which comes loud and clear both internally, where he endures the most depressed economic conditions in Latin America if not the world, and externally where he has been a virtual pariah to be exploited and then discarded.

The deportation of over eight thousand Haitians from Cuba in 1934 and the massacre of several thousand settlers on the Dominican boundary in 1937 are but two cases of the general contempt in which this nation has been held by its neighbors, in the Caribbean and in Latin America. Recent concerns over the island's fate are recognized by Haitians for what they are: self-centered fears over cold war issues which have a minimal relevance to the Haitian. Land erosion, illiteracy, malnutrition, a booming population growth, and the black man in a white-dominated world—these are the concerns of the Haitian. And, in that respect the majority seem to agree that Papa Doc Duvalier has been, if no better, certainly no worse, than past governments.

Much of the nineteenth century history of Haiti's immediate neighbor, according to more than one Dominican scholar, was shaped by that society's fear of the Haitian "menace." Considering the actions of the Haitians, who invaded and held the Dominican Republic from 1822 until 1844, one can easily understand this fear. Be that as it may, the Dominican Republic differed from both Cuba and Haiti in its socioeconomic development. Cattle ranching was the main support of Dominican economy. Since it was not a labor intensive enterprise, Dominicans had little need for massive slavery. The lower class formed the other sector. Sugar, then, did not play, as it did not play in independent Haiti, a major part in the shaping of the social structure and the quality of interpersonal social relationships.

When sugar did enter as a major part of the economy it was with North American capital (by the 1920s 80 percent of the total) and heavy supplements of Haitian labor. This was late in the nineteenth century and other changes were also at work. The Dominican class structure had already crystallized, the shaping forces being the traditional agrarian upper class and its new rival for power, the urban commercial and import-export sector. The traditional group had its main lease on the second city, Santiago de los Caballeros, which remains to this day a traditional city. The capital city, Santo Domingo, was the one which experienced the real competition between the two sectors when it became the center of political and commercial activity of the new group.

It was during the three-decade reign of Rafael Leonidas Trujillo (1929–1961) that the Dominican society began to be reshaped for the second time. A man of relatively humble and racially mixed heritage, Trujillo harbored a deeprooted hatred for the upper class which had ostracized him socially. Even as commander of the army he had found it impossible to gain membership in one of the capital's exclusive clubs. Trujillo eventually dealt this class, especially the landholding aristocracy whose lands he coveted, severe political, economic, and social setbacks. A new group, rising through the ranks of the military and public sector in general, gained a strong foothold during this period. Trujillo's achievements in acquiring American-owned banks, public utilities and sugar mills are not to be understated. The context of post-1961 Dominican politics was formed by this nationalization, or personalization, of the economy.

Society in post-Trujillo Dominican Republic is characterized by a struggle between more than just political groups; it is the struggle of the old aristocracy to regain its expropriated lands, the new groups to hold on to their positions, and a reformist faction which desires to restructure the whole picture. And this picture is not a reassuring one for the lower classes. In a large sample taken from the slum areas of the capital city, where a full 50 percent of the urban lower classes live, the Belgian sociologist André Corten and his wife found the average expenditure on food per day to be 20 *centavos* per person, and that this represented 70 percent of their total income. Using a series of explicit objective measures they discovered that 50 percent of their sample lived in "bad" conditions, 25 percent in "infrahuman" conditions, and the rest in "decent" conditions. One wonders what a rural sample would indicate since these are largely migrants streaming into the city to seek better opportunities and conditions.

Even though race, or at least color, plays something of a role in the stratification system, it is certainly not an overriding issue. The upper class tends to be white, the middle, white and mestizo, and well over 90 percent of the nation's Negroes (12 percent of the total population) are in the lower class. All classes, however, have members of all races. The issues are economic and political and have to do with the distribution of the national patrimony, now largely in state hands being used for the benefit of the government's allies.

No one can read the many books by ex-President Juan Bosch with their tortured soul-searching and the great ambiguities and fears about his social status, even while President, without being made aware of the problem of the democratic reformer. To read ex-Ambassador John Bartlow Martin's *Overtaken By Events* is to confirm the extent and scope of these difficulties: Bosch, socially insecure and in self-imposed isolation from social and university circles, was invited to meet the nation's upper class for the first time. The dinner was arranged by Ambassador Martin. Bosch's predicament, social and political, was not enviable. His dependence on Martin was tragic. The broader dependence is further reflected in the plural "we" used by Martin to describe Dominican events: "If we had survived that night [of the coup which overthrew Bosch in 1963], we might have survived another, and another, and somehow muddled through."

Dominicans have historically rejected any notion of belonging to an "African" Caribbean; more than any Caribbean society, their politics and society have been cast in Latin American terms. But the nation's structural problem, as distinct from its cultural orientation, is clearly that of the dependent small nation. At this level it is Caribbean.

## Where Race Defines Function

To shift from the works of ex-President Bosch to those of Trinidad's Prime Minister Eric Williams is revealing. On the surface their concerns seem totally different, but there is a deeper level on which

the similarities are striking. Both are concerned with describing the historical evolution of their nation's societies, both tend to see that evolution in deeply personal terms. Both strike out at colonial social structures and foreign intervention. Their bitterness and resentment, their frustrations assault the reader from virtually every page. To Bosch it was because he was not born in what he calls *"los de primera,"* the cream of the upper class; to Williams it was the fact that he was colored in a racialist colonial society. If Bosch expresses the frustrations of the reformer in the Hispanic Caribbean, Williams expresses those of the early black nationalist in the British West Indies and Trinidad in particular.

Although surely similarities could be found with writings of any Third World statesman, geography and geopolitics have placed the Dominican Republic and Trinidad in the same sea, in the same sphere of influence and geared more and more towards the same markets and sources of capital. Social movements in both nations have tried, and thus far failed, to change all this, except of course that which man cannot change, geography. The historical development of Trinidad has been quite different from that of any of the nations so far described although there are strong parallels to the Cuban case.

No one has described society in the British Caribbean in general and Trinidad in particular with such accuracy as the Trinidadian, V. S. Naipaul. His short tale "The Baker's Story" is worth citing at length because it lays bare the island's social structure and the kind of thinking that structure has produced. It goes a long way in explaining Williams' frustrations on the one hand and the reasoning of those who advocate a complete change in social structure. The story deals with a Grenadian Negro who wants to go into business in Trinidad.

> You know, it never cross my mind in those days that I could open a shop of my own. Is how it is with black people. They get so use to working for other people that they get to believe that because they black they can't do nothing else but work for other people.
> . . . I start praying and God tell me to go out and open a shop for myself. . . . I baking better bread than the people of Arouca ever see, and I can't get one single feller to come in like man through my rickerty old front door and buy a penny hops bread. You hear all this talk about quality being its own advertisement? Don't believe it, boy. Is quality plus something else. I begin to wonder what the hell it could be.

And so the protagonist, faced with economic crisis, set out to do some sociological work to uncover "what the hell" that something else could be. One day by the Savannah (park) he noticed a black man selling coconuts. "And you wouldn't know how funny this was, unless you know that every coconut seller in the island is Indian." Keen observer that he was, our Grenadian couldn't help noticing that the black coconut seller was, "forgetting looks, just like a Indian." Talking Hindustani, "putting away curry," and in general little different from the rest of the coconut vendors except, as stated, for his looks. To the Grenadian that sight had meaning, but its real importance had not yet dawned on him. It was not until his abusive black Trinidadian friend (Trinidadians are not particularly fond of Grenadians) asked him to suggest a place for lunch that light fell on the subject.

> So I tell Percy we could go off to a parlour or a bar. But he say "No, no. When I treat my friends, I don't like black people meddling with my food." And was only then that the thing hit me. . . . Then the thing hit me, man . . . And then I see that though Trinidad have every race and every colour, every race have to do special things.

And so our enterprising Grenadian decided to become a "Black Chinee" as a means of succeeding in the bakery business.

> I never show my face in the front of the shop again. . . .

> Was hard in the beginning to get real Chinese people to work for a black man. But money have it own way of talking, and when today you pass any of the Yung Man establishments all you see behind the counter is Chinee. Some of them ain't even know they working for a black man.

How and why did Trinidad develop so uniquely in one sense, yet confront today the same crisis conditions shared by the area?

Because of its peculiar economic, social and cultural configuration, Trinidad became the first "experimental" Crown Colony in the West Indies, consistently given less local autonomy than any other West Indian island. After a hectic and anti-British nineteenth century the island produced one of the first truly West Indian radical nationalists, Captain Arthur Cipriani, then went on to be the scene of the most violent labor movement of the 1937–1938 West Indian "Riots." The progressive black nationalist politics of the pre- and post-independence period is today being challenged by what is perhaps the most articulate and organized Black Power movement in the Caribbean. In the realm of culture Trinidad has the most varied folklore of the non-Hispanic Caribbean. The songs (calypso) and dance (jump-up, limbo, shango, bel-air) identified as "West Indian" are originally Trinidadian and its national musical instrument, the steel pan, has no equal in ingenuity, and some would say in beauty of sound, in the area. Before the steel band there was bamboo-tamboo and before that the *cuatro*, string bands with their *parang* serenaders. Trinidad's pre-Lenten carnival finds competition only in Rio de Janeiro's in terms of costumes, size and just complete popular expressions of joy.

Trinidad's satiric humor (*picong*) is remarkably similar to the Cuban's *choteo*. Creole culture, as M. G. Smith calls it, has found its most complete and rich expression in Trinidad. Nowhere in the Caribbean are middle class parlors as alive with apprehension and foreboding as in Trinidad, and in few places with more reason. Yet the

*mamgai* (ridiculing) atmosphere still accompanies discussions in most sectors. This state of affairs is directly related to the history of the island and the type of society which developed. In a sense the social climate seems similar to that of Cuba in the 1950s, though clearly in 1970 Trinidad could not by any stretch of the imagination be called a dictatorship.

The other sugar islands of the British Caribbean had long reached and passed their peak as sugar producers when Trinidad was wrested from the Spaniards and became an English colony in 1797. Intensive cultivation was still in the future for these relatively unpopulated two thousand square miles of fertile land. But if the sugar economy was not fully developed, such was not the case with other aspects of the society. Trinidad was in fact a fully developed "Latin" or Mediterranean society by 1797. The elements that formed this society were two: Spanish government and laws, Spanish and French planters white and colored, and French-speaking slaves.

The French had arrived in considerable numbers in the 1880s from the neighboring islands, especially Grenada and Martinique; their numbers were boosted by exiles from St. Domingue in the 1790s, arriving with their slaves under a special *cédula* or law emitted by the Bourbon King of Spain in 1783. Free colored families were given exactly half that given their white counterparts, but even this discriminatory provision was a handsome concession at the time. They came in even larger numbers than did the whites. The French of both races joined the Spanish in becoming small sugar, cocoa, coffee and cotton farmers. An occasional Corsican, Catholic Irishman or Englishman joined in at the trading end in the new port of Port-of-Spain which soon became the real seat of government in lieu of the old one, San José de Oruña. The second largest city, San Fernando, became the center of a lively society of the free colored, mostly French-speaking, and, of course, also slave-owning.

Roman Catholicism, with all its concomitant cultural practices (including a lively pre-Lenten carnival), was the common religion and Spanish code law governed master and slave alike. Miscegenation was widespread as was the practice of *coartación,* or allowing a slave to buy his freedom on installments. In a sense these two practices, miscegenation and *coartación,* were related since it was most often the progeny of a master-slave union that was given the opportunity to free her- or himself. Older slaves whose hardworking days were numbered also were often permitted to avail themselves of this custom. Initial settlement and Spanish practices, thus, had augmented the colored middle sector of society, a sector which, because of the abundant fertile land available, was able to acquire the economic means of educating their children in the professions. Because of racial prejudice, however, this colored sector formed very much of a subgroup with their own particular claims on and aspirations for the society.

By the time the English conquerors arrived in Trinidad, the island had a fairly self-conscious Spanish-French cultural identity. The following figures on the island's population in 1803 give an idea of the heterogenous racial and cultural population:

|         | Whites | Free Colored | Slaves |
|---------|--------|--------------|--------|
| English | 663    | 599          |        |
| Spanish | 505    | 1,751        | 20,464 |
| French  | 1,093  | 2,925        |        |
| Total   | 2,261  | 5,275        | 20,464 |

Grand Total        28,000

It is important to add that most of the slaves were French-speaking; the island's colorful dialect, *patois,* hardly spoken anymore, was a product of the cultural mix. This population was fairly spread out because of the diversified, though relatively undeveloped, economic structure. The following scheme gives an idea of the diversity of crops and settlement:

| Crop | Region | Ethnic Group |
|------|--------|--------------|
| Larger Sugar Estates | Port of Spain area and South | French Spanish |
| Cocoa and Coffee | Central Trinidad and Southwest | French, White & Colored Spanish Free Blacks |
| Cotton | South and Southwest | French |
| Commerce | Port of Spain | Irish Spanish English Corsican French |

The "British" Party, as the new conquerors were labelled, had their own ideas for the island and little trust or sympathy for the Spanish-French "old colonists," much less the colored sector. The social history of English Trinidad up to 1850 is the history of the struggle between the Roman Catholic Spanish-French sector and the Anglican English establishment. The former's resistance to any attempts at Anglicizing the island was a critical aspect. In analyzing the "conflict" between these two sectors it is important to understand several things:

1) The lenient "Articles of Capitulation" of the English guaranteed the property of the conquered, their religion, teaching in their language, and, in general, their existence as a community. Spanish law and the *cabildo* (town meeting) were not replaced until the 1840's. The open door policy on immigration was continued.

2) All three major sectors, the Spanish-French, English, and Free Colored
had a vested interest in continuing the existing economic structure,
specifically slave labor.

3) The Free Colored supported the white French-Spanish sector in their
battle with the English only in so far as the questions concerned
common interests such as religion and education. In general they
formed a separate group discriminated against by white society.

By mid-century several economic changes had wrought important
shifts in the island's social structure and dynamics. First, large inflows
of English capital began to modernize and increase the island's sugar
production and the large sugar estates started to edge out the small
scale producer. The smaller farmers, mostly old colonists and colored,
moved into the hills and interior areas where they added their numbers to those already in cocoa and coffee cultivation. This trend was
accelerated by the crisis in credit capital of 1847–1848 which affected
the whole economy but which bankrupted many small planters with
no ties to the metropolitan money markets. The sharp division between the cocoa-coffee sector and the sugar sector was also accentuated
by emancipation and its aftermath. The freed blacks left the plantations and occupied crown lands which in Trinidad, as distinct from
Barbados, for instance, were plentiful. They also found seasonal work
on the easy-going and patriarchically run cocoa plantations. The sugar
industry on the other hand, bereft of its labor, sought a solution in a
plan of indentured labor. The Cuban pattern comes to mind.

Chinese, Portuguese, and even some Northern Europeans were imported. None of these experiments worked as designed, but they had
unexpected effects on the society. A solution was finally found in the
indenture of British Indians. The importation of the East Indians, as
they are called in the West Indies, soon reached massive proportions.
It is not without reason that the East Indians' traditional claim to
having saved the sugar industry on the island, reaping so few of the
benefits, has made an impression on young Indians today.

East Indian immigration, which was not terminated until the end
of World War One, added several new dimensions to the island's
society. It added a non-Christian element to a Catholic-Protestant
population; it added a new "racial" element (anthropologically, of
course, Indians are Caucasian), and it added new fuel to the large
planter (mostly sugar)–small farmer (mostly cocoa) conflict. By 1871
the Indians composed 25.1 percent of the island's total population of
109,638, and were beyond question the backbone of the sugar industry
which by that time was nearly totally English owned. In order to shift
the financing of the immigrants from the English treasury to the
island's, a special stamp tax on every planter and an excise tax on rum
were imposed much to the non-sugar sector's chagrin.

Creole society perceived no economic gain from the immigration system. It had no identification with the Hindu and Muslim Indians and resented being taxed to support the "expatriate" sugar planters. The freed blacks saw in the Indians an attempt to perpetuate the system of slavery. This was but an early case of conflict between the mass of Trinidadians and a governmental economic policy in which they felt no participation. The Indian was discriminated against by all sectors of Creole society; this, in addition to the Indian's own separatist feelings, made his integration into Creole society virtually impossible.

By the end of the nineteenth century, therefore, the basic structure of Trinidadian society of the twentieth century had been set. The white sector was divided into English sugar planters and the officials of British colonial government on the one hand, and the "old colonist" sector which came to be known as French Creole (the term "Creole" indicated their links with general Creole culture) on the other. The colored sector formed a distinct middle class also of Creole culture. The black population formed the largely urban lower class with the Indians remaining as rural workers. The small groups of Portuguese and Chinese found their niches as rumshop and general store owners, the latter being more disposed to moving out of the capital city and into plantation areas.

Each group had a strong cultural identity and often was internally split by religious differences. The Indians at first divided themselves along caste lines. Whether shipped from Calcutta or from Madras, there was a wide mixture of castes in all groups. The English historian, Donald Wood, reveals that of the 21,288 immigrants registered in Calcutta for Trinidad for the years 1876–1885, 17,741 were Hindus, 3,535 were Muslims and 12 were Christians. The Hindus in turn were divided into Brahmins and other high castes, 18 percent; agricultural castes, 32 percent; artisan castes, 8.5 percent and 41.5 percent recorded as low caste. Later the Hindu-Muslim differences became more important, further emphasized by the urban residence of the Muslims as compared to the rural Hindus. The Portuguese were sharply divided between the Catholics and the Presbyterian followers of a Scottish missionary, Dr. Robert Reid Kalley. A victim of religious persecution in Madeira, he and his followers chose the island because of its religious freedom. Some 725 Catholics and 573 Kalleyites settled in Trinidad.

The upshot of this mass of varied immigrants was a teeming society in which the various groups jealously protected what was considered their patrimony and, of course, their rights. The history of the island's journalism clearly reveals the heterogeneity of opinions and viewpoints. At times in the nineteenth century the island had no less than ten different weekly and daily newspapers publishing simultaneously. English, Spanish and French were the most common languages. Edgar Mittleholzer's novel *A Morning at the Office* reconstructs a scene in a typical Port-of-Spain office in the twentieth century in which Englishman, French Creole, East Indian, colored, and Negro —each in traditional assigned roles—get through a morning of work and social interaction.

British colonial policies never managed to stifle dissent and opposition in Trinidad, never managed to suppress the Creoles' irreverent humor and wit, never could convert them into colonial Englishmen. The existence of a multiracial, strong cocoa economy, which, by the end of the nineteenth century briefly outstripped sugar as the island's main export, provided the means of maintaining Creole culture alive and vigorous. However, this sector could never truly affect policy in the Crown Colony. Despite the fact that by the 1920s cocoa had been virtually destroyed by disease, West African competition and financial troubles, the counterpoint between that white and colored Creole sector and the English sugar economy had left its legacy, cultural and political. Culturally the main aspects of Mediterranean-African traditions—music, dance, humor, and, outstandingly, carnival—were kept. This was Creole culture. Politically, a tradition of outspoken opposition politics which had reflected itself in the Water Riots of 1903 and the movement led by the son of a bankrupt cocoa planter, Arthur Cipriani, of the 1920s, was never squashed.

There was one thing, therefore, which stood as a formidable barrier to the final unity of Creole society—race consciousness. Faced with the concern over racial purity of both the Spanish and English colonial masters the French Creole found it best to assert his already pronounced pride in an unmixed racial heritage (which as time passed became more of a myth than a biological reality).

Economic circumstances, however, had forced the French Creoles into different roles. The catastrophe of the cocoa industry which began in 1902 and finished off the survivors in the 1920s, meant the end of their unity as an important group. An aristocracy of skin color and names without an economic base usually has a short reign. Lacking education and special skills outside that of cocoa planting, they were at the mercy of the true possessors of power in the society, the English entrepreneurs. Their "union card" was their white skin which they traded at the expense of their tenuous alliance with the colored Creole sector. Their traditional opposition was also undermined by a wave of British Commonwealth "nationalism" engendered by World War One. When large groups of French Creoles rushed to join the British Army, while their colored and Negro countrymen were being denied participation in what was still a white gentleman's "duty," the end of the alliance had been reached. The intellectual sterility of the commission agent world to which they returned following World War One further marginated them from the trends of Creole society. The colored sector responded to official and private discrimination by asserting its own superiority.

Outside Creole society the racial divisions were accentuated by stark cultural-religious differences. Indians, called "coolies" by Creole society, looked askance at association with blacks, and the "Portugee" (a separate "race" to most Trinidadians even today) and "Chinee" kept to themselves. Because race mixing continued, the offspring of mixed parentage took on the attributes of neither race but formed separate groups. Thus "Doogla" (or "bastard" to the Hindu) usually refers to a Negro-Indian mixture, Chinee-Creole to a Chinese-Negro mixture. The 1960 census reported the following racial distribution: Negro, 358,588; white, 15,718; East Indian, 301,946; Chinese, 8,361; Mixed, 134,749; Lebanese-Syrian, 1,590; other, 6,714; not stated, 291. Roman Catholics, Hindus, Anglicans, and Muslims are the four major religious groups in that order.

The social clubs of Trinidad clearly reflect this racial division. When recently the government ordered an official enquiry into racial discrimination at the country club, and then extended the enquiry to all social clubs, it was discovered that the white country club was one of the few which did not have a racial clause in its admissions laws. It did not need to. Racial lines reflected the economic ordering of the society historically. Social clubs were means of confronting the system, with all its challenges and potential rewards, as a group or race.

Open conflict had long been avoided in the island because of the ready availability of land and, later, the discovery of oil and the establishment of a refinery. While the East Indian had largely remained rural and on the sugar estates, black labor moved toward the oil complex in southern Trinidad, and formed also the Civil Service sector of the urban centers, including minor Civil Service and police. Competition for jobs, thus, had been reduced by the demographic distribution of the labor force. But this division of economic functions further accentuated the racial-cultural divisions, a fact easily exploited by the first cycle of political leaders of independent Trinidad. The two-party system of the 1956–1970 period was a purely black-Indian dichotomy with the French Creole sector siding with the Indian party.

In this respect Trinidad follows a different pattern from that of Guyana, which has a similar racial composition. In Guyana the white sector has been English and Portuguese. Nearly ten times as many Portuguese went to Guyana than to Trinidad; today they are the backbone of the urban commercial sector. The Portuguese have formed their own party which is not a racial party (The United Force) but a conservative one, stressing laissez-faire economics and Christian morality. The East Indian sector of Guyana is, paradoxically, both property-owning (most rural lands) and supportive of Cheddi Jagan's Marxist party, the People's Progressive Party. On the other hand, the Negro sector, which is largely urban and propertyless as in Trinidad, supports the more moderate People's National Congress. The emergence of these groups as participants in the system is relatively new in Guyana. Up to World War Two that nation had had none of the history of anti-establishment agitation Trinidad had experienced. Its Creole culture does not compare to the dynamism, expression and exuberance of Trinidad's. Guyana's history has been the story of an uninterrupted sugar economy, its multiple racial groups having to adjust to that reality.

While Trinidad's unique historical development accounts for its special cultural configuration, economic realities at work in the whole Caribbean area have been at work in Trinidad as well. A society built around a traditional order, no matter how colorful that order might be, is more often than not incapable of confronting new economic realities without an accompanying crisis. Because each racial group was assumed to have its own "fixed" niche in the social structure, little was done to modify that social structure in any radical way. To be sure, independence brought the black and colored middle class to political power. It did not, however, affect the fate of the lower classes, black or Indian. A good index of that fact is the structure of education of the island:

### (1965–1966 Figures)

| | |
|---|---:|
| Total Population in 5–18 age group | 355,260 |
| Total in school in all grades | 219,679 |
| Total who finish 5 years of primary | 31,000 |
| Total who finish 7 years of primary | 11,000 |
| Total who finish high school | 669 |

These figures are interesting in light of the fact that government spending on education has risen from BWI $10.5 million in 1956 to BWI $45.2 million in the 1970 budget.

Between 1956 and 1969 the government has distributed nearly 12,000 acres of land to farmers; established 225 dairy farms. The government has also purchased the large Orange Grove sugar estate and 51 percent of the shares of Caroni, Ltd. (the sugar mill). State expenditures on agriculture rose from BWI $2.5 million in 1956 to BWI $237 million in 1969. Nevertheless, the distribution of land in heavily agricultural Trinidad is still lopsided. Of a total of 35,800 holdings, 60 percent or 25,860 are 1 to 9 acres in size and occupy only 18 percent of the cultivated land, while 42 estates are larger than 1,000 acres and occupy fully 25 percent of the land. The continued importation of foods (BWI $10 million of milk, $11.5 million of meats, $4 million of fish, and $8.5 million in rice in 1968) are some indication of the use of that land.

The growing concern over the island's development program is partly explained by a quick glance at some official statistics:

|                        | 1956                        | 1969          |
|------------------------|-----------------------------|---------------|
| Government Revenue     | $ 88.5    (million          | 303.6         |
| Government Expenditure | 86.5      BWI)              | 333.6         |
| Persons with Jobs      | 250,100                     | 318,300       |
| Persons without Jobs   | 17,000 (7%)                 | 50,100 (18%)  |

Since this trend has been present for over a decade it might be fair to state as a proposition that in Trinidad as government income and expenditures increase so does unemployment. (The actual figure on unemployment in 1969–1970 was between 20 and 25 percent.) One can hardly argue any longer, as nineteenth century laissez-faire economists did regarding pauperism, that unemployment is a structural necessary concomitant of development. The definition of "development" is being changed too drastically for that. There are, however, no easy solutions to this particular problem of unemployment. As the present Cuban government is discovering, Caribbean societies' hardened attitudes towards certain low status jobs often keep even the unemployed from taking them. Cane cutting is one such job and consequently the apparently paradoxical fact of Barbados having to import cane cutters from St. Vincent and St. Lucia while Barbadians cut cane in Trinidad and put up with the atrocious migrant camps of Florida's sugar farms. The problem extends to other areas: black West Indians are not supposed to be good businessmen, yet West Indians in general and Jamaicans in particular succeed surprisingly well in businesses in New York and Connecticut.

The problem is one of motivation, a social-psychological one, not economic. This problem of attitudes as they affect the well-being of the nation is reflected in the middle and upper classes also. In the Caribbean a motor car is an expensive luxury, yet in Trinidad in 1960 there were 10,000 more motor car owners than income tax payers; by 1963 the number of obvious tax dodgers rose to 20,000, the difference between private vehicles and income tax declarations. Only by 1964 did the absolutely logical occur: the number of taxpayers surpassed that of car owners. While this was an improvement, it was not cause for pride. In 1967, 45,000 citizens owned private automobiles, yet only 32,219 individuals declared taxable incomes of more than BWI $1,000 (US $500).

Tax evasion is only one expression of the upper and middle classes' attitudes toward the society. But, when (as in the 1960s) only 137 individuals declare taxable incomes in the range of BWI $18,001 to $22,000; no one declares in the $60,001 to $66,000 bracket; and only one in the above $66,000 bracket, the attitude becomes seriously detrimental to the nation.

Bearing these facts in mind, two conclusions can be derived from the island's social history:

1) The existence of a parallel economic structure to that of sugar allowed the survival of a vigorous cultural-religious sector which gave birth to Creole culture and kept alive a tradition of opposition to the established order in the island. The similarity to the Cuban case is striking.

2) The traditional structure of the society is in crisis. No longer can conflict-avoiding innovations like that of Naipaul's black Grenadian baker be expected. "Black Power" means merely the inverting of racial references. The masses (up to this point the clamor has come from the black masses; East Indians will no doubt be heard from soon) want to participate in the prerogatives of citizenship—not despite their race, but precisely because of it.

It might appear enigmatic that while point number 2 holds true, though less emphatically, for Barbados, the first one does not. Barbadian society is strikingly different from that of Trinidad. The particular historical evolution of Barbados is similar to that of Guyana in one fundamental respect: sugar reigned supreme and unchallenged throughout its history. What Barbados never received, however, were the infusions of different racial and cultural strains which make Guyana what it is.

It was fundamental to the crystallization of Barbadian social structure that that island never changed hands after settlement by the English in 1625. The island had the third earliest House of Assembly in the New World, and this representative system of the whites was never replaced by a Crown Colony system as it was in other West Indian islands in the middle of the nineteenth century. Barbados was, therefore, less subject to variations in British politics than were the other Crown Colony islands. Sugar had converted a one-time settlement of small farmers into a series of white-owned, slave-worked, and manager-administered estates. The Caribbean process of an expanding sugar economy paralleled by a diminished ownership base was true also of Barbados. It was not rare to see a new sugar estate, where formerly up to forty families lived and labored. Though absenteeism was not as high as in Jamaica, it increased as the smaller estates failed.

The white upper class could shape Barbados economically, politically and socially. One should add religiously to that series as well, since the Church of England had little competition on the island. What this meant was that as the sugar economy evolved, comprehensive political, social and cultural power passed to a smaller and less representative sector, solidly English, white and Protestant.

Emancipation in Barbados in no way changed the structure. Lacking land to occupy, the black man necessarily stayed on the estate; even the city business was sugar-related and tied to the estate somehow. Wages could be easily controlled by the few producers since labor had no means of controlling the supply and demand system.

Up to World War Two not more than five percent of Barbadian

arable land was planted in food crops. World War Two forced a change in that system but up to today the island imports most of its food. With one of the highest population densities in the world (1,600 per square mile), Barbados seems even more crowded to the eye because a full four-fifths of the area is planted with sugar, leaving over 450,000 people to somehow live on one fifth of the 166-square-mile island.

Barbadian society is the most rigidly stratified of the Caribbean. Perhaps only in Martinique are there such rigid, nearly caste-like, barriers between the white upper class, nearly totally English, and the rest of the population. Nowhere else in the West Indies can one find a social club of the likes of Bridgetown's Savannah Club which for its exclusivity could comfortably exist in its North American namesake city. Horse racing and polo exist today as they did over a century ago with but little change in style or participating families. Boarding schools such as Lodge School and Codrington High School (established in 1710) have traditionally educated the island's and neighboring islands' and mainland's upper class whites.

A style of life associated with plantation days continues in this island, and serves to illustrate the tremendous tenacity of certain structures, even long after they have become archaic in the region as a whole. The completeness and comprehensiveness of white domination over such an extended period had created a traditional and parochial black population. Is it any wonder that the protagonist of the largely autobiographical work of Barbados' foremost novelist, George Lamming, *In the Castle of My Skin*, discovers his true "identity" as a black man in Trinidad where he, like so many of his countrymen, went to seek work?

Barbados' little diversified economic life, its sharply bifurcated social structure is reflected in many ways. Positively, it has meant a hard working, religious, honest and thrifty population. Bridgetown is as neat as a pin, "Bajans" as courteous as any people in the world. In general it can be said that the island's social structure has created a culture which reflects the most salient features of the Protestant ethic.

This in turn has a negative aspect. This ethic on the part of the masses has not meant their successful participation in the benefits of the island's economic life, while on the other hand it has left them without much of the folklore enjoyed by other West Indians. Barbados is singularly bereft of original music, dance, carnivals, popular folklore in general. What tourist magazines highlight as distinctly Barbadian are invariably those aspects which the upper class treasures: the port police in their 18th century Nelson uniforms; the Zouave military musical band with the uniforms Queen Victoria admired so greatly; the old plantation houses which are now tourist resorts; the beautiful white beaches, now largely foreign owned.

A monolithic economic structure created a distinctly bifurcated social structure in which two social classes sharply correspond to two different races, and in which "every man knows his place." Political mobility since the 1950s has not fundamentally changed the social structure.

In a sense this is true also of Jamaica, except there the social structure is much more complicated, as is, in fact, its economic structure. Nowhere else in the British Caribbean is there so much concern over shades of color as in Jamaica.

But whether we are speaking of Barbados, Jamaica, or the islands of the Leeward or Windward groups, an irreversable phenomenon of replacement of the white world by "blackness" as the reference group is occurring. American and Canadian events, more than African ones, are having an important effect on these societies, reversing the old pattern of West Indians carrying the message of black pride to the United States. It is not a new theme in the Caribbean as the cases of Cuba and Haiti demonstrate, but it is a Caribbean theme, at last.

## Curaçao

Most of the cases thus far illustrate the apparent paradox of Caribbean development. As these societies began to "modernize," to supply foreign sugar markets through foreign owned means of production, the worst features of the social structure emerged. Social and economic inequalities and an economic and psychological dependence were the most characteristic legacies of this process.

Curaçao is a clear example of the dangers of some forms of modernization. Up to World War Two the island had existed more or less peaceably with a society composed of widely differing groups. The upper class was Sephardic Jewish of Portuguese descent and Protestant of Dutch descent. The middle class was colored and Catholic. The lower class was Negro. Curaçao has long had a well-developed cultural identity. All native classes communicate in Papiamento, Dutch being the much disliked official language. They all appreciate the beauty of the local music and dances—Waltz di Corsow, mazurka, and tumba—and, in general, are a sophisticated and completely urban and urbane population. The island enjoys, with Surinam and the other Dutch Antilles, associated membership in the European Common Market. None of this, however, deterred the Caribbean trend of modernization followed by unemployment.

The growth of the oil refinery since World War Two brought an influx of large numbers of Dutch technicians and managers and Portuguese Madeira island laborers. The Dutch lived isolated in a compound appropriately called "Isla" and managed in many ways to invite the hostility of the population, whom they invariably held in contempt. Calling the Dutch *makamba* was the *yu di Corsow's* (son of the land in the Papiamento tongue) way of retaliating. Eastern European Jews began arriving after the war and in two decades controlled much of the commerce not already in Sephardic hands. Chinese and Arabs began cornering the general store and dry goods business, and finally, the 1960s witnessed the development of a large tourist sector in North American hands.

Politics was dominated by a democratically elected group from the white Protestant sector which, after a decade and a half in power, had become blatantly nepotistic and oligarchical. As time passed this ruling group gave the impression of working more for the benefit of the foreign sectors and their own economic interests than for the people. The very election of this white party had been an indication of the racial tolerance of the majority Negro population. Unfortunately, that trust was not reciprocated.

On May 30, 1969, this highly educated, cosmopolitan and racially tolerant (though very color conscious) society exploded. Close to one third of the businesses in the capital city, Willemstad, were burned to the ground on that day. Fatigue-clad workers began to roam the island. Dutch troops arrived and the omnipresent American fleet turned up off the coast.

It is important to note that although the *Frente Obrero i Liberashon* which emerged as a mass-based political party was predominantly Negro and nationalistic, it was not a racial, much less racist, movement. As a matter of fact, Stanley Brown, a top leader and foremost ideologue of the movement, is a white school teacher. Nor was it anti-semitic; the Sephardic Jews were not particularly singled out. Their attacks were directed against the Dutch *makambas* and North American firms which were attempting to undercut union-based wage scales; the Eastern European store owners (*Judio Polako*) who were notorious for their low wages; the tourist industry and its wage and racial policies; and the leadership of the ruling party and its oligarchical tendencies.

Modernization of the oil industry had brought about an increase in the island's population by attracting many foreigners. As the process of modernization changed towards automation, the labor market began to contract, unemployment set in. Of course, it was the Negro lower class which formed the mass of unemployed. Tensions in the island reached a high pitch in 1969 with the aforementioned consequences. The fact that the main sources of production are in white foreign hands is that much more oil on the flame of nationalistic discontent still burning on the island.

## Conclusion

Fernando Ortíz explained the development of the Cuban society and culture in terms of the counterpoint between two types of economic development. One type he called centrifugal development; the sugar industry was such a case. Capital, skills and planning came from the outside; what developed inside was purely for the sake of profits to be exported. Such development, he maintained, left nothing but misery and frustration. Centripetal development was just the reverse. It sprang from native capital and knowledge, planning and marketing remaining in local hands; it tended to enrich culture by ennobling owner and laborer alike. This had been the case of tobacco cultivation in Cuba.

The cases of Trinidad and Cuba show how a sector such as tobacco or cocoa, which developed centripetally, managed to offset the deadening impact of monocultural sugar cultivation. In both cases, to be sure, the native economic sectors eventually succumbed to interests created by a centrifugal development pattern. But they accomplished their historic task: to build into the social structure sectors independent enough to find within their own society the spiritual strength for change and reform. Fundamentally this meant groups and individuals unwilling to remain content with the system as it eventually developed and who aspired to a better order of things. The healthy flame of constructive opposition, of concern for the broader society, was kept alive in these countries.

The recent hectic, but very exciting and hopeful, developments in these societies reflect that background.

Other societies such as Barbados and the French Antilles never developed enough internal strength to compete with the overwhelming outside forces. Their contributions to the formulation of a future Caribbean society have so far been few. But even there society can no longer remain isolated and removed from the general trends in the area. Indications are that they are feeling the stimulation emanating from the area's major dynamic centers.

The case studies analyzed here would indicate that the variety of historical patterns have created a wide range of cultural orientations. It might, therefore, be too much to hope for a Caribbean culture sometime in the near future. But these case studies also indicate that throughout the area there is increasing recognition that centrifugal development programs have contributed little to the fiber and health of these societies. Too large a sector has been totally marginated from the benefits without any real redeeming values accruing to the rest. These people are, of course, also aware that isolated internal development is no longer possible given the realities of international economics and the weaknesses of each island unit. Some form of autochthonous development in each island, however, will have to take place before the historical balkanization of these societies can be ended.

# CARIBBEAN PROBLEMS

Ben S. Stephansky

# Puerto Rico

## The Commonwealth

The Commonwealth of Puerto Rico, about two-thirds the size of Connecticut but almost equal in population with 2.7 million inhabitants, is America's island border state in the Caribbean. It was established through a series of acts between 1950–52. Beginning in 1950, in response to a Puerto Rican request, the United States Congress adopted Public Law 600 which, "in the nature of a compact," enabled the people of Puerto Rico to organize a government of its own under a constitution of its own. During 1950–51, a Puerto Rican constitutional convention drafted and adopted a constitution, which was ratified by popular referendum. In 1952, the constitution was approved by Congress and President Truman with a few changes. The changes were accepted by the Puerto Rican legislature; and when the whole procedure was again ratified by popular referendum, the "Associated Free State," as it was called in Spanish, or the "Commonwealth of Puerto Rico," as it was named in English, came into existence in 1952. Created, thus, through steps resembling the enabling act procedures that had for over a century admitted states to the federal union, the case of Puerto Rico introduced a novel relationship into the American federal system. The relationship was that of a sphere of constitutional self-government in Puerto Rico, not integrated into

*In 1964–67* BEN S. STEPHANSKY *was executive secretary of the United States– Puerto Rico Commission on the Status of Puerto Rico. Dr. Stephansky has also been United States ambassador to Bolivia (1961–63) and deputy assistant secretary of state for Latin America (1963–64) as well as deputy United States representative to the Organization of American States. At present he is associate director of the W. E. Upjohn Institute for Employment Research, and director of the Institute's Washington office.*

the federal system as in the case of the federated state, but rather connected to the federal system by the applicable parts of the federal Constitution and by a specially adopted Federal Relations Act.

It is the connected, rather than the integrated nature of the federal relationship, in the view of those who devised the Commonwealth, that could permit a change to either conventional statehood or independence. The key to the relationship is the "compact" which can be changed by mutual consent. On the other hand, the compact established the Commonwealth as a permanent and evolving relationship, if neither the federal government nor the people of Puerto Rico prefer a change in status.

Under its own constitution Puerto Rico elects and is governed by its own bicameral legislature and its own governor. The governor appoints his own cabinet officials, makes other key executive and administrative appointments, and appoints also the Commonwealth judiciary, including the members of the Commonwealth Supreme Court. The Legislative Assembly approves the governor's proposed budget, makes appropriations, and legislates for the whole range of Commonwealth affairs. The Commonwealth's large educational establishment —primary, secondary and university—is exclusively under Commonwealth control and administration. Spanish and English are the official languages of Puerto Rico, with Spanish customary. The language of instruction in the public schools, and in the main, at the University of Puerto Rico, is Spanish, but English is a required subject from the first grade through the second year of college. Spanish is the language of the home, of business, of government; all but one of the newspapers are in Spanish, and most radio and television stations broadcast in Spanish.

Under the Federal Relations Act, the federal authority applicable to Puerto Rico is defined. For example, Puerto Rico is within the United States tariff wall and all tariffs apply. On the other hand, federal income tax laws are not applicable to Puerto Rico. Puerto Ricans are United States citizens, but by their own choice do not participate in federal elections. They are represented in Congress by a non-voting resident commissioner who has a voice but no vote in the House of Representatives. Foreign affairs and defense are under the federal jurisdiction, although there may be potential spheres of trade, commercial initiative, and participation in international agencies that have not been fully explored and developed. These could be increasingly important for Puerto Rico in relationship to the growth of trade and development in the Caribbean.

The establishment of the Commonwealth signified more than a novel political discovery under the American constitutional system to eliminate a long standing semicolonial relationship. It provided an institutional framework that liberated energies to achieve one of the world's great modern experiments in development.

The outlines of the achievement are generally known to those who have come to understand with what difficulty progress comes to developing countries: rapid economic growth that transformed a backward agricultural island into a modern industrial economy; widespread social change that dramatically elevated the level of human achievement; a growing popular participation in the community's political life that has created an open and hopefully stable democracy; and a cultural transformation, induced by the confrontation of Spanish and American cultural values, that has launched Puerto Rico on a disquieting but fruitful search for its modern identity. Puerto Rico has indeed undergone a revolution since 1952, and perhaps the most remarkable achievement of all, in view of the depth and breadth of the revolution, is that, thus far at least, it has been a peaceful one.

## A New Chapter in Puerto Rican History

Puerto Rico's general elections of November, 1968, opened an unprecedented chapter in the island's political experience. For the first time in the history of Puerto Rico's relations with the United States, the proponents of federated statehood for Puerto Rico won the opportunity to pursue their objective from a seat of political power. Not unexpectedly, the internal pressures of the statehood party, enhanced by the exuberance of a first taste of victory, dictated the adoption of a militant strategy to obtain a mandate for statehood. On the other hand, the statehood party came to power with less than a majority of the popular vote, and against the background of the 1967 status plebiscite, in which a large popular majority had opted for the continued development of Commonwealth. Thus, whether to ignore the results of the 1967 plebiscite and proceed to advance the cause of statehood; whether to attempt to fulfill the role of custodian of the Commonwealth's continued development; or whether to fashion a policy which in some manner would seek to balance both objectives— these alternatives constituted the statehood party's paradoxical problem of government. Since it was unlikely that the statehood party would adopt any course other than that of pressing its advantage, its stay in power promised the resurgence of Puerto Rico's unresolved status question in a particularly acute and complicated form.

What shaped the outcome of the 1968 elections was the political accident of a leadership crisis, which during some 2 years preceding the voting had corroded the unity of the Popular Democratic Party. Until the crisis erupted, the PPD appeared to be invincible. It had governed Puerto Rico for nearly 30 years. It had authored "Operation

Bootstrap" and "Operation Serenity," had engineered the island's social revolution, and had crowned these achievements with the innovation of the self-governing Commonwealth within the American constitutional system. Confident of its success—and of its maturity—the PPD had even taken the uncommon step of initiating a voluntary transfer of leadership to a younger generation. In 1964, persuaded that the time had come for induction of the new generation the PPD had nurtured during its long tenure in power, Luis Muñoz Marín, founder and leader of the PPD and governor of the Commonwealth for four successive terms, declined to be a candidate for a fifth term. He defended his decision against his party's strong reluctance to part with a tested, charismatic winner, but his political judgment appeared to be impeccable and his confidence in the PPD wholly confirmed, when his handpicked younger successor, Roberto Sánchez Vilella, for whom he had campaigned vigorously, polled even a greater majority of the popular vote in the 1964 elections than Muñoz had won four years earlier.

It will be a matter of lasting interest to political historians of Puerto Rico to account for the underlying factors that crumbled the PPD's unity at a moment when it seemingly was at the height of its power, without any profound ideological differences, and when it had undertaken, in an apparent atmosphere of internal harmony, an enlightened transition in leadership. Perhaps the root causes will never be fully explained, since many of them were traceable to the inexplicable rupture of the personal relationship between Sánchez and Muñoz after 1964. That relationship had been marked by the most intimate confidence and loyalty during the sixteen years that Sánchez had served as Muñoz' most trusted aide. In any event, by 1966, serious differences that were wholly unpredictable in 1964 had erupted between Governor Sánchez and the leaders of his own party both in the Legislative Assembly and around the island over a wide range of issues. These problems were compounded by the governor's erratic behavior during his last two years in office. Thus, he announced in March 1967 that he would not seek reelection and withdrew from participation in the Commonwealth's first status plebiscite in the summer of 1967. In the spring of 1968, however, he reversed his decision on reelection, announcing he would seek the PPD nomination when it was already obvious that he could not obtain it. And, after an overwhelming defeat at the PPD's 1968 convention by the Senate majority leader, Luis Negrón Lopez, one of the leaders with whom he had feuded, Sánchez launched a new People's Party with a Commonwealth platform not much different from that of the PPD, undoubtedly aware that the PP could at best be only a minority party. Sánchez, of course, headed the PP ticket as candidate for governor.

In launching his splinter party, Sánchez plunged the PPD's prolonged leadership crisis into the 1968 electoral campaign. The damage sustained by the PPD was severe. Not only did it lose the votes drawn off by the PP—which ran somewhat stronger than was expected—but the PPD also lost a bloc of independent votes and, most important, an uncounted but significant number of its own followers who had been disheartened by the spectacle of their party's split and abstained. Thus, although the PP polled only ten percent of the vote, that margin was sufficient to assure the success of the PPD's major opposition, the New Progressive Party (PNP).

The PNP was a newly constituted party favoring federal statehood for Puerto Rico, whose candidate, Luis A. Ferré, had unsuccessfully run against Muñoz Marín in 1956 and 1960, and against Sanchez Vilella in 1964, as the candidate of the Republican Statehood Party (PER). With only 45 percent of the total vote and a narrow 36,000-vote margin over the PPD, the PNP won the governorship, the post of resident commissioner in Washington, the mayoralties of Puerto Rico's two largest cities—San Juan and Ponce—and, by a margin of one member, the House of Representatives of the Legislative Assembly. The PPD, with 41.8 percent of the total vote won only the Senate by a margin of three members.

The victorious statehood party had been organized after the status plebiscite of 1967 by Luis Ferré. As vice-president of the Republican Statehood Party, Ferré strongly advocated participation of the PER in the plebiscite, against the stand of the PER's president, Miguel A. García Mendez, who advocated a boycott. The issue was decided at a special PER convention in January 1967, when García Mendez, who tightly controlled the PER machinery, obtained a large majority for the boycott. Ignoring his defeat, Ferré proceeded to establish a non-political organization, the Organized United Statehooders, that campaigned for the statehood option in the 1967 plebiscite under his leadership. The plebiscite was won by supporters of Commonwealth with 60.5 percent of the vote; but Ferré harvested enormous prestige from the campaign, particularly after his United Statehooders gained almost 39 percent of the vote, a solid 4.5 percent more than the Republican Statehood Party polled in the 1964 elections. Since the results of the plebiscite demonstrated that statehood proponents had supported Ferré's position to participate in the plebiscite rather than the boycott position of García Mendez, Ferré utilized his newly gained prestige to transform the machinery of his United Statehooders into the New Progressive Party, formally registered in January 1968. Although the PNP wisely refrained from campaigning in 1968 on a statehood platform, not only because it was too soon after the plebiscite, but mainly to capitalize on the divisions within the PPD, the results of the election left no doubt that the PNP had totally replaced the Republican Statehood Party as Puerto Rico's new statehood party. The PER polled a humiliating 0.2 percent of the vote—in contrast to the 34.6 percent it won in 1964—and lost its legal standing.

## The 1967 Status Plebiscite

The 1967 plebiscite had stirred some modest expectations that the status question, which had agitated Puerto Rico's internal politics and its relations with the United States for more than half a century, could, for a time at least, occupy a quieter corner of the political stage. The expectations were possibly unrealistic, for similar hopes had been raised in 1952 when the Commonwealth of Puerto Rico came into existence, widely acclaimed as a persuasive demonstration of the ability of American federalism to accommodate creatively the need of a dependent territory for self-determination. The very novelty of the Commonwealth, however, generated a new status debate. Those who continued to aspire to statehood alleged that Puerto Rico was still technically an "unincorporated territory" to which a generous grant of local self-government had been accorded by Congress without altering its fundamental status. Independentists, with much the same arguments, still regarded Puerto Rico as a colony, alleging that Congress had not divested itself of authority over Puerto Rico, including the authority to alter its status. The designers of the Commonwealth contended that the process through which it was created—the laws enacted by Congress and their approval by the people of Puerto Rico by referendum—had ended the territorial status and had established the legal, political and moral foundations for a new, quasi-autonomous political relationship within the American federal system. The relationship was admittedly not a finished one, it was argued, but it could evolve its own special character over time by mutual agreement between Puerto Rico and the United States from the foundations that had been laid.

The debate over Commonwealth settled nothing during the 1950s; indeed the positions of status partisans hardened and inhibited any growth of the Commonwealth relationship. Nor was there any enlightenment from the mainland, for neither Congress, the President, nor the Supreme Court found the occasion to offer any clarification of the issues that had been raised on the island. The Popular Democratic Party made one major effort in 1959 to end the debate by proposing in the Fernos-Murray Bill of that year a design for a "culminated," permanent Commonwealth. The hearings on the bill only succeeded in presenting to Congress a confusing spectacle of the profound divisions among Puerto Ricans over the status issue. The Bill died in committee.

It was from a second major effort to put an end to the status debate that there emerged the device of the status plebiscite. The proposal for a plebiscite was advanced in an exchange of letters on July 25, 1962, between President Kennedy and Governor Muñoz Marín commemorating the tenth anniversary of the Commonwealth. The correspondence took note of Puerto Rico's rapid economic and social growth, but also stressed, in contrast, the lagging institutional growth of the Commonwealth relationship. It was agreed that to determine whether further development of the Commonwealth could be undertaken, the people of Puerto Rico should be given the opportunity to express a status preference among the three alternatives of a more fully developed commonwealth, statehood or independence. When subsequent efforts to formulate definitions of the status alternatives and a procedure for a referendum were unsuccessful, a new impasse was avoided by the establishment in 1964 of a joint United States-Puerto Rico Commission on the Status of Puerto Rico. The leaders of the three contending positions were represented on the Commission, which was to conduct a comprehensive review of the status issue and to make recommendations that might conceivably lift it out of the political morass into which it had descended during the previous decade. One of the Commission's main recommendations was that a status plebiscite could intelligently advise both the Congress and the people of Puerto Rico of the prevailing sentiment on the island and thus provide an informed basis for future policy.

The Commission's work extended over a period of two years during which it conducted extensive public hearings in Puerto Rico, carried out a number of special studies, and examined the legal, economic, social, and cultural factors involved in the status question. Its unanimous report in 1966 legitimated the Commonwealth, which, along with "Statehood and Independence are within the power of the people of Puerto Rico and the Congress to establish under the Constitution." Whether the Commonwealth could be a "final," permanent status was reserved for a decision by the people of Puerto Rico at a future, unspecified time. For the present and immediate future, the Commission saw the Commonwealth as an "open-ended" status, capable of its own development but also, because of its proved capacity for economic growth, able to set the stage for either statehood or independence, if either was desired by Puerto Ricans.

In the economic sphere, the Commission found that any "immediate or abrupt change in political status would involve serious economic risks and dislocations," which could only be offset by carefully designed plans of transition. Projections as to when Puerto Rico could be "ready" for a change to either statehood or independence were admittedly imprecise, although for the former, "professional estimates begin at a minimum of 15 years to a much longer period"; and for independence, "even longer . . . unless there is more rapid economic development and integration of this hemisphere than can now reasonably be expected." The Commission also found, however, that "as Puerto Rico continues to develop, a time will come when the economic structure can more readily absorb the impact of a change to statehood or independence." It concluded: "It is therefore in the interest of proponents of such change to maximize Puerto Rico's economic growth, for as further growth is achieved the people of Puerto Rico will be able to weigh more realistically the economic costs and advantages of each of the status alternatives."

In the social-cultural sphere the Commission found a different "ideological dimension" in each of the three status positions—that "each involves a concept of the identity of the people of Puerto Rico, an interpretation of history, a way of life and an aspiration for the future." While each of the alternatives was committed to the preservation of Puerto Rico's cultural values and the Spanish language, it was recognized that each alternative would require a different form of adjustment to fulfill its commitment, and that "insofar as . . . ideology . . . culture and language are involved in arriving at a consensus regarding their future political status, it is the people of Puerto Rico themselves who must resolve these questions."

It was against the background of the Commission's report—widely circulated and studied in Puerto Rico—that the plebiscite was conducted in July of 1967. The Commission had also recommended a mechanism of joint United States-Puerto Rican "ad hoc committees" to follow the plebiscite and carry out its mandate. The mechanism was designed to permit each status alternative to develop its own "agenda" of specific measures to be studied and adopted in the event it won the plebiscite, in order to assure evolutionary rather than abrupt changes in the progress towards the victorious status. Two-thirds of Puerto Rico's electorate registered for the plebiscite; 60.5 percent voted for a continuation of the Commonwealth, that status to be further developed; 38.9 percent voted for statehood; independentists for the most part boycotted the plebiscite and the independence alternative polled only 0.6 percent. The mechanism of the ad hoc committees, however, was never activated by the Commonwealth regime. By mid-1967, Governor Sánchez had broken with the PPD leadership and no agreement on an agenda for the development of Commonwealth was possible. In 1968, the PPD split had worsened and all attention turned to the upcoming political campaign.

## The Strategy for Statehood

The PNP in power after the election of 1968 chose not to take custody of the Commonwealth's development to carry out the mandate of the 1967 plebiscite. On the contrary, the logic of its first victory compelled the PNP to exploit its opportunity for an intensive drive to obtain a mandate for statehood. Perhaps because of Governor Ferré's profound and sincerely felt conviction that statehood was the greatest good that could come to Puerto Rico, the PNP appeared disposed to pursue an open strategy. In any case, the outlines, at least, of the PNP plan of action were a matter of general public knowledge by the end of 1969.

The strategy for statehood appeared to consist essentially of two operations, one on the mainland and one in Puerto Rico. The operation on the mainland was designed to develop and extend support for statehood. Ferré undoubtedly attached great importance to this operation for he conducted it as a personal campaign. During his first two years in office he travelled to the mainland with unprecedented frequency, making at least twenty voyages. He was an indefatigable envoy for statehood, promoting the cause on every possible occasion, public or private, official or informal. At two meetings of state governors— he never missed these conferences—Ferré succeeded in getting unanimous resolutions adopted favorable to statehood. Already known as "Mr. Statehood" to mainlanders, Ferré may well have been stealing a page from the Popular Democratic Party's style on the mainland, and after two years was beginning to demonstrate a kind of skill in cultivating a friendly Republican Administration that Muñoz Marín had developed to a fine art with friendly Democratic administrations.

The object of the PNP operation in Puerto Rico was to convert the PNP from a minority to a majority party and set the stage for a major electoral victory in 1972. This was a legitimate purpose for any party in power; however, the PNP had a further purpose, announced in 1969. This was to conduct a new plebiscite after 1972 in the hope of obtaining for the first time a majority vote for statehood and perhaps even a large popular mandate. A strong 1972 electoral victory was, of course, a necessary prelude to a new plebiscite, not only to give support to a plebiscite from the seat of power, but also to win the Senate from the PPD where plebiscite action could be blocked. Thus, as early as 1969, the scene was ready for what in all likelihood would be one of the most fiercely contested electoral campaigns in Puerto Rican history.

The campaign in Puerto Rico aimed at a statehood victory in 1972 centered in large part on the courtship of mass target groups. Labor was courted with a commitment to a policy of raising the Puerto Rican minimum wage to the level of the mainland—a commitment which could greatly discourage investment if carried out before 1972. At one point, Ferré appeared to consider a policy of permitting tax exemption only in cases where mainland minimum wages were paid. Civil servants and teachers were other target groups, and the poor sectors were promised greater participation in welfare programs financed by United States federal funds; in fact, a special study was commissioned by the

PNP administration in 1970 to locate all federal programs for which Puerto Rico was eligible but not fully participating.

Without doubt the most significant single stratagem launched by the PNP in its statehood operation, directed at both Puerto Rico and the mainland, was the activation of an Ad Hoc Committee to study the feasibility of Puerto Ricans voting for the president and vice-president of the United States. This was the first ad hoc committee invoked under the procedure recommended by the Status Commission. In September 1969, the governor announced that he had requested the president to form the joint committee; but it was not until April 1970 that the fourteen-member committee of seven Puerto Ricans and seven mainlanders was formally announced. At the time of the announcement, Ferré noted that he considered the work of the Ad Hoc Committee a step in the growth of Commonwealth since the PPD's own agenda for Commonwealth development included the presidential vote. The general view, however, was that he had found a way to employ the heretofore unutilized mechanism of the ad hoc committees to effectuate a basic step toward statehood. The PPD argued that it would have been proper for the PNP to consult the Commonwealth party before beginning with as sensitive a measure as the presidential vote to develop Commonwealth. It also argued that the presidential vote, isolated from the rest of the PPD's agenda for Commonwealth development, necessarily meant a step toward statehood; and that only in the context of an integral program, and balanced by other steps for greater Commonwealth autonomy—for example, in the applicability of federal legislation, in the administration of the Commonwealth government, in foreign trade, immigration, and shipping—could the presidential vote be regarded as a measure for the further development of Commonwealth. The Ad Hoc Committee held its first formal session in Washington, D.C. in October 1970. It announced the appointment of an executive secretary who was charged with the task of formulating the Committee's program of research and public hearings.

There were probably more serious issues awaiting the Committee than even those anticipated in Puerto Rico. From the comments of several of the mainland members at the time the Committee was proposed, it was evident that questions would be raised regarding the relationship between the presidential vote, representation in Congress, and exemption from federal taxation. If these questions arose, it was almost inevitable that a new, full-fledged status debate was in the offing. Equally sober was the eventual prospect that even if a referendum on the question was held—a measure the Ad Hoc Committee could recommend—Congress would not feel bound by the result; nor was it likely that Congress would declare itself in advance to accept either the recommendations of the Ad Hoc Committee or the results of a referendum. Finally, an affirmative recommendation of the Ad

Hoc Committee or an affirmative result of a referendum would require an amendment to the United States Constitution—a lengthy, difficult process.

There were, of course, other non-status problems of government that were faced by the PNP administration during its first two years: the celebrated Culebra affair (the use of Culebra island as a firing range by the United States Navy), which shook the island and accomplished the first instance of close collaboration between Ferré and Muñoz; anxieties about the drop of tourism, and more important, the drop in mainland investments; drug addiction; serious student disturbances; fire bombings of commercial establishments; and others. Undeniably, however, the heavy accent of the PNP during its first two years was on the statehood target to a degree that often touched the nonstatus issues. Thus, for example, in a strong speech in September 1970 in support of lowering the voting age to eighteen, a high statehood official not only discussed the merits of the measure, but took occasion to report that a recent poll conducted by the PNP showed that most of the island's eighteen-year-olds favored statehood.

THE EFFECTS OF STATEHOOD STRATEGY

The PNP's aggressive statehood strategy, as would have been expected, exerted a polarizing effect on the traditionally divided Puerto Rican political spectrum. Status lines hardened. For the PPD the pressure may well have had the salutary effect of intensifying efforts to reunite the party. Independentists appeared to be gaining strength, finding more frequent occasions for cooperation among their various factions; and by the spring of 1970, the militant independentist newspaper, *Claridad*, was reported to have reached a circulation of 15,000. The noticeably growing distance between the PNP and the other parties evoked the comment from a columnist writing in the *San Juan Star*—Puerto Rico's English-language newspaper supporting statehood —that during the PNP's first twenty months in office,

> The new Progressive Party has learned . . . there is a big difference between winning an election and governing. The party, whose basic ideological tenet is statehood . . . found it had to govern not only statehooders, but commonwealthers and independentistas as well. Trying to come to grips with these two groups has come to be the PNP's biggest challenge.

Evidence of the growing polarization on status appeared in the results of a year-long study of Puerto Rican attitudes and aspirations on a comprehensive range of contemporary issues, conducted by the University of Puerto Rico's Social Science Research Center and published in August 1970. The study, based upon intensive interviews of a selected sample of 1,300 Puerto Rican adults in all parts of the island, included questions on political status. Asked to express their preference

for one of three status solutions, 45 percent favored a further development of Commonwealth, 33 percent favored statehood, 13 percent
favored independence with close ties to the United States, and 9 percent were undecided. These results, must, of course, be distinguished
from the results of the 1967 plebiscite, in that they probably more
clearly reflected committed attitudes rather than pragmatic choices.
Since the 1967 plebiscite, for example, was expected to be followed by
action guided by the results, the Commonwealth option as an open-
ended alternative not precluding a future opportunity for choice of a
"final" status may well have harvested support from independentists
and others opposed to statehood. The attitude survey can thus be taken
as a reading of more clearly polarized status preferences, with independence running surprisingly high, and the undecided reflecting the
genuinely perplexed.

The evidence of polarized attitudes tends to be enforced by additional data presented in the study tabulating responses when two
status choices were offered, instead of all three options. In the following
table, which combines the results of the 1967 plebiscite with the Social
Science Research Center's status data, it is evident that when paired
options were offered, those opposed to either of the choices or those who
were in doubt increased significantly. Thus, when the choice of Commonwealth versus statehood was offered, a total of 17 percent was
opposed or doubtful; when Commonwealth versus independence was
offered, a total of 27 percent was opposed or doubtful; and when statehood versus independence was offered, a total of 38 percent was opposed or doubtful. It is interesting to note that even in the pairings of
Commonwealth versus independence and statehood versus independ-

Composite Table on Political Status Combining Results of 1967
Plebiscite and 1970 Social Science Research Center Study

| Status Preference | 1967 Plebiscite[1] 3 Options | Data from Social Science Research Center Study[1] | | |
| | | 3 Options | Paired Options | |
| | | | CW vs. S | CW vs. I | S vs. I |
|---|---|---|---|---|---|
| Commonwealth (CW) | 60.5 | 45 | 51 | 62 | — |
| Statehood (S) | 38.9 | 33 | 32 | — | 46 |
| Independence (I) | .6 | 13 | — | 11 | 16 |
| Opposed to Either Option | — | — | 10 | 20 | 27 |
| Doubtful | — | 9 | 7 | 7 | 11 |
| TOTAL | 100.0 | 100 | 100 | 100 | 100 |

[1] Expressed in percentage of total votes or responses.

ence, where both commonwealth and statehood scored higher than
they scored in the 1967 plebiscite, the opposed and the doubtful also
registered their highest levels. The general conclusions that could be
drawn from the Social Science Research Center study were that the
PNP's energetic statehood strategy had produced no tide of consensus
for statehood; that it had apparently stimulated a resurgence of independentist strength; and that, if anything, status differences had probably both widened and stiffened.

If there was any preoccupation in PNP ranks concerning the evi-
dences of growing status polarization, there were few outward indications. The secretary of education, Dr. Ramon Mellado, in an address
on July 4, 1970, proposed a union between commonwealthers and statehooders on the grounds that both believed in permanent union with
the United States. The suggestion appeared to have been ignored. One
voice that could not be ignored, however, was that of Senator Justo
Mendez, minority leader of the Senate and the PNP's first vice-president. In a major address in Miami on July 25, 1970, the anniversary of
the Commonwealth Constitution, Senator Mendez proposed a policy
of consensus for the PNP, based upon the further exploration of the
Commonwealth's potentialities, as a way of coming to terms with the
status divisions in Puerto Rican society. The senator endorsed the
Commonwealth as a "contribution to modern federalism," and recognized the "compact theory" that underlies the Commonwealth's relationship to the United States. He questioned the value at this stage
in Puerto Rico's history of what he referred to as a policy of "blind
assimilation," and suggested that island leaders needed to reorient
their thinking toward answering the demands of the people for "more
authority and liberty over their own lives," and toward "providing our
people with instruments that guarantee their own personality." The
senator called upon the people to develop Commonwealth "in a new
dimension without requiring greater loyalty than that of serving the
people," and proposed that both commonwealthers and statehooders
join in a search for common ground to promote the growth of Commonwealth. To his own party, Senator Mendez suggested a longer
perspective—that statehooders need not fear greater Commonwealth
development because "as we grow and develop the time will come to fix
which class of political union with the United States best suits Puerto
Rico."

It was not likely that Senator Mendez's design for a new approach
presaged any precipitate review of PNP policy. To committed statehooders it undoubtedly appeared to be an invitation to squander the
fruits of the 1968 electoral victory; and it was almost inevitable that
the PNP's militant statehood strategy would run a longer course. Yet,
the senator, a high leader in his own party, had sounded a deep note
of skepticism that with a divided people aggressive status politics

offered any solution. His appeal to the PNP for a longer-range perspective to permit longer-range factors to work themselves out—and during an indefinite interval, for Commonwealth to be developed in a way that avoided or compromised the sensitive or decisive issues of status— could conceivably be relevant at a later time.

## The Realities of Puerto Rico's Status

At some point in the future, when the PNP's militant strategy for statehood has run its course, it will have learned—or, better, relearned from its seat of power—that status politics, particularly polarizing status politics, will not resolve Puerto Rico's long-standing identity crisis. It will have also learned that the real "enemy" to statehood is not the Commonwealth, nor for that matter the smaller number of independentists, although the latter could conceivably muster the strength to frustrate a statehood petition to Congress in a last-ditch stand. The real "enemy" to statehood is the Puerto Rican who is not yet ready to be assimilated into statehood. He belongs to a majority in Puerto Rico that must yet come to terms with their own modern identity before making a final decision about the cultural world to which they belong. Thus, a final political status cannot be forced or imposed. It can only evolve as Puerto Rico evolves its identity.

All three of the status parties are on record for the preservation of Puerto Rico's cultural identity. Before the Status Commission, the proponents of statehood testified that it was wholly compatible with the maintenance of Puerto Rico's linguistic and cultural identity; indeed, since that time the PNP has adopted the slogan of "Jibaro Statehood" to denote that statehood would not sever Puerto Rico's cultural roots. For independentists, Puerto Rico's culture is an integral part of its nationalism, to be preserved at all costs. And among commonwealthers, there is great satisfaction that Puerto Rico's autonomous status permits full cultural self-determination.

But Puerto Ricans "have been members of what may be the most rapidly modernizing society in the twentieth century," wrote Professor Arnold S. Feldman, who collaborated with Professor Melvin Tumin in their monumental study of social change in Puerto Rico during the decade 1954–64, *Social Class and Social Change in Puerto Rico.* The vast scope of the changes that have come to Puerto Rico drain the meaning from the political rhetoric for cultural preservation. Puerto Rico is light years distant from the "folk culture" the United States found in the desperately poor and illiterate island it took in 1898. It is no longer—if it ever was—the romantic culture of Pedreira's *Insularismo,* in which the rarified Hispanic values needed only to be free from American materialism in order to be restored. Nor is it any longer the "Jibaro" culture exalted by the Popular Democratic Party and belatedly borrowed by the statehooders. Puerto Rico is rapidly becoming a highly literate urban, class-structured, industrial culture, with all the good and all the ills that modernity creates. It is a culture being shaped by the impact of far-reaching changes in all departments of Puerto Rico's life, political, economic, and social—changes induced by Puerto Rico's special relationship with the world's most powerful country. These are the changes with which Puerto Ricans will need to come to terms as they settle the matter of their modern identity; and these are the changes, therefore—as they are understood, assimilated, controlled and given purpose—which will be the determinants of Puerto Rico's political status. The task for Puerto Ricans is beset by intricate and sensitive difficulties, both in Puerto Rico and on the mainland. But the fact that Puerto Rico's concern with the definition and preservation of its own identity has come to permeate its life is evidence that Puerto Rican development is not an end in itself, but is serving as a means of continuing self-discovery.

## Economic and Social Change

The quantitative measures of the economic and social changes that are creating an industrial and highly mobile society out of a former sugar-island society are as always impressive to review.

In Puerto Rico per capita income for the first time in 1967 exceeded $1,000—the exact figure reported was $1,047 on July 1, the month when the Commonwealth celebrated its fifteenth anniversary. In its annual report on the incomes of 158 nations, the World Bank reclassified Puerto Rico as a "rich nation," slightly poorer than Russia, but richer than Italy, Japan, Spain, Greece, and all of Latin America. Puerto Rico's per capita income was over $1,200 in 1969, still rising at an annual rate of better than ten percent. In 1940, the per capita figure was $120.

During the first fifteen years of the Commonwealth, Puerto Rico's annual gross national product quadrupled, increasing from $755 million to $3,336 million. During the same period the island's population increased from 2.2 million to 2.6 million, exclusive of migration to the mainland. The labor force rose from 680,000 to 780,000, while employment grew from 601,000 to 716,000. Mainly through the efforts of the Economic Development Administration (known as Fomento), more than a thousand new manufacturing plants entered the island. The net income from manufacturing increased from $90 million to $635 million, or from 12 percent to 24 percent of the value of production. As a result employment in manufacturing more than doubled, increasing from 60,000 to 130,000. Employment in agriculture was reduced by one half, declining from 200,000 to 95,000. As an index of the changing composition of Puerto Rican manufacturing between 1952–1967, the very low-wage home needlework industry, nearly the largest employer in 1952, had almost disappeared by 1967. Manufacturing employment, at 18 percent of total employment, had surpassed employment in agriculture, which stood at the level of 14 percent of total employment in 1967. Tourism during the first fifteen years of the Commonwealth became a major industry. In 1952 an estimated 70,000 tourists spent about $10 million in Puerto Rico. By 1967 an estimated 815,500 visitors spent $158 million. Primarily as a result of growth of manufacturing in Puerto Rico, trade with the mainland rose steeply between 1952–1967. Puerto Rico's exports to the mainland in 1967 were valued at $1,321 million, more than four times the level of 1952. Purchases from the mainland in 1967 reached $1,800 million, almost four times the level of 1952, and surpassed those of the United States' best customers in Latin America, Venezuela and Mexico. In fact, on a per capita basis, Puerto Rico's purchases exceeded imports by Canada, the principal U.S. market in the world.

There were other noteworthy indexes of the Commonwealth's progress in its fifteenth anniversary year, reflecting the great shifts in population on the island and the rapid upward mobility of the population. Between 1952–67 Puerto Rico's urban population surpassed its rural population for the first time. Life expectancy, reaching better than 70 years, edged ahead of that in the United States. Illiteracy dropped below 13 percent, making its complete elimination an obtainable objective. Reflecting, as in many developing countries, a strong commitment to formal education, elementary and secondary school enrollment more than doubled in fifteen years, and college enrollment, standing at close to 48,000 in 1967, was doubling every 10 years. Housing had grown by 30 percent in fifteen years, more than 96 percent of the urban housing had electricity, and electrification of rural housing had leaped from 25 percent in 1952 to 75 percent in 1967. The leading causes of death in 1952, diarrhea and enteritis and tuberculosis—the diseases of the poor which together accounted for 28 percent of all deaths in that year—dropped to a combined total of 8 percent in 1967. The number of telephones per 1,000 inhabitants increased more than four and a half times, from 16 per 1,000 in 1952 to 76 per 1,000 in 1967; and the number of registered automobiles had risen in 1967 to 330,000 from a level of 62,000 in 1952.

Between 1952–1967 about 400,000 Puerto Ricans left for the mainland, continuing the large scale migration of Puerto Ricans to the United States which began to develop after World War II. Migration was a fluctuating phenomenon, reaching a peak of almost 70,000 in 1953 and registering a net return migration in the years 1961 and 1963 and almost a net zero rate in 1964. By the fifteenth year of the Commonwealth, total net migration to the mainland was estimated at a level of more than 1 million. Since Puerto Rico's own resident population in 1967 was about 2,600,000, the migrant group living on the mainland comprised more than 30 percent of all Puerto Ricans, in and out of the island. Despite a considerable backward movement for permanent resettlement on the island, it appeared that about one-third of Puerto Ricans resident on the mainland had been established as a permanent phenomenon. In the light of this heavy mainland residence, and of the resettlement in Puerto Rico as well as the habit of frequent return visits to the island, it was noteworthy that between 1952–1967 the number of Puerto Ricans on the island able to speak English increased from about 28 percent to about 50 percent. The number of Puerto Ricans who can be described as bilingual in the sense of having mastered both Spanish and English is small. But the growing number of Puerto Ricans who can speak English comfortably has undoubtedly been the result of migration as much as of formal education.

Reaching for competence in the realm of sophisticated technology, Puerto Rico established an Atomic Energy Commission in 1957. In less than a decade, Puerto Rico was using atomic energy for power production and was planning larger units in 1969. In 1968, a scientific and technological center was established in Mayaguez, modeled after Oak Ridge, to attract and develop young scientists. A marine biology laboratory was established in the same year. The petrochemical industry took a giant leap in 1967 with the decision of a group of companies to invest over $400 million in new and expanded facilities; and one of the larger companies installed its research facilities in the Mayaguez center. Puerto Rico is experimenting with educational television, with "ocean farming," and with desalinization. Finally, for a densely populated island, with 800 persons per square mile, Puerto Rico is experimenting with new and cheaper building materials and plastics to help supply the ever increasing need for housing. It is instructive to recall in this connection that it was in Puerto Rico that Dr. Gregory Pincus first proved the reliability of what has come to be known as "The Pill."

THE REACTIONS TO CHANGE

From merely a reading of the quantitative measures of social and economic change—and many were omitted in the preceding summary—one can gain an appreciation of the great task confronting Puerto Ricans who need to "find themselves" in the midst of a vast transformation of their society. One systematic effort to do so was noteworthy. In 1965, the Puerto Rican Senate established a "Commission to Study the Purpose of Puerto Rico," which after three years of research delivered its report in 1968. The central issue to which the report addressed itself was contained in the introduction: "The success that our Puerto Rican society has had in creating new wealth impels us to consider it fully for the purpose of our people emphasizing not only progress but cultural values." On this theme, the report proposed a ten-year program to give purpose and direction to the progress of Puerto Rico. The report appears to have been ignored by the new administration, but it is still a useful document providing insights into the issues with which Puerto Ricans are wrestling to assert their cultural "personality" in a modernizing society.

Perhaps the central issue—not dealt with explicitly in the Commission's report, but one that pervades it throughout—is an issue not confined alone to Puerto Rico, but applying to all small states with large populations and severely limited resources. The small state, for its growth and development, finds it imperative to seek vital linkages with external sources of growth. Unlike the larger underdeveloped state, which can look toward a future, however distant, of self-sustained growth, the small state requires vital external linkages of a permanent nature, for its continued growth can only be externally supported rather than self-sustained. There is, therefore, in a small state, a permanent concern of abandonment or indifference. At the same time, the small state—precisely because of its dependence—is concerned about assimilation or domination from the very source of its growth, the larger external power. These are the contradictory moods of the small state, and without an understanding of this contradiction it is impossible to deal successfully with the small state.

In Puerto Rico, for any but the outright assimilationists, this contradictory mood is directed toward the United States. In the economic sphere, Puerto Rico has become, as it were, another region of the American economy. Its industrial sector is largely a "value added" economy, with raw and semi-finished materials imported, value added, and the products exported almost exclusively to its American market. The institutions of what amounts to a common market, a customs union, a common currency, a common legal structure, a common capital market, a free flow of labor and capital resources, and particularly the special tax incentives, all operate to facilitate the economic growth of Puerto Rico. The growth is a source of great satisfaction; yet there also is the preoccupation that Puerto Rico in its industrial development may be reduced to the role of a spectator. The report of the Commission to Study the Purpose of Puerto Rico thus noted that in the manufacturing sector mainland enterprises accounted for 62 percent of the employment and 77 percent of the total investment on the island in 1968. It therefore recommended an effort to achieve a 50 percent balance of both during the next ten years.

Puerto Ricans are also concerned about the almost exclusive dependence upon the United States, with few ties elsewhere in the Caribbean and Latin America. There is concern with mainland competition in consumer products in cases where Puerto Ricans are attempting to establish enterprises to manufacture local products. For example, in the first six months of 1970, three Puerto Rican beer companies lost 16 percent of an expanding market while sales of beer imported from the mainland rose by 85 percent. Puerto Rican professionals have taken steps to limit mainland competition. Doctors need to be licensed and attorneys must pass the bar examination in Spanish in order to practice in Puerto Rico. There is preoccupation over former nationals from other countries freely entering Puerto Rico after obtaining United States citizenship. An estimated twenty thousand Cubans have entered Puerto Rico in the last decade, and are now prominent in television broadcasting, tourism and restaurants, and retail trade.

In the social sphere, Puerto Ricans are deeply concerned with a range of issues. A high, persistent rate of unemployment has not been solved, running at an official rate of about 11 percent in 1969, but probably much higher, for only Puerto Ricans "actively seeking jobs" are counted as unemployed. Although levels of income are generally higher than they were two decades ago, a serious maldistribution of income has appeared, with 38 percent of the families of Puerto Rico reported at the poverty level in 1967.

Although Puerto Rico's fiscal autonomy—its own power to tax at a higher level because of exemption from federal taxes—yielded an annual budget of close to $1 billion in 1969, Puerto Rico was still spending less than Mississippi for the educational needs of a growing young population. One of the major preoccupations of Puerto Ricans is that, although federal funds for social welfare programs are often generous, the programs themselves have been formulated for the mainland and are not readily adaptable to Puerto Rico without bureaucratic friction. There are still large slums in Puerto Rico. The "drug culture" has entered. The large number of women workers entering the factories has disturbed the traditional family structure. The large tourist industry—as in most places—grates on Puerto Rican sensibilities. Free access to Puerto Rico's beaches—a long-standing policy—became a disturbing issue in 1970.

The large migration of Puerto Ricans to the mainland has raised new and disquieting problems for Puerto Rico. Long recognized as a "pull" migration, most Puerto Ricans have raised their levels of income on the mainland compared to their prior earnings in Puerto Rico. Their concentration in and around ghetto areas, however, and the discovery for the first time that large numbers of migrants were "black," have made of migration anything but a blessing. For them and for the next generation of mainland children, the question of their "identity" has been raised in an acutely painful form. Moreover, the pressures to adjust into the mainland milieu are minimal; for Puerto Rico is less than four hours away by air from New York and attachment to the island is retained. Language has been a particularly difficult problem, and only in recent years has bilingual teaching capability been introduced in New York. Puerto Ricans' problems on the mainland have been of such range and magnitude as to have provoked the comment of a noted sociologist that there may well be as many Puerto Rican independentists on the mainland as there are on the island.

In the political sphere of Puerto Rico's relationship to the United States, Puerto Ricans have long been disturbed over the lingering imperfections in the Commonwealth vis-à-vis the federal authority. Dr. Carl J. Friedrich conveniently summarized the imperfections in his 1959 essay, *Puerto Rico: Middle Road to Freedom*:

> There are essentially five shortcomings in the present federal relations of Puerto Rico. There is first the failure to provide for active Puerto Rican participation in the process of federal legislation (including constitutional amendments). There is second the failure to provide for participation in the shaping of foreign and defense policies. There is third the failure to envisage a contribution of Puerto Rico to the federal treasury. There is fourth the failure to give Puerto Rico the same freedom as other states regarding a number of clearly local matters, such as citizenship and the debt. There is finally the need of associating the government of Puerto Rico with the execution of those laws which have been and which will in the future be made applicable to the island.

Much more can be said on this complex subject, but the essence of Dr. Friedrich's critique—a view widely shared in Puerto Rico—is that in the absence of any significant evolution in the Commonwealth relationship since 1952, it has come to operate in the American federal system like a conventional, but truncated state—a "one-armed" state, as Governor Ferré recently described it. For statehooders, of course, the answer is full statehood; but for those who wish greater autonomy without statehood, Dr. Friedrich's five deficiencies constitute an agenda for innovations yet to be created within the American federal system.

### THE FUTURE

These, then, are some of the issues with which Puerto Ricans are grappling as they seek to adjust their cultural inheritance to their modern identity in the age of Puerto Rico's transformation. The process requires time to absorb the changes, to find the purpose and the direction of their society, and time to experiment with the great American power to which they are vitally tied and whose insensible assimilation they resist. The first vice-president of the statehood party may well have had this need for time and experimentation in mind when, in his address of July 25, 1970, he cautioned against a headlong rush to statehood and called for the search for common ground between statehooders and commonwealthers to develop the further growth of the Commonwealth. Dr. Jaime Benítez, rector and president of the University of Puerto Rico for more than a quarter of a century and one of the great architects of Puerto Rico's modernization, also stated the same case for time and tolerance before the Status Commission in 1965:

> I regard Commonwealth as an evolving, flexible, elastic form of political relationship. One of its highest merits consists in that it is unencumbered by the dogmatism of formulas which were developed in bygone days and which, under present conditions, hinder the full flowering of culture, social and human interchange of growingly interdependent communities. . . . I believe that one of the advantages, I repeat, one of the advantages of Commonwealth is that it neither calls nor makes any Puerto Rican a traitor. Quite the contrary. It is much more respectful of differences and more tolerant of them than all other alternatives. . . .

## Puerto Rico's Role in the Caribbean

Puerto Rico is one of a "family" of nine associated states in the Caribbean. It was the first to be established. If it was not utilized as a model, it was undoubtedly a source of encouragement for the establishment of the other eight associated states inasmuch as it attracted wide attention and interest in 1953 when the United Nations General Assembly approved the joint Puerto Rican-United States actions that established the Commonwealth. In 1964, the Kingdom of the Netherlands established the associated states of the Netherlands Antilles and Surinam. In 1966, Great Britain established the five associated states of Antigua, Dominica, Grenada, St. Kitts-Nevis-Anguilla, and St. Lucia; and in 1970 St. Vincent. Since there are three constitutional structures involved, the American, the Dutch and the British, the associated states function in different ways, thus affecting the role that each can play in the Caribbean. In the case of Puerto Rico, the status question again appears as the source of both Puerto Rico's potentialities as well as its limitations in defining its role in the Caribbean.

Puerto Rico's phenomenal development has exerted an important "demonstration" effect in the Caribbean. But its unique relationship to the United States prevents it from being used as a model for development in the region. Puerto Rico can, however, design a role for itself in the development of the Caribbean, unless—as has already begun to happen—an internally polarized struggle over status exacts the external cost of destroying institutions that Puerto Rico managed to create as it was evolving its Caribbean presence during the past decade.

The status tensions did not ease Puerto Rico's task in exploring relations in the Caribbean. There has long been a stubborn notion among committed statehooders that to establish a role for Puerto Rico in the Caribbean would undermine statehood as a future option. Intransigent independentists, on the other hand, regularly conducted their ideological campaigns throughout the Caribbean region, and during the 1960s from Cuba as well, on the theme that any Caribbean state entering a relationship with a non-independent Puerto Rico—

and incredibly this line found a following even among enlightened Caribbean statesmen—would make itself vulnerable to United States "imperialist penetration." Despite these internal and external obstacles, Puerto Rico did participate in the Caribbean Commission and provided the headquarters in 1961 for its successor institution, the Caribbean Organization. After the latter was disbanded in 1964, Puerto Rico created a Caribbean Development Corporation (CODECA) in 1965, through which it encouraged inter-Caribbean trade and kept in touch with the continuing development efforts in the Caribbean.

One of CODECA's more interesting projects was the *Entendimiento,* initiated in 1967 with the Dominican Republic, a cooperative plan to establish complementary industries in both communities and explore possibilities for a common market. But CODECA's most promising effort to link itself to a newly evolving Caribbean development institution was its offer, in 1968, accepted by the countries establishing the Caribbean Free Trade Association (CARIFTA), to participate as a contributing but non-borrowing member of the Caribbean Development Bank, with an initial contribution of $6 million. Both the *Entendimiento* and Bank projects were pursued with careful deliberation and with careful attention to Puerto Rican and Caribbean public opinion. Particular care was taken in the case of the Bank, not only because of its anticipated major contribution to the growth of the CARIFTA countries when it began to operate in early 1970; but also for the reason that the United States, following the precedent it set in the case of the Central American Bank in 1962, decided to limit its participation to loans to the Caribbean Bank, rather than membership. This was a gratifying decision for Puerto Rico, for it permitted the United States and Puerto Rico to function independently in relation to the same institution.

But it was an unhappy commentary on the resurgency of status tensions in Puerto Rico since the elections of 1968, that CODECA's carefully developed programs were suspended by the PNP administration within a few months after it took office, and CODECA itself was converted largely into a tourist-promotion agency. These casualties of intensifying status politics came at a moment when the region was preparing to launch some of its most important development institutions and when the Economic Commission for Latin America had made a decision to offer the kind of assistance to the Caribbean that it had successfully done in the case of the Central American Common Market. There was, thus, denied to Puerto Rico a participative role in the Caribbean's pioneering steps toward regional integration.

PUERTO RICO'S DEVELOPMENT EXPERIENCE AND THE CARIBBEAN REGION

Any comment on the scope and applicability of Puerto Rico's development experience to the Caribbean region should note that, wholly apart from the status question, the very fact of Puerto Rico's development has had a more pervasive impact upon the Caribbean region than has been generally appreciated. The demonstration that the Caribbean species of the small state, beset by the characteristic Caribbean constraints of small size, limited resources, monoculture, overpopulation and low level of human achievement, was capable of development and not doomed to eternal backwardness constituted a psychological breakthrough for the whole region.

Furthermore, Puerto Rico's growth was rapid, even dramatic, much of it compressed into the last two and a half decades when it grew at an average annual rate of better than ten percent. Its basic social transformation, political development, and improvement in the quality of human resources were joined with the process of economic growth. With severely limited natural resources, Puerto Rico developed a modern industrial complex not confined to manufacture for import substitution but extended largely to manufacture for export. All these factors combined to raise the aspiration and emulation levels of many of the small states in the region. The proof is that virtually all of the transferable features of Puerto Rico's development experience have been borrowed and applied extensively throughout the region often without acknowledgment, but more often under Puerto Rico's active tutelage. This is because Puerto Rico made itself a readily available workshop for instruction in development techniques, planning, tax incentives, industrial promotion, tourism development, administration, technology, transportation, education, and its other useful instruments. It has been a rich resource for the Caribbean in those features of its own development that were readily transferable and applicable to the other small states of the region.

Recognition that Puerto Rico has provided both the encouragement of a small state's development example as well as a generous dissemination of its transferable techniques does not, however, qualify Puerto Rico as a model for Caribbean small-state development. The reason is that the vital source of Puerto Rico's development is its unique politico-institutional relationship to the United States. The relationship, which made possible the creation of a customs union, common currency, an ample budget for public expenditures, a broad range of fiscal autonomy and flexibility, a significant access to capital markets, and a secure legal framework, is not a transferable one. This relationship required aggressive exploitation—left alone between 1900–1930, it produced only a distorted sugar economy on the island—and the aggressive exploitation came when Puerto Rico acquired the self-government necessary to invent and utilize the abundant range of what have been referred to as the transferable or the readily applicable instruments for development. But the fundamental integration of Puerto Rico into the American growth system is not transferable and thus

Puerto Rico cannot offer itself as a model for Caribbean development. Nor has Puerto Rico offered itself as a model for the Caribbean; and the fact that it cannot nor has not done so should alleviate at least one source of anxiety or suspicion that Puerto Rico's Commonwealth relationship to the United States can be utilized with hidden purposes. In the Caribbean world, Puerto Rico cannot be a broker for the United States to sell its unique relationship; and similarly, within Puerto Rico, partisans of other status positions may be secure that Commonwealth partisans cannot advance their cause by any claim to general applicability of the Commonwealth status to the small states in the Caribbean.

### THE PUERTO RICAN ROLE IN CARIBBEAN DEVELOPMENT

Puerto Rico's special link to the United States does not disqualify it from participation in the development of a region replete with other unique relationships. On the contrary, while tied to the United States and evolving with its growth, another part of Puerto Rico's development necessarily belongs to its own geographic and cultural habitat. Although Puerto Rico has indeed developed remarkably, its level of life and its style of life are not those of the United States; and while they are not as "Caribbean" as they formerly were, the style and the level of Puerto Rican life belong more to the region than to the mainland. Realistically, both Puerto Rico and the Caribbean region could pursue their own paths of development without each other; but the prospects for the further development of both would be improved with their mutual participation.

Thus, for example, in the cases of the Caribbean Bank and of the *Entendimiento* with the Dominican Republic, Puerto Rico would have both contributed and benefited. And this would be so if Puerto Rico's future role in the Caribbean evolved, not only as a disseminator of techniques and experience, but as a participant in the new development institutions now being created and those yet to come in the region. For a variety of institutions Puerto Rico could be a source of capital for both public and private ventures. It could be a source of technology, a general servicing center, a hub of communications and transportation. It has technical assistance capacity in education, administration, banking, science, and other fields. It has its market to offer to an expanded regional market. It could participate in bilateral and multilateral cooperative ventures in tourism, undersea exploration, satellite communications, transportation and communication innovations and in the development of complementary industrial processes. Puerto Rico could, in short, participate in development banks, public and private; in bilateral and multilateral trade arrangements; in OAS technical bodies; and in selected institutions of economic integration. Perhaps the only activity closed to Puerto Rico would be full membership in a customs union of Caribbean states protected by a discriminatory external tariff. There may be other limitations, too; but the fact remains that Puerto Rico can evolve a broad and varied role in the Caribbean, aligned with its own and with the region's development needs and institutions.

PUERTO RICO'S CARIBBEAN ROLE AND FUTURE STATUS OPTIONS

It cannot be over-emphasized that Puerto Rico's possible role in the Caribbean does not imply the elimination of future status options. Although in some cases an international negotiating situation would arise, the fact that the State Department or another federal agency would either need to participate or delegate negotiating authority to Puerto Rico bears no status implications. It has long been recognized that in the United States-Puerto Rico relationship, as in the case of other associated states in the Caribbean and elsewhere, ultimate responsibility for foreign affairs along with defense lies with the federal authority. But there are a great variety of ways in which grants of local authority, for specified as well as for broader categories of international transactions, have been and can be worked out.

There are no insuperable problems, if there is no skittishness on the matter of status. Yet, it is precisely for the reason that international relations are involved in a Caribbean role for Puerto Rico that the committed statehood position perceives a "danger" to its future aspiration. The "danger" has never been fully spelled out in specific terms, but one can readily gather that for the hard statehood position, Puerto Rico's participation in a group of international institutions would imply that statehood had indeed been by-passed. The issue, of course, is more political and even symbolic than substantive; for in the event that the people of Puerto Rico opted for statehood in the future, all prior relationships in conflict with statehood, when it came, would need to be altered. The controlling fact would be Puerto Rico's choice, not a Caribbean relationship which the people would have chosen to modify or discontinue. It would be contrary to every principle that underlies the relationship established in 1952 between Puerto Rico and the United States to suppose that a Caribbean role would supersede an explicit decision by Puerto Rico to modify or alter its political status.

Upon reflection, it should be apparent that a Caribbean role for Puerto Rico is compatible with any of the three status options still open to Puerto Rico: independence, statehood, or an improved and possibly, in time, a permanent Commonwealth. There can be no quarrel with a role in the Caribbean if one contemplates an independent future for Puerto Rico; although as a sovereign state, Puerto Rico would need to revamp completely its relationships to the Caribbean. If one contemplates a statehood future for Puerto Rico it would be

hopelessly provincial to believe that Puerto Rico could isolate itself
from its geographic neighborhood. As a state, Puerto Rico would not be
in the heartland of the United States, but would be a new border state
in the Caribbean. And just as other border states have a variety of
special relationships with Mexico and Canada—from border commissions, dams, conservation programs, cultural exchanges, and labor migration arrangements to very major undertakings in which the states
participate, like the St. Lawrence Seaway's compacts—Puerto Rico
would necessarily have to arrange special relationships with the nations
on its "borders." One can indeed make the case that if the Commonwealth developed a role in the Caribbean it would as readily be
preparing for future statehood as for any other future status.

Thus, there should not be any quarrel with a Caribbean role under
the present Commonwealth relationship. Not only is no future status
precluded, but the present status could be enriched. A Puerto Rican
role in the Caribbean under the present Commonwealth would improve the Commonwealth; it would recognize Puerto Rico's cultural
duality, being at once of America and of the Caribbean. And, most
important, a Caribbean role for Puerto Rico would make use of the
Commonwealth in its most enlightened conception: to contribute some
of the development acquired from its association with the United States
to the Caribbean community of which it is also an inseparable part.

George Volsky

# Cuba

## Revolutionary Cuba

Cuba, the largest and most populous of the Caribbean island nations, officially became a Communist state on May 1, 1961. But the most important event in the country's recent history occurred 28 months earlier, on January 1, 1959, when the aging dictator, Fulgencio Batista, suddenly fled the island and the young guerrilla chieftain, Fidel Castro Rúz, then 33 years old, assumed power.

This event marked the onset of the most profound social revolution in the Western Hemisphere since the Mexican Revolution of 1917, and the start of a historical process that 11 years later was still far from running its course, remaining a source of concern as well as hope for Cuba and much of the world around her.

From the outset, Castro skillfully asserted his authority. Under his leadership Cuba underwent deep political, economic, and social transformations, shedding the popular image of the pleasure island she had acquired after gaining independence from Spain in 1902. Having rushed from relative obscurity into the maelstrom of international politics, Castro's Cuba produced an indelible imprint on contemporary history. She not only caused serious and frequently exasperating problems for the Hemisphere—the Castro experiment unleashed revolutionary trends in Latin America and even among radicals in the United States—but, during the October 1962 missile crisis, she also brought the American and Soviet superpowers for the first time to the

GEORGE VOLSKY, *research associate at The Center for Advanced International Studies, University of Miami, lived in Cuba 1947–61. Consultant on Cuban affairs for various research organizations, including RAND Corporation, he has written about Cuban developments for various United States publications and is currently preparing a book on the Cuban economy since 1959.*

brink of nuclear confrontation. Late in 1970, the use of Cuban waters
by Soviet atomic submarines set off another crisis between Washington
and Moscow.

REVOLUTIONARY STRUGGLE

Although Cuban official publications have attributed to Fidel Castro
and his guerrillas all the credit for the overthrow of the 1952–1958
Batista regime, many factors converged to make the dictatorship's
downfall inevitable. Besides the efforts by other revolutionary groups
in the mountains, and the relentless struggle of the anti-Batista city
underground, what really enabled Castro to become the undisputed
leader of his country was the disintegration of the Cuban professional
army. This process began in 1933 when Batista, a 33-year-old army
sergeant, led a successful uprising of noncommissioned officers and
soldiers against their tradition-conscious élite officers. By December
1958, the army was no longer an effective military force.

The 1933 sergeants' rebellion, in which many officers were killed,
broke the army's *esprit de corps* and altered its constitutional role.
Within a few years, many of the victorious sergeants, corporals, and
soldiers became generals, colonels, and majors. The principal characteristic of Batista's new officers' corps was its lust for wealth and
power. Militarily second rate, the army ceased to be a moderating
force in Cuba's political life. The paltry efforts by the democratically
elected government of Presidents Ramon Grau San Martín and Carlos
Prio Socarrás to raise the civic responsibility of Cuba's armed forces
were ended by Batista's new *coup d'état* in 1952. Encouraged by the
ease with which Dr. Prio was overthrown, the Batista military came to
regard the country as their own domain. High-ranking army officers
were frequently rewarded with lucrative public works contracts, and
scores of their friends and relatives were given government sinecures
and other perquisites. Corruption among Batista's civilian officials was
equally widespread.

Early in 1956, a dozen senior officers plotted to remove the dictator.
But betrayed by one of their fellow conspirators, they were arrested,
tried, and condemned to long prison terms. With the liquidation of
this group, called *Los Puros* (The Pure Ones), the Cuban army tied
itself inexorably to the fate of the Batista dictatorship.

While many high-ranking officers became rich almost overnight, the
lower ranks shared little of that wealth. When, years later, they had to
fight Castro's guerrillas in the mountains, the junior officers, NCO's and
soldiers understandably showed no enthusiasm for risking their lives
to preserve the privileges of their superiors who hardly ever left
Havana. Batista's army thus already carried the seeds of self-destruc-
tion when Castro landed in Cuba several months after the trial of *Los
Puros* officers.

Castro, whose bid to be elected to Congress was thwarted by the 1952 coup, always believed that Batista would never step down voluntarily. Dedicated to the concept of armed struggle, he organized a small group of youths, who on July 26, 1953, attacked Camp Moncada, a strongly defended military headquarters in Santiago de Cuba. The attack failed. Castro was captured and 84 of his 126 men were killed. But despite this fiasco—criticized by virtually all the other opponents of Batista (and the Cuban Communists, who described him and his followers as *"petit bourgeois,* adventurers and putschists")—Castro quickly acquired national stature. With his superb political instinct, he turned the Moncada defeat into an actual victory. He converted his own trial into an indictment of the Batista regime and a springboard for his revolutionary organization, the 26 of July Movement.

Castro was sentenced to a fifteen-year term, but did not stay in prison long. Freed under the 1955 political amnesty, he left Cuba, promising to return to continue the fight. On December 2, 1956, he and an 82-man invasion force, sailing from Mexico aboard a small yacht named *Granma,* landed on the southern coast of Oriente Province. But Batista's army immediately reduced the invading force to 12 men. Castro, his brother Raul and Argentine-born Ernesto "Ché" Guevara, the expedition's top leaders, were among those who escaped and reached the haven of the Sierra Maestra mountains.

For most of the next 25 months, Castro's slowly growing guerrilla force waged mainly psychological warfare, striving above all to become a symbol of anti-Batista resistance. Although Castro called his small detachments "columns," his entire force the "Rebel Army," and its operation areas "fronts," the guerrillas' encounters with government troops were few and infrequent. Castro followed the basic guerrilla tactic of avoiding battle and of striking only when the enemy was outnumbered. After 1959, much was written in Cuba about the "battles" of Castro's "Rebel Army columns," never larger than 100 men each and equipped with an assortment of mostly obsolete weapons. But those rare encounters hardly produced more than a dozen fatalities. The rebel losses during the 1956–1958 struggle were never announced by Havana. According to Castro, his guerrilla force in August 1958 totalled only 300, including a handful of women. Batista's army was estimated at about 50,000 men.

It was the urban underground that carried the brunt of the daily and largely unpublicized war against Batista's police, losing in the process many of its best men. Yet, events played into Castro's hands. One by one, his potential city rivals for top revolutionary leadership were killed or lost political stature due to failures. While the Fidelista guerrillas stayed in their relatively safe mountain hideouts, the underground performed the dangerous task of corroding the dictatorship's morale through sabotage and other clandestine activities.

One group, significantly, suffered few, if any, losses during the anti-Batista insurrection. The *Partido Socialista Popular* (PSP), the Cuban Communist party, took no part in the struggle, neither in the mountains nor in the cities. Only in September 1958, when Batista's fall was regarded as a question of time, did the PSP send a few leaders into the hills.

## CASTRO ASSUMES POWER

Even though the fate of the regime was sealed several weeks before January 1, 1959, few Cubans expected the precipitous flight of the dictator, his cabinet, and high-ranking military leaders. Though he, too, was taken completely by surprise, Castro instantly reacted to Batista's departure. He proclaimed a nationwide general strike and set up a new government in Santiago de Cuba, naming Dr. Manuel Urrutia Lleo, a judge, as provisional president. He appointed himself "Commander-in-Chief" of the Cuban armed forces. But on January 8, when Castro arrived in Havana after a six-day "Victory March" along the entire length of the island, there was no doubt who was the real ruler of the country.

Virtually everything that happened in revolutionary Cuba after that first day in January was directly influenced by the personality of Fidel Castro. He had all the qualities of a charismatic leader. His explosive entry on the amorphous Cuban political scene sharply contrasted with the confusion and unhappiness that permeated Cuba under Batista. The seven-year-long dictatorship had seriously debilitated the fabric of the Cuban society, never well-knit or resilient. The Batista coup, carried out only a few months before the 1952 general election (regarded as the real test of Cuban democracy that might have solidified the country's weak institutions), produced a mood of bitter frustration in the bewildered nation. This feeling deepened as the dictatorship turned increasingly venal and repressive.

Under Batista, graft was an open practice. There was hardly any position in the executive, legislative, and judicial branches—let alone in the armed forces and the police—that was not used for personal gain. To be able to operate, industrialists had to pay off government and labor union officials. Even small merchants were at the mercy of greedy inspectors of every kind. A number of supposedly independent newspapermen regularly received large monetary "gifts" from the Presidential Palace. Some of the country's best-known intellectuals and artists also were on the government payroll. Prominent members of the Roman Catholic hierarchy were known as Batista sympathizers, making the Church less than popular in the eyes of many Cubans. As the spreading rebellion further damaged the economy, the dictatorship recruited thousands of unemployed Cubans as police informers and soldiers. It seemed as though Batista was determined to leave nothing unsoiled in the Cuban society.

The participation of several traditional political parties in the rigged 1954 elections and in the subsequent political negotiations with Batista aimed at a non-violent solution to Cuba's institutional crisis served to discredit their leaders. Opposition centered among the middle class and the students, who generally were strongly nationalistic, but not necessarily Marxist or anti-American. It was a shapeless coalition of forces pinning its hopes on the leadership of Fidel Castro as he boldly moved to fill the post-Batista vacuum.

Endowed with an exceptional gift of oratory, an excellent memory and amazing energy, Castro could speak extemporaneously for hours. He was able to articulate ideas in simple terms easily understood by all his audiences. But Castro was unpredictable and moody. He also could be suspicious, merciless, and proud. As many of his friends and enemies were to find out, he rarely forgot grudges. He was wary of men who could challenge his position of "Maximum Leader of the Revolution." As in so many authoritarian countries, a powerful second-in-command or even a collective leadership never developed in Cuba. There were few brilliant advisers around Castro. Few officials were known to publicly voice objections to his views. Those who dissented did not remain in their posts for long. Castro had very few, if any, close friends. Little was known of his personal life other than that his marriage ended in divorce in 1956 and that his only son, Fidel, lived in Cuba, his health impaired because of a serious automobile accident.

Castro's charisma, his stature as a victorious guerrilla leader—in addition to his pledges to solve Cuba's endemic problems—enabled him to secure absolute power. The overwhelming majority of the population enthusiastically accepted his leadership. While, at the outset, his authority was derived mainly from his personality, he soon created the real and lasting instruments of power as well. Batista's armed forces were quickly disbanded and the Rebel Army enlarged. An important branch of the Rebel Army was its intelligence service, the G-2, which rapidly extended its activities into civilian life. From a relatively small force, the G-2 quickly grew into the powerful Ministry of the Interior, controlling the regime's state security apparatus.

Castro was determined to be the supreme leader, unconstrained by constitutional limitations and a fixed elective mandate. He erased his previously proclaimed democratic promises. He incarcerated and ordered executions of many men, some of whom had been his close associates and supporters. Major Huber Matos, a top guerrilla leader, was sentenced in December 1959 to twenty years' imprisonment for denouncing Communist infiltration in the revolutionary government. Major Humberto Sorí Marín, Major William Morgan, and other Rebel Army officers who conspired against Castro were shot.

*Castro's Ideology*—Since the early 1960s, the anti-Batista struggle was portrayed as a *sui generis* Cuban social revolution inspired by

Marxist-Leninist ideas. Although the ideology of the 26 of July Movement was at best hazy, it certainly was not Marxist. In his statements before 1959, and shortly after taking over power, Castro advocated a democratic and elective form of government. He reassured Cubans that any revolutionary changes enacted by his government would be subject to a free referendum.

Castro had repeatedly denied he was a Marxist. "I have never been and am not a Communist. If I were, I should have the courage to say it," he declared in 1958. But on December 1, 1961, Castro indicated he had always been a Marxist-Leninist and said he would remain a Marxist "until the last day of my life." Later he expanded on the statement: "Of course, had we said from Turquino Peak (in the Sierra Maestra mountains) that we were Marxist-Leninists, we might possibly never have been able to descend to the plains below." On April 22, 1970, Castro formulated his credo in the following fashion: "I am Marxist-Leninist and anti-liberal. To me all bourgeois philosophy and all bourgeois liberal ideas are like old superstition, long since outmoded. The 26 of July Movement was not a Communist movement. What could be said is that some of us who had organized that movement were strongly influenced by Marxist-Leninist ideology . . . and that the conception that inspired the revolutionary strategy which resulted in the 1959 victory was the . . . hybridization of the essential ideas of Marxism and Leninism with the peculiar experiences of our country."

## CUBA'S POLITICAL AND ECONOMIC TRANSFORMATION

On February 16, 1959, Castro formally became prime minister of Cuba with full executive powers. Three months later, he enacted the first important revolutionary measure, the Agrarian Reform. The May 1959 reform marked the beginning of the confiscatory period of the revolution, which lasted until the middle of 1961. During that time, big and medium agricultural estates and most of the industries, businesses and commercial establishments were expropriated. The revolutionary government made few demands on the people. Castro was constantly assuring the country that abundance was just around the corner and would be attained if only everybody would trust his judgment and support his revolutionary measures.

While transforming Cuba's economic and social institutions, Castro introduced his own style of governing which, he said, "reminds us of the Greek democracy where people in a public square discussed and decided upon their destiny." At multitudinous rallies and Castro's marathon television appearances, critics of revolutionary measures were vilified, with most venom reserved for those in the United States.

The most enthusiastic supporters of the reforms included the leaders of the Cuban Communist party, and Castro soon realized the usefulness of the party machinery. Communists unquestioningly praised his ideas; they attacked his detractors; and they provided disciplined cadres for carrying out his revolutionary laws. Soon Castro and Communist leaders, with Moscow's blessings, joined in an alliance.

But it was a liaison full of mutual suspicion and mistrust. Top PSP leaders, appointed to important posts in the Castro regime, almost immediately tried to undercut the premier's hitherto unchallenged authority. They not only replaced a number of Fidelistas— even in the army—with known PSP members, but also began to denounce, without mentioning Castro, the cult of personality and advocate collective leadership as the only proper form of government for socialist Cuba. In 1961, Blás Roca, head of the PSP, travelled to Moscow and was received with the highest honors by Soviet Premier Nikita S. Khrushchev. Roca's book, *The Foundation of Socialism in Cuba*, became the country's best seller with 700,000 copies printed. Lazaro Peña, another veteran Communist, became secretary-general of the Cuban Confederation of Labor. All new government appointments had to be cleared through the office of Aníbal Escalante, former organization secretary of the PSP, who in July 1961 was placed in charge of organizing Cuba's unified Marxist party.

In March 1962, Castro struck back. He dismissed Escalante, charging him with "sectarianism and dogmatism," and accusing him of trying to secure a dominating influence for the veteran Communists in the party and state organizations. A few years later, Castro eliminated practically all the Communist "Old Guard" leaders and their underlings from positions of power. Some of them were even jailed, among them Deputy Defense Minister Joaquín Ordoqui in 1964, and Aníbal Escalante in 1968. The latter was accused of anti-party "microfaction" activities.

The 1960 visit to Havana by Anastas Mikoyan, then first deputy premier of the Soviet Union, made feasible the radicalization of the revolution. It brought about the establishment of close political, economic, and military ties between Havana and Moscow and the rest of the Communist bloc. Now Castro no longer had to fear United States reprisals as he proceeded to sharpen his revolutionary aims. Later in the year, Committees for the Defense of the Revolution, watch-dog groups organized in every city block, were created to assist the G-2 in repressing anti-Castro conspiracies. Later, as the committees grew in size—by 1970 they had over three million members—they were given additional, multifaceted social and economic duties. Together with other "mass organizations" (among them the Federation of Cuban Women), the committees became Castro's basic tool for trying to accomplish his economic and social goals by a participatory, collective effort and for solving the difficulties confronting the revolutionary government. The educational system, the labor unions, and student and professional organizations as well as all the news media were put under state control. By the end of 1961, when Cuba's ruling Marxist-Leninist party was organized, the existence of a Communist state in the Caribbean became an established fact.

The party was organized by several stages and, as elsewhere in Communist countries, underwent several purges. In June 1961, the 26 of July Movement, the *Partido Socialista Popular* (Communist), and the 13 of March Student Directorate (an anti-Batista student group) merged to form the Integrated Revolutionary Organizations (ORI). Escalante, named ORI's organization secretary, proceeded to build its structure according to the Soviet model. After the dismissal of Escalante (who was also blamed by Castro for introducing chaos in the government and giving jobs to PSP members "who were hidden under their beds during the struggle against Batista"), ORI was thoroughly purged of "Anibalitos" and renamed the United Party of the Socialist Revolution (PURS). In October 1965, PURS became the Communist Party of Cuba (PCC), and in the process the party's membership was again revised. There was another party purge following the discovery, arrest, and trial of Escalante's Communist "microfaction" in 1968.

The defeat of the April 1961 Bay of Pigs invasion by a group of exiles equipped and supported by the United States strengthened the Castro rule, then increasingly harassed by internal opposition. While the Rebel Army and the militia battalions destroyed in three days the poorly-trained force of about 1,700 exiles, Castro's security forces arrested some 100,000 men and women throughout the country. Even though most of them were released after two or three weeks, the anti-Communist underground, which before the invasion had been gaining momentum and self-confidence, was smashed. Following the Bay of Pigs, no meaningful, organized opposition to Castro developed again in Cuba. Occasional hit-and-run actions by exiles, often helped by the Central Intelligence Agency, had only limited tactical objectives and produced no noticeable political effects.

THE GOVERNING PROCESS IN CUBA

After 1961, with Cuba's socioeconomic upheaval practically completed, the Castro regime settled down to the task of governing. But economic difficulties tended to increase rather than diminish as time went on. Some of the prestige Castro won by defeating the invasion was lost in 1962 when the Soviet Union, disregarding his views, withdrew its ballistic missiles from Cuba to avoid a confrontation with the United States. Cuban-Soviet relations cooled noticeably, Castro talked publicly of his "differences" with Moscow, and declared that he would never have "given in" as Khrushchev had done.

To be sure, Castro wanted the Cuban revolution to be always on the move, constantly experimenting. He proclaimed that Socialism and Communism were simultaneously being built in Cuba where, he said, the first new "Socialist man" would be created, an abnegated, selfless individual liberated from the vestiges of the former materialistic, easy-going Caribbean mentality. "The Revolution has to be necessarily audacious, it cannot follow a lengthy, unending course of action," Castro observed. He argued that a "true revolution" must be in a state of continuous change, permanently in a process of catharsis. To instill that sense of motion, Castro constantly travelled throughout the country. He supervised ongoing projects, set up agricultural and social "pilot" plans, praised and criticized officials, listened to complaints and gave his political and economic "orientations." But there was little method in Castro's own peripatetic *modus operandi,* which was adopted by many of his close collaborators. Castro, who admittedly dislikes paperwork, had no permanent staff of any size, nor a fixed office to conduct government business. His office, he would say, is where he happened to be at a given moment. Thus he became increasingly involved in time-consuming administrative details on the lowest level, often risking the loss of nationwide perspective. The effectiveness of his itinerant way of governing had to be limited because of his unusual ways. Castro appeared to operate on the premise that energy was more efficient than efficiency. And some Cuban officials conceded that the "revolutionary enthusiasm" actually generated by Castro's brief presences at factories or state farms tended to fade away shortly afterwards.

Unlike most Communist countries, which go through the motions of elections and approval of government and party policies by elected representatives, in Cuba it was the Council of Ministers, appointed and directed by Castro, that held alone the executive, legislative and often judicial powers. The council's decrees-laws were usually published without forewarning. Some of them were announced, however, by Castro at public rallies, and the applause greeting his announcements was the only tangible expression of approval. Traditional corruption was practically eliminated after the revolution. Yet the squandering of public resources—due to "ignorance," as Castro put it—continued and was as costly as Batista's malfeasance. In terms of public administration, therefore, one set of problems was replaced by another.

The Communist Party of Cuba was the country's only political organization. With some 100,000 members in 1970, it was structured according to the European Communist model. Its highest executive bodies were the eight-member Political Bureau and the six-member Secretariat, both headed by Castro. They were supposed to carry out the directives of the party's 100-member Central Committee. But the Central Committee—almost two-thirds of its hand-picked members were army officers—did not meet formally after its creation in 1965,

contrary to the model. Party secretariats were set up in each of Cuba's
six provinces as well as in every region, municipality, and city ward.
Party committees were organized in practically all factories, state
farms, offices, larger military units, etc.

Party members were selected chiefly from among "exemplary" production workers. Since this selection method put a premium on physical accomplishments of Cuban Communists, the party had some 80
schools for "elevating political, cultural and technical level" of its
members. No exact line of authority was drawn between the party
and the administration. At the top, the party theoretically was to
direct the government. At the intermediate and lower levels, its members had the duty of supervising the execution of administrative orders. Factory and farm administrators were generally party appointees,
with the prime criterion being their political reliability rather than
technical capacity. But since they were usually better trained than
the party's *aparatchikis,* there were constant frictions between them.
All the ministers, most of the highest-ranking army officers, and many
administrators were party members.

The Communist Party of Cuba had a highly vertical power structure, tightly controlled at the top by a quasi-military oligarchy. Soviet-
style democratic centralism was not introduced in Castro's Marxist
organization. Rank-and-file Communists had no visible channels for
intra-party discussion. The party's theoretical monthly, *Cuba Socialista,* which between 1962 and 1965 had shed some light on divergent
opinions on national and international issues, was closed down allegedly because of the lack of newsprint. Castro's penchant for supervising the most insignificant details of the governing process and for
participating personally in low-level decision-making inevitably weak-
ened the party apparatus.

The First National Congress of the Communist Party of Cuba, an
event which for Communist national organizations everywhere represents a landmark in party life, was postponed twice, most recently in
1970. Thus there could be no wide-ranging examination of the revolution's basic problems, including the question of the legal framework of
revolutionary Cuba. In May 1961, Castro had declared that the 1940
constitution, which, in a slightly amended form had been declared the
law of the land by the revolutionary government in February 1959,
was no longer valid and that Cuba would soon have her "Socialist
Constitution." (On that occasion, the premier also stated that elections
were no longer necessary in Cuba.) In 1965, the party's Central Committee named a constitutional commission, but it suspended its deliberations three years later without announcing any results. Judicial
procedure followed the general maxim of "the good of the people."
Arbitrary arrests and summary punishments of citizens continued to
be common practice. Consequently, Cuba was one of the few Com-

munist countries without a constitutional and clearly defined legal framework.

The intervention of the state in daily life was total. From an early age, the Cuban lived under the shadow of the state. When boys and girls entered elementary schools, they were channelled into "Cuban Pioneers," an organization that taught them rudimentary notions of Marxism-Leninism. As they grew older, they were increasingly involved in extracurricular activities with more Marxist indoctrination. At ten, school children participated in the harvesting of coffee, cotton, and fruit crops, attended public rallies, marched at official parades, etc. At fifteen, a large number joined the Union of Young Communists, the Cuban equivalent of the Soviet Komsomol.

For adult Cubans, membership in a number of government-controlled "mass organizations" was practically unavoidable as the state was the only employer in the country. Joining the trade unions was obligatory. Many women were members of the Federation of Cuban Women. All citizens were urged to belong to the Committees for the Defense of the Revolution, which, in 1970, claimed over three million members.

Cubans were subjected to a constant barrage of state propaganda, telling them what to think, whom to love or hate. Their life was a highly regimented one. They were instructed where to buy food, which "volunteer" work to perform and when, how much and what to produce. The secret police, helped by the defense committees, watched over their activities and warned them if they fell out of line. Opponents of the government were harshly treated. Between 1959 and 1970, Cuban newspapers printed the names of over 1,000 persons who had been executed. Although no precise figures were available, foreign observers estimated that in 1970 there were no less than 20,000 political prisoners in Cuban jails and labor camps. Castro himself put the number at some 15,000. Cubans who asked permission to leave the country were dismissed from their jobs and, except for the old and sick, sent for lengthy periods to special working "agricultural battalions." They were treated as second class citizens and, when allowed to leave, had to deed to the government all their possessions, with the exception of a few personal belongings.

ECONOMY OF REVOLUTIONARY CUBA

From the outset, the government's principal concern was the task of organizing and administering the island's state-directed economy. As soon as socialization got underway, Cuban leaders discovered that it was easier to expropriate private companies than to run them efficiently and profitably. The shortage of trained managerial personnel was the first problem that adversely affected the performance of the growing state economic sector. Middle-class Cubans—the administra-

tors, technicians and professionals, the *gusanos* (worms), as Castro
called them—began to leave the country in 1960 by the thousands.
They were replaced in their jobs by Castro's unconditional supporters,
often lacking technical or educational qualifications.

In the meantime, the regime had to face a major demographic
transformation. Cuba's population, which totalled about 6.5 million
in 1959, reached 8.3 million by the end of 1970, despite the departure
of some 500,000 citizens. Since December 1965, under an agreement
between the United States and Cuban governments, about 45,000
refugees had been arriving annually on the mainland. The island's
annual birth rate increase was estimated at 2.2 percent, in the absence
of any known government-sponsored birth control program. According
to an official Cuban source, the divorce rate in the first six years of
the revolution increased by more than three hundred percent.

Castro's problems, which were only beginning in the early 1960s, were
often of his own making for Cuba is an extremely rich island. Described by its discoverer, Christopher Columbus, as "the most beautiful
country human eyes have ever seen," the 44,278-square-mile island,
about the size of Pennsylvania, has a moderate and stable climate and
is covered by a perpetual green mantle of lush vegetation giving it a
semblance of a tropical garden. Plentiful and valuable minerals, mainly
nickel, copper and manganese, are the wealth of the subsoil. Primarily
an agricultural country, Cuba produced in abundance fruit, vegetables, coffee, tobacco, and principally sugar. Cognizant of the island's
wealth, Spain tried to hold on to it by force and thus Cuba was the
last Spanish colony in the Americas to gain independence.

In spite of intermittent political turmoil, between 1902 and 1958,
Cuba achieved remarkable economic and social progress due as much
to the great potential of her resources as to the resourcefulness of her
inhabitants. There was practically no class or racial friction in the
country. Social and economic upward mobility was customary and
racial mixture was a common and long-accepted practice. But the
island had chronic socioeconomic problems. The economy was too
dependent on sugar, although this dependence started to diminish
after the Second World War. Unemployment in general, mitigated
by seasonal employment during harvests, was relatively high, especially
in the countryside. Even though Cuba's per capita income compared
favorably with other Latin American countries, the wealth was unevenly distributed. Illiteracy was high and education funds were often
squandered or misappropriated by venal politicians and government
officials.

One of the first problems facing Castro was how to end the economic recession produced chiefly by the two years of military and
political strife. He, therefore, proposed a two-point program: to
diversify agriculture to free the country from overdependence on sugar

and to speed up industrialization to reduce imports, principally from the United States. At the same time, government decrees drastically cut rents and increased wages. A public works program was launched, substantially reducing unemployment. Later, unemployment, an endemic Cuban problem, was eliminated altogether by the revolutionary government. Under the Agrarian Reform, big estates were broken up to be converted into peasant cooperatives.

The creation of the Central Planning Board in February 1960 signaled the start of the Socialist phase of the Cuban economy. Western European and Latin American Marxist economists, among them Frenchmen Charles Bettelheim and René Dumont, came to Cuba to serve as top economic advisers and to aid in setting up state agencies to absorb confiscated private enterprises. Organizational models of the European Communist countries were adopted in most cases. Guevara's Ministry of Industry took over major industrial installations. The Institute of Agrarian Reform had control over the seized land. It soon transformed worker cooperatives into state farms—the Cuban counterpart of the Sovkhozes. (Additional small-sized farms were expropriated in October 1963, leaving only a fraction of arable land in private hands. But owners of small farms had to sell their produce to the state, which told them what to cultivate and how.) Private service, trade, and artisan activities—even those carried out by individuals—were outlawed in 1968.

But as he rapidly transformed Cuba's private enterprise system into a centrally-directed state economy, Castro led the country into inflation and monumental bureaucratic chaos. By 1961, agricultural production declined sharply and late that year food rationing was introduced for the first time in the nation's history. (It was later expanded to embrace all foodstuffs and manufactured products, although on occasions perishable staples, when available, were sold freely.) The country entered a stage of perennial economic crises, even though revolutionary leaders continued to announce grandiose development plans.

"Industrialization" became the basis of the revolution's economic policy. In 1962, Guevara assured the nation that by 1965 Cuba would be the most industrialized country in Latin America, leading the continent in per capita production of electric power, steel, cement, and tractors and in petroleum refining. Blaming sugar for most of the country's economic ills, Castro and, especially, Guevara became obsessed by what they later described as "the anti-sugar spirit." Consequently, hundreds of thousands of acres of the best sugar land were cleared for other crops that failed to materialize, at least in the quantities planned.

By 1963, Castro realized that his industrial and agricultural plans were simply not working. Cuba became more economically dependent on the Soviet bloc than she had ever been on the United States. Production in all sectors was steadily declining and so was labor productivity. Moreover, the Soviet bloc countries were unable or unwilling to supply Cuba with factories, machinery, and the technical assistance they had promised. As a result of hasty Cuban-Soviet planning, costly blunders were made. Several small factories were installed, but it developed that no provisions had been made for the importation of raw materials essential for their operation. Lacking hydroelectric potential or oil deposits, Cuba was totally dependent on Soviet petroleum that had to be ferried for weeks over more than 6,000 miles, while her earlier sources, the United States or Venezuela, were only a few days away. In 1960, when Soviet oil shipments began arriving in Cuba, the government said that Russian petroleum was cheaper than what it had been purchasing before. It was not known whether that price remained the same ten years later. In 1970, there were no figures available on total Cuban-Soviet trade.

At the same time, serious flaws in Cuba's economic organizational structure became visible. No necessary investments in infrastructure were made or planned. Foreign Marxist advisers began to leave the country, voicing their disappointment over the inefficiency of a huge and rigid state apparatus, which controlled the entire economy from Havana. Bettelheim blamed Guevara for most of the difficulties. He described state agencies created by Guevara as "aberrations," and stated that Guevara's insistence on enforcing the principle of "moral incentives" to stimulate production was "idealistic voluntarism." In spite of this criticism—and other less than enthusiastic comments by Soviet bloc economists—Castro not only doggedly continued to endorse the principle of moral incentives, but also insisted that reverting to material incentives was to stray from Marxism. In 1968, he said:

> . . . We should not use money or wealth to create consciousness. We must use consciousness to create wealth. To offer a man more than is expected is to buy his consciousness with money . . . Communism cannot be established if we do not create abundant wealth. But the way to do this, in our opinion, is not by creating consciousness through money or wealth, but by creating wealth through consciousness.

Faced with the inevitable, and probably pressed by the Soviet Union, Castro abandoned his much-publicized industrialization plans. In 1964, after a trip to Moscow, he reversed his economic policy. Under a plan elaborated with Khrushchev and unveiled in 1965, high sugar production became Castro's principal economic goal. The two leaders announced that according to the principle of "Socialist division of labor," Cuba was to become the Communist bloc's main supplier of sugar. The country's annual sugar output was to increase progressively from 6.5 million metric tons in 1966 to 10 million tons in 1970. During that five-year period, Cuba was to produce 41 million tons of sugar, of which more than half was to be delivered to the Soviet Union, with additional quantities for other Communist countries. Plans for agricultural diversification were postponed to expand sugar-cane plantations. On his part, Khrushchev formally pledged to solve Cuba's problem of declining farm labor productivity by supplying Soviet-made cane-cutting and loading combines to rapidly mechanize sugar-cane harvesting, a promise he failed to keep.

The about-face in Cuba's economic policy was a bitter defeat for Castro and above all for Guevara. In April 1965, shortly after the new sugar plan had been officially unveiled, Guevara left Cuba. He was killed two years later leading a guerrilla force in Bolivia. Following his departure, the Ministry of Industry was divided into several smaller ministries. Most of his trusted aides were promptly replaced. The reasons why Guevara abandoned Cuba and his high and honored position will probably remain forever a secret. Overtly, there were no political or personal disagreements between him and Castro, who had respect and deference for his Argentine-born companion. But Guevara may have become bored with routine plodding as an administrator. A firm believer in the revolutionary domino theory, as applied in Latin America, he might have thought that Bolivia would represent the first stage of a continental Socialist upheaval. He might have reasoned that, if successful, he would become the top revolutionary leader of Latin America.

The 1965–1970 sugar plan did badly. State bureaucracy continued as rampant as ever. The government's urgent calls for harder work fell on deaf ears. Absenteeism and labor inefficiency increased constantly. Outward expressions of popular support for the Castro regime at government-organized rallies were not matched by conscientious and productive daily work. Many Cubans may well have resented being ordered to work extra hours "voluntarily" without pay. An exodus from the rural areas to the cities, principally caused by the government's failure to meet more fully the needs of the countryside populations, created labor shortages at the state farms. The government reacted by sending thousands of city dwellers to work on the farms, sometimes for months. But the efficiency of these agricultural "volunteers" was poor at best; they were unhappy over periodic separations from their families. Weariness and dissatisfaction spread throughout the country, compounded by the realization that, Castro's optimistic statements notwithstanding, things were not getting better.

Confronted with what appeared to be a massive but unorganized passive resistance of the population, the government launched in 1968 a "Revolutionary Offensive" attempting, as it said, to strike "the final blow at the remnants of the bourgeois society." As part of the "offensive," all public bars, nightclubs and other places of amusement

in the country were closed. Imposing a regime of "revolutionary austerity," Castro declared that Cuba would become a truly "equalitarian
society," with all citizens working hard and sharing the rewards of
their labor.

Although many government officials did work hard without high
salaries or bonuses, the Cuban "equalitarianism" was something of a
myth. Communist party leaders and high-ranking armed forces officers
were more equal than the rest. They did not have to stand in line
for hours for their daily food rations. They lived in the best homes
which once belonged to the exiled middle-class Cubans and they drove
their automobiles. When those cars wore down, they were awarded new
Alfa Romeos imported from Italy by the government.

Meanwhile, the Cuban *guajiros,* the humble peasants, continued to
live as before the revolution: in thatched-roofed huts *(bohios)* with
dirt floors and no sanitary facilities. In the cities, as Castro himself
also acknowledged, there were countless shacks made of scraps of
wood, old metal signs, and other odd materials the dwellers managed
to secure. In July 1970, Castro said that "the tremendous shortage of
housing" was one of Cuba's major social problems. Stating that "those
miserable *bohios* are everywhere," the premier said that there was a
deficit of one million housing units in Cuba. A month later, the Cuban
official newspaper *Granma* said that housing construction in Santiago,
Cuba's second city, "has been almost totally abandoned to concentrate
[building] efforts on other economic tasks."

But, undoubtedly, the bulk of the revolution's popular support—
whose depth and solidity are always difficult to gauge—still came from
industrial and agricultural workers. While the majority of peasants
and workers received few rewards for their toil, they did not have to
worry about unemployment. They benefited from free social services,
such as medical care and education for their children, and, often, free
rent and meals at work. From this social group the government selected
the lower echelon of its officialdom: administrators of state enterprises
and factory and state farm supervisors.

Castro, who came to power mainly with the support of the middle
class and the peasants, significantly downgraded the importance of
the latter. Even though during the revolutionary struggle organized
labor was generally indifferent to his movement, he said on July 26,
1970, that "the industrial proletariat is the truly revolutionary class,
the most potentially revolutionary class" in Cuba. Castro strove to
instill in his working-class supporters a sense of pride and dignity
from having defied the most powerful nation in the world—the United
States—and gotten away with it.

But, inevitably, the nation was taking much for granted. Many
young Cubans had forgotten that without the revolution they would
have had no free education nor assured employment once out of school.

As "Viator," an observer who revisited Cuba after ten years of Castro wrote in the January 1970 issue of *Foreign Affairs,* "a sense of frustration may well have developed among young people who can find no outlets for their aptitudes in an educational system which ignores the humanities." And adult workers, having heard so many promises of a better life, were pressing for quicker progress and material rewards.

## THE NEW ECONOMY

There was one important factor which, even according to European Marxists, contributed to the steady worsening of the Cuban economic situation: Castro's growing personal involvement in planning and executing his government's economic policy. Whatever his attributes as a political leader, Castro, trained as a lawyer, displayed a limited understanding of economics, of the needs of a semi-developed country like Cuba, and of the necessity for basic scientific research in directing a modern society. Yet, on his orders, nationwide projects were launched without adequate previous scientific studies, often against the advice of Cuban and foreign experts. Almost invariably, these projects turned out to be failures. The Voisin episode is a case in point.

Early in December 1964, André Voisin, a French gentleman-farmer and amateur agronomist, arrived in Cuba at the invitation of Castro who had read his book on rotational grazing. After two weeks, during which he delivered several lectures on cattle breeding in Cuba, Voisin suddenly died in Havana. But his short presence convinced Castro of the correctness of what most agronomists regard as a pseudo-scientific approach to animal husbandry. Following Voisin's advice, Castro ordered rotational grazing paddocks throughout the country and placed cattle in them. Castro also had Voisin's lengthy book on grazing and ecology serialized for months in all Cuban newspapers and magazines. Since Voisin's theory did not take into account Cuba's unpredictable rain precipitation and the lack of irrigation and silage facilities, millions of head of cattle starved during the exceptionally dry 1965 and 1966 seasons. Only when cattle mortality reached large proportions in 1967 was the Voisin plan abandoned. The experiment is believed to have cost Cuba at least $50 million.

Despite the Voisin fiasco, Castro continued to consider himself the country's principal cattle expert and, subsequently, he ignored the opinions of British scientists whom he brought to Cuba to work on livestock development. At the May 1969 Congress of the Cuban Institute of Animal Science, Castro brushed aside documented studies by several British and Cuban cattle specialists, declaring that their experiments and findings did not take political factors into consideration. Science and politics are inseparable, Castro asserted, and pronounced the latter more important than the former in charting the country's economic policy.

The recent history of Cuba abounds in Castro's costly economic failures and haphazard plans. His economic recklessness, according to some Marxist critics, was due to his certainty that no matter what the scope and cost of the blunders, the Soviet Union would always come to his rescue. And, indeed, the Soviet assistance to Cuba kept growing. In the 1964–1968 period, Soviet aid, designed to keep the Cuban economy afloat, was estimated at some $350 million a year. By 1970, it reportedly increased to almost $600 million annually, with Cuba's total debt believed to be over $3 billion, excluding military aid. The Soviet Union was receiving from Cuba mainly sugar—a commodity Russia did not need as a sugar exporter herself—and was paying for it a premium price of 6.11 cents a pound, about twice the average price on the world market.

Castro assured himself of the continuation of that support by endorsing, with some reservations, the Soviet 1968 invasion of Czechoslovakia and aligning himself with the Kremlin leadership in its stand against Peking. Until 1968, Castro had repeatedly underlined Cuba's freedom from foreign tutelage and had spoken disapprovingly of his Soviet bloc allies. "This Revolution will maintain its absolute independence . . . and follow its own path," Castro said in 1967. "This Revolution will never be a satellite of anyone nor will it ask permission of anyone to maintain its ideological position, externally and internally," he declared. But by supporting the Russian move into Czechoslovakia and following the Soviet line afterwards, his revolution appeared to have lost the independent image Castro had been striving to preserve.

Castro's endorsement of the Soviet invasion, which came three days after Russian soldiers occupied Prague, was not expected by most Cubans. During those initial days, the controlled Cuban press and radio had maintained a posture of neutrality, giving equal space to Soviet justifications of the invasion and the Czechoslovak condemnations of it. Apparently encouraged by what on the balance appeared to be a show of sympathy for the Czechoslovak Communist reformist movement, Czech technicians in Havana reportedly marched through the streets of the capital shouting patriotic and anti-Russian slogans and receiving vocal support from cheering *Habaneros*. But the brief evenhandedness ended after Castro's speech. The premier conceded that many people in Cuba had reacted strongly against the occupation of Czechoslovakia by foreign troops, but he termed this a "romantic and idealistic posture." He recognized that the decision to invade Czechoslovakia had no legal basis, yet emphasized that the action was necessary to prevent the Czechoslovak Communist party under Alexander Dubček from "marching toward a counter-revolutionary situation, capitalism, and into the embrace of imperialism."

Having failed to reach the first four production targets of his 1966–

1970 sugar plan, Castro staked his government's prestige on fulfilling the plan's final stage—10 million tons of sugar in 1970. Meeting that goal was a question of "the honor of the Revolution," Castro said, adding that to produce even one pound of sugar less than the 10 million tons would be a defeat. He assured the country that every contingency had been foreseen to make the harvest a success and to convince the world that his government could keep its word.

In July 1969, to give the country ample time for the harvest, Castro put the Cuban economy on war footing with practically all the available labor force mobilized for cane cultivation and cutting. Sugar mills were enlarged and the transportation system was overhauled. Over $200 million were invested in improvements of every kind in the sugar industry, not counting the cost of expanding cane-growing areas which had been repeatedly fertilized to ensure high sucrose yield.

But in May 1970, Castro dejectedly announced that he had lost. He attributed the failure to the "ignorance" of the revolutionary leadership, including his own. At the same time, he disclosed that efforts to mechanize sugarcane harvesting proved to be unsuccessful and that practically all cane cutting had to be done manually. At the end of the harvest, in July, 8,535,000 tons of sugar had been produced, making the total output for the 1966–1970 period 28.8 million tons instead of the planned 41 million tons. The 1966–1970 production was actually not much higher than the output of the preceding five years, when the crops were harvested without elaborate preparations and in much less time. Still, the 1970 harvest was the largest in history.

On July 26, 1970, in a speech commemorating the anniversary of the 1953 Moncada attack, Castro delivered a *post mortem* of the sugar harvest and an analysis of the Cuban economic situation. According to Castro, the failure of Cuba's "great leap forward"—as the ten-million-ton harvest had been called—not only made the revolutionary government suffer a "moral defeat," but it also wrought havoc in virtually every segment of the nation's economy. The concentration of practically all the human and technical resources on one economic objective increased the long-existing strains within the country as it was left with few resources to tend its basic social needs. Bleak as Cuba's economic situation was in 1970, he said, it was not going to begin improving until 1975, with a promised change for the better noticeable only by the end of the decade.

The housing situation was critical, Castro admitted. Cuba urgently needed one million new dwellings, but would not get even a fraction of that number in the next five years. There was a great shortage of schoolrooms and teachers. In 1970, only 32 percent of Cuba's population was employed, Castro said, and this low ratio would not increase at least until 1975. The premier commented:

Our enemies are saying there are difficulties [in Cuba]—and they are right; our enemies are saying we have problems—and they are right; our enemies are saying there is discontent—and they are right; our enemies are saying there are irritations—and in reality they are right.

But while he took personal blame for the economic and social disarray in the country, and even half-seriously offered to resign, he did not propose any fundamental changes either in his economic policies or the revolutionary leadership which still seemed to have the potential to instill a sense of dynamism in the nation. "Unfortunately the problems cannot be solved by replacing revolutionary leaders . . . we don't bring magic solutions. Only through the will of the people our problems will be solved," Castro said.

THE IMPACT

Even though Castro sought to soothe the tensions with pledges of changes in the political system and by promising to make it more responsive to popular needs, many Cubans, particularly in the middle-age groups, became increasingly disillusioned, their hopes eroded by the passage of time and their standard of living declining.

The premier himself admitted that workers were largely unresponsive to his exhortations. In September 1970, he said that about 400,000 workers, twenty percent of the country's labor force, were "shirkers." At a Havana factory meeting, which according to the official announcement was convoked to discuss "mounting absenteeism," Castro criticized "indifference, irresponsibility, disorganization, chaos, incompetence and inefficiency" in a number of production centers:

> The Revolution is going through a moment of crisis, perhaps because of having advanced too much. It is like advancing too deeply into enemy lines with troops that are still insufficiently trained and with poor commanders. Let me say that neither this nation's economy, nor that of any other nation can tolerate the corrosive, demoralizing and disruptive action of 400,000 shirkers. What I am sure of is that 20 percent of these loafers can ruin the work of 80 percent of the people if we do not become aware of this and do not win the battle against them.

Despite a concerted effort to combat "absenteeism and laziness," launched by the Cuban government in early September 1970, little visible progress was made. In November, Havana reported that absenteeism in some production centers rose to over 40 percent, and that the bureaucratic system of "passing-the-ball," under which officials avoid making decisions and thus taking responsibility for possible mistakes, also was more widespread. By the end of 1970, many government officials became, as Castro put it, "demoralized," and the loss of the revolutionary élan was noted by official Cuban commentators. In 1959, Cuba's leaders were by-and-large young, vigorous, and enthusiastic. Twelve years later, they had become middle-aged and dis-pirited—"worn out and shriveled," as Castro described many of them in his July 26, 1970, speech.

But he still seemed to have much of the youth with him—young persons who were children when he took power and who grew up under and with the revolution. To them, the social and nationalist revolution remained a shiny dream.

Measured in terms of its contribution to the economic well-being of the Cuban people after twelve years in power, Castro's revolutionary government, even by its own account, fell short of the goals it had set in 1959, and which it later revised downward. It could not match promises with performance. According to the best available estimates by Western economists (after 1966 Havana stopped announcing specific production figures), Cuba's gross national product in 1970 was about $3.5 billion, only slightly higher than in 1958 when the country had two million fewer inhabitants. As suggested by Castro in his July 26 speech, the Cuban economy had neither capital, technological know-how, nor well trained political and administrative leadership to make appreciable progress in the foreseeable future. The premier indicated that his government's 1970–1975 economic policy would focus on im-proving the efficiency of state farms and factories, and on making "micro-investments"—purchases of inexpensive machinery abroad to eliminate "production bottlenecks."

Structurally, Castro's Cuba remained a political dictatorship, with most of her institutions organized along military lines and many of them run by army officers. The allocation of the nation's resources was in the hands of Castro, who decided what the population ate, what clothing it wore, where it worked, and what leisure it enjoyed. The police apparatus easily disposed of the most vociferous protesters, though popular grumbling and dissatisfaction, a Cuban trait, went on.

Considering the resources the government said it invested in social programs during the 1959–1970 period, the results seemed to fall below expectations. Commendably, a determined effort was made to wipe out illiteracy. Full scholarships were provided to hundreds of thousands of young Cubans of both sexes, many of whom otherwise would have probably begun working at an earlier age or not gone to school at all. But Communist Cuba's educational system was yet to show its ability to train skilled administrators and technicians. According to Castro, the majority of officials in charge of state-owned agricultural and industrial enterprises in 1970 had less than six years of elementary education. In 1970, an army major was appointed the minister of education and another major was made his first deputy.

"Our teachers have multiple weaknesses of a technical nature, and it is true that they lack pedagogic experience," former Education Min-ister José Llanusa said in 1969. More important, Llanusa disclosed that out of a total of 1,800,000 students in Cuban elementary and high schools during the 1968–1969 school year—a high number by Latin American standards—about 140,000 dropped out altogether after enrollment. Absenteeism among students between the ages of six and sixteen, he said, reached 400,000. But this rate certainly was not worse than elsewhere in Latin America. Llanusa also declared that, "more than 700,000 students at the elementary and high school levels give evidence of retardation that can be regarded as the equivalent of more than two academic years." Llanusa's call for "improving the quality of educators" was echoed by Major Belarmino Castilla Más who replaced him in July 1970, and who again emphasized the problems of "school desertions" and of "the deficit of teachers and professors in the country." In October, the official newspaper *Granma* reported that in Oriente Province alone there were some 80,000 youths between thirteen and sixteen years of age who neither studied nor worked.

Cuba's universities had their share of troubles, too, inasmuch as their precise fate as institutions of higher learning was uncertain. Under a plan announced by Castro in 1970, the country's three separate universities were to be abolished and their facilities converted into new centers of advanced study and research. The basic undergraduate teaching was to be conducted at industrial and other production centers where future engineers would study and work at the same time. Cuban universities, as one Chilean sympathizer of the revolution observed in 1970, "ceased to be the critical conscience of the country." Under the 1967 concept of "integral education," Cuban youth became part of the country's labor force when agricultural work was made an intrinsic part of the curriculum.

The government has made a relatively large financial effort to develop a cultural establishment. In the early 1960s, the Castro regime not only sought to suggest that the revolution had stimulated an effervescent artistic vitality in Cuba, but it also demanded that the country be recognized by the hemisphere's leftist intellectuals as Latin America's cultural and artistic leader. Yet the revolutionary cultural rejuvenation proved to be ephemeral and soon Havana's official artistic circles submerged into ennui and stagnation. In 1965, as Ché Guevara wrote, there were no artists "of authority" in Cuba. Revolutionary Cuba did not serve as a catalyst for artistic creation, and failed to develop a cultural image of her own.

Considering the basic wealth of the island and the great patriotic fervor and energy generated by the downfall of the Batista dictatorship, Castro could have turned Cuba into a country where all citizens would have "bread without terror." But he seemed to have lost a rare historical opportunity to forge a new socially-advanced democratic order in Latin America. Instead, he turned to Marxism-Leninism for ideological justification of his system and to the Soviet bloc for economic and military support. His reluctance to delegate authority and his insistence on exercising absolute power made him the irreplaceable incarnation of the Cuban revolution. While underlining the towering strength of his personality, it represented a potentially dangerous weakness for the regime.

The revolution's strong de-emphasis of material incentives and rewards represented a departure not only from the deeply entrenched values of the Cuban people, but also from modern Marxism as practiced in nearly every other Communist country. In his strenuous effort to reshape the easy-going Caribbean mentality of the Cuban people, Castro failed to produce a political and administrative organization able to steer revolutionary enthusiasm into productive channels. The premier unquestionably maintained a degree of personal popularity and was capable of dealing with international problems, but his vertical administrative structure could not properly organize garbage collection, distribution of milk, shoe repairs, or the fixing of a roof. Fidel Castro, as James Reston wrote in *The New York Times,* "has mastered the art of being popular, but not the complicated problems of growing cane, exporting and importing, or governing the urban and rural populations of his island."

Neither did Castro solve the problem of succession. With the Communist party weak and the administrative apparatus still in disarray, the Cuban armed forces loomed in 1970 as the strongest, if not the only element of organized power. But the political sentiments of the Soviet-equipped and well-trained army were a mystery. How would the army react to post-Castro popular pressures? Would it maintain the verticalization of the power structure, or allow a limited freedom of dissent from the government? These were some of the new questions. The army could conceivably look for new economic and social models. It could—within the present social context—favor a form of government more responsive to popular aspirations. If so, it would have to carry out a basic revision of the whole system replacing personal rule with a collective broadly participatory approach and charisma with impersonal and eclectic political and economic pragmatism.

## Cuba and the Caribbean

Except for a short period after 1959, Castro appeared to have shown little active interest in the Caribbean. Possibly because, while a student, Castro took part in an abortive expedition in 1947 against Dominican dictator Rafael Leonidas Trujillo, he set out to bring about his downfall as soon as he came to power. In June 1950, a small expedition left Cuba for the Dominican Republic. Led by Rebel Army Major Delio Ochoa, the invading force was quickly exterminated by Trujillo's troops. In August 1959, a Cuban attempt to overthrow the government of Haiti also failed with the death or capture of about 30 Cubans who tried to invade the little Caribbean republic. With the fiasco of these two invasions as well as subsequent unsuccessful expeditions against Panama and Nicaragua (all four were organized by Ernesto "Ché" Guevara), Castro's attempts to intervene directly in Caribbean affairs ended.

Although Cuba has strong ethnic ties with the Caribbean—many Cuban blacks were imported from Haiti and Jamaica and, later, others came voluntarily for sugar harvesting—her culture was always oriented toward Spain and the economy toward the United States. After the 1959 Caribbean fiascos, Castro chose to emphasize the Latin American character of the Cuban revolution. The thrust of his speeches was thus directed at audiences in the large Spanish-speaking Hemispheric nations.

Even though Cuba's subversive potential varied with time, the Caribbean countries regarded the Castro regime as a threat to their security. But the relatively low-key propaganda effort directed by Havana at its Caribbean neighbors demonstrated that the Castro government realized that it was not likely to become a development model for the region's overwhelmingly English-speaking countries. Because of the uncertainty over the effectiveness of his propaganda—and possibly afraid of the consequences of renewed interventions—Castro treaded lightly in the Caribbean.

No known attempts to infiltrate Haiti—across the narrow Windward Passage from Oriente Province—were made after 1959, despite the presence of a sizable Haitian population in Cuba from which, conceivably, "volunteers" could be recruited. While Havana Radio continued to broadcast in Creole to Haiti—telling Haitians that their "principal task is to organize their revolutionary violence so as to destroy [President François] Duvalier"—these broadcasts seemed perfunctory and even less violent than Radio Moscow's own Creole programs.

There is no evidence that Cuba influenced the 1965 Dominican civil war. Constitutionalist leader Francisco Caamaño Deño, who vanished from sight in October 1967, while serving as Dominican military attaché in London, was later reported in Cuba. But he failed to appear on the Dominican scene to disrupt the 1970 presidential election, a role that might have been assigned to him by Castro.

To be sure, Castro had many friends in the Caribbean, though their zeal for the Cuban cause was not overly noticeable. In January 1966, when the Latin American Solidarity Organization was created in Havana, its members included representatives from Guadeloupe, Guyana, French Guiana, Haiti, Jamaica, Martinique, Puerto Rico, the Dominican Republic, Trinidad-Tobago, and Surinam. But their subsequent activities were limited in scope.

On the other hand, there were no indications that any of the Caribbean nations registered concern over Cuba serving as a Soviet military base in the region. To the contrary, Trinidad-Tobago's Premier Eric Williams urged in February 1970 that the Hemisphere reconsider its political ostracism of the Castro government, a proposal also advocated by Mexico and Chile, even before the election in the latter of Marxist President Salvador Allende Gossens.

While Cuba's impact on Caribbean economic life was negligible over the years, mainly because of the similarity of the regional economies, the Castro government moved in 1970 to establish trade relations with some of its neighbors. A Cuban agricultural delegation visited Trinidad-Tobago in August to increase the small commerce between the two countries and set up permanent links for the exchange of scientific information. Simultaneously, Jamaican Prime Minister Hugh Shearer suggested that the Organization of American States establish some contacts with Cuba. A month later, a bill was introduced in the Jamaican Senate to upgrade the relations with Cuba from consular to full diplomatic level, and to exchange trade missions with Castro.

## Cuba and the United States

Despite signs in 1970 that many Caribbean and South American nations would favor a change in the United States' Cuban policy, Washington's posture toward the Castro government remained unchanged in its hostility. In broad terms, the American policy sought to isolate revolutionary Cuba ideologically, preventing her influence from spreading to other Latin American countries. Moreover, by applying the so-called policy of economic denial, Washington strove to make the island's development as difficult as possible and its support by the Soviet Union equally costly. The policy of "interdiction of Cuba," as former Assistant Secretary of State for Inter-American Affairs Covey Oliver termed it in 1968, was generally successful, although its success could be attributed in equal measure to Castro's own political and economic mistakes.

After the revolutionary victory, Castroism loomed as the wave of the future in Latin America. In the early 1960s, Castro was unquestionably a hero to many Latin Americans. His slogan, "the duty of every revolutionary is to make revolution," was echoed in several Latin countries where guerrilla groups, encouraged and materially supported by Cuba, gradually emerged. In January 1966, under the aegis of the Cuban government, the Latin American Solidarity Organization was founded in Havana, essentially to stimulate Latin rural guerrillas. But by 1970, the organization appeared to have lost its viability. Cuba-backed guerrilla groups were vanishing while other

methods of revolutionary struggle—principally urban guerrilla movements frowned upon by Castro—were gaining more followers among
the Hemisphere's extreme left, from Guatemala to Uruguay. The
failure of "Ché" Guevara in Bolivia was due as much to his own as to
Castro's lack of understanding of local social and political conditions
and to their erroneous belief that the Cuban revolutionary experience
would inevitably repeat itself in other Hemisphere nations. United
States aid in training special Latin American anti-guerrilla military
units was an important factor in dismembering Castroite guerrilla
groups in several countries of Central and South America.

The effectiveness of Washington's economic denial policy was conditioned by Cuba's financial situation rather than by the Yankee
diplomatic ability to isolate the Castro government economically. The
United States was thus unable to prevent Cuba from trading with
Canada, Western Europe, Japan and, in 1970, with Chile. The scope
of Cuban commerce with non-Communist countries was always limited by her production potential. With the exception of sugar and
nickel, Cuba had few goods to sell. Agricultural products like beef
and fruit were available for export only as a result of drastic reduction
in the home consumption. Significantly, on July 26, 1970, when he
acknowledged deep and widespread economic difficulties, Castro did
not mention the "Yankee boycott" as a factor in his problems.

Ironically, the United States—rather than Cuba's subsequent Soviet
ally—was the most sympathetic at the outset of Castro's revolutionary
struggle. As early as 1957, the United States government expressed its
concern over political unrest in Cuba. In 1958, Washington suspended
arms shipments to Batista (then trading with the Soviet Union),
charging that he had used American weapons to combat Castro's
rebels in violation of an agreement with the United States. When the
Castro regime came to power, the Eisenhower administration regarded
it with some warmth. It promptly recognized the new revolutionary
government, welcoming its promises of political freedom and social
justice for the Cuban people. In April 1959, Castro visited the United
States. Although the administration expressed its willingness to discuss Cuba's economic needs, he forbade members of his entourage to
engage in any conversations concerning possible American aid to
Cuba.

Even before the end of 1959, it became obvious that Cuba and the
United States were on a collision course. Washington was becoming
apprehensive over growing Communist tendencies in the Castro
regime. Havana, for its part, attacked the administration for allowing anti-Castro activities by Batista supporters in Miami and New
York. By mid-1960, practically all United States properties in Cuba
were seized, and Washington responded by suspending Cuba's sugar
quota in the subsidized American market. On January 2, 1961, Castro

gave the United States 48 hours to reduce its Havana embassy staff from over 100 to 11 persons, and one day later President Eisenhower broke relations with Cuba.

The April 1961 Bay of Pigs invasion further exacerbated United States-Cuban relations, and Castro, calling the United States his principal enemy, declared that Cuba could live without trading with her northern neighbor. In the spring of 1962, President Kennedy imposed an embargo on exports to Cuba, except for medicines, and on imports of Cuban goods and those manufactured elsewhere with products of Cuban origin. At the same time, the United States imposed restrictions on travel by Americans to Cuba. Yet journalists and scholars—on a selective basis—and young supporters of the revolution were able to visit the island.

Shortly before the 1962 missile crisis, Cuba began to broadcast a "Radio Free Dixie" program directed at the black population in the United States. The program was conducted by Robert Williams, a radical American black leader who had been given political asylum in Cuba. A few years later, Williams went to Communist China and from Peking accused Castro of preaching racial equality, but practicing racial discrimination in his country. In 1969, members of the Black Panther Party who had visited Cuba charged that their leader, Eldridge Cleaver, was isolated, if not practically imprisoned, during his stay in Havana.

The Cuban government's efforts at attracting white American radicals were more successful. In 1970, about fifteen hundred members of the so-called "Venceremos Brigade" traveled to Cuba via Canada to participate in the sugar harvest and other agricultural work.

While constantly attacking the United States government, Cuba maintained normal diplomatic and limited trade relations with Canada. The Cuban purchases in Canada included breeding livestock, spare parts for United States equipment in use in Cuba, automobiles, pharmaceutical and other products. Cuba also received on several occasions large quantities of wheat bought for her in Canada by the Soviet Union. While likewise maintaining diplomatic relations with Mexico, Cuba's trade with that country was very small. The twice-weekly flights between Havana and Mexico City by Cubana de Aviación, the Cuban government airline, were the only regular air transportation link between Cuba and the Americas. But the Mexican government cancelled the air agreement with Cuba in August 1970, reportedly because of Cuba's refusal to extradite several hijackers of Mexican commercial airliners.

THE MISSILE CRISIS AND CUBAN-AMERICAN RELATIONS

The role played by Premier Castro in the 1962 missile crisis was never made clear, although it is presumed that he was more than a willing instrument in Premier Khrushchev's strategic move against the United States. To the very last, Cuba denied that any Soviet missiles had been installed on the island, describing President Kennedy's charges of their deployment as "falsehoods and slanders."

The October crisis again affected Castro's attitude toward the United States. Whereas, initially, he regarded the United States as a "paper tiger" and repeatedly assured his nation that the "co-relation of forces" had become favorable to the Communist bloc, he came to respect the military might of the United States after the 1962 confrontation and to recognize begrudgingly that Cuba was only a minor factor in the global contest between the two superpowers.

In the early 1960s, questions were raised by certain writers as to whether the Cuban revolution had taken an anti-American and pro-Communist character because Washington had not shown sufficient patience and understanding for the Castro regime. But with the benefit of hindsight, it may be concluded that the socialization of the revolution was inevitable and that hostility toward the United States was inherent in the dynamics of the revolutionary process.

No major changes in the United States policy toward Cuba were discernible as the new decade began. One reason was Castro's evident lack of interest in any rapprochement with Washington. In the early 1960s the question of Cuba was fairly high on Washington's priority list. In 1970, with Castro's threat diminished and more important problems at home and abroad preoccupying American policy-makers, the interest diminished greatly.

After 1962, Cuba became of marginal importance strategically to the Soviet Union in view of technological advances in ballistic weaponry. In October 1962 Moscow acquiesced, over Castro's vigorous objections, to the American aerial surveillance of Cuba. Castro accepted the American overflights as a consequence of the failed missile gamble. Neither did he try to raise again the issue of the United States Guantanamo naval base, the lease on which expires in 1999 and cannot be terminated unilaterally.

The two explicit United States conditions for reestablishing diplomatic and commercial relations with Cuba remained the abandonment by Havana of support for Latin American guerrillas and subversive elements and the severance of military ties with the Soviet Union. In April 1970, Castro indirectly replied to the American conditions. "Our political and military ties with the Soviet Union will never be broken," he said. "On the contrary: As far as we are concerned, we will always be ready to increase our military ties with the Soviet Union." In the same speech he estimated the value of Soviet military aid to Cuba at $1.5 billion. Denying that Havana had eased her revolutionary posture in Latin America, Castro added: "Cuba has not refused nor will she ever refuse support to the revolutionary movements."

Castro's readiness to strengthen his military ties with Moscow was not taken lightly in Washington. Concern arose that Castro might allow the Soviet Union to establish a naval base in Cuba, possibly in Cienfuegos, a port on the southern coast of the island, some four hundred miles west of the Guantanamo base. In July 1969, a squadron of Soviet warships sailed for the first time in the Caribbean Sea. Soviet naval units again visited Cienfuegos and Havana in May and September of 1970. In November 1969, the Soviet defense minister, Marshal Andrei Grechko, toured Cuba for nine days. Several months later, non-stop flights to Cuba by Soviet TU-95 long-range reconnaissance aircraft began on a sporadic basis.

Few American officials expected the Russian air and naval buildup in Cuba to accelerate quantitatively at the 1962 pace. But because of the rapid Russian naval construction program and the Kremlin's emphasis on using seapower as a foreign policy tool, the Soviet military presence in the Caribbean became an accomplished fact in 1970. In November 1970, reportedly through secret diplomacy, the United States reached an understanding with the Soviet Union under which plans for building a Russian submarine base at Cienfuegos were abandoned. Reports about Soviet-directed construction activities in the Cuban port were widely publicized in the West weeks prior to the Washington-Moscow agreement. Yet Castro—who in the past had always been quick to publicly react to discussions of Cuban affairs by foreigners, particularly by the United States—refrained from making any statement about Cienfuegos.

It appeared, therefore, that as a result of Cuba's growing economic dependence on the Soviet Union, Moscow's grip on the Castro regime was tighter than ever. Thus the possibility that the Soviet Union would establish in Cuba permanent supply and recreational facilities for its growing navy became quite real. Such action would create a new military situation in the Caribbean—traditionally regarded by the United States as its *mare nostrum*—putting additional strains on Cuban-American relations.

*Frank McDonald*

# The Commonwealth Caribbean

Throughout the island and mainland states of the Caribbean, a new nationalism is emerging, a nationalism that not only spurns the implied racism ("rent-a-villas come with rent-a-cooks, rent-a-maids, rent-a-nannies") of tourist-brochure images of the region as a tropical playground for North Americans, but one that also increasingly rejects the economic domination of North Atlantic investment patterns. This nationalist movement is nowhere more evident than in the English-speaking Caribbean where, during the past year and a half, the rise of the Black Power movement and a series of nationalist rebellions have altered forever the region's traditional politics.

As the 1970s began, for example, uneasy governments of the Commonwealth Caribbean were already initiating proceedings against Black Power leaders. In Barbados, Grenada and St. Lucia, there was a ban on all Black Power activity. In Jamaica, racial tension and state repression made confrontation there a way of life. In Guyana, East Indians and Afro-Guyanese maintained an uneasy peace as the politics of Black Power began to radicalize the black population there. And then, most significant of all, in Trinidad-Tobago, a mass movement of students, unemployed blacks, under-employed East Indians, powerful trade union leaders, and a rebellious army nearly succeeded in creating what might have been the Caribbean's second social and nationalist revolution following Cuba. This near-miss at a Black Power revolution has resulted in a series of sedition trials that have involved over one hundred defendants.

*Educated in the United States at the Universities of Notre Dame and Chicago and abroad at the Universities of Oxford and Paris,* FRANK McDONALD *is a fellow of the Institute of Current World Affairs, specializing in the emerging states of the Caribbean. He has also been associated with the United Nations Institute for Training and Research.*

For the Commonwealth Caribbean, therefore, not a smile, but clenched fists are the images of the time. And the reasons are clear enough. After three hundred years of political dependency coupled with economic exploitation, the black, brown or red people of the islands object to the poverty of their present conditions. They know, that in spite of constitutional independence and the emergence of Afro-Caribbean politicians, they remain essentially an economically colonized people. More precisely, the mass of West Indians have begun to realize that the resources of the region and the manner in which those resources are utilized are North Atlantic prerogatives, that the proportion of the Caribbean's wealth that does accrue to the local population is limited, primarily, to the white or Afro-Saxon sectors of the society, to those who are acting as representatives of North Atlantic interests.

Such conditions, underscored by an economically structured racism (white capital, black labor), have resulted in an increasingly active pan-Caribbean movement for change, a movement that seeks to promote the direct interests of the four million black people of the area who are suffering the poverty of the system most severely. The radical alternative to contemporary political and economic conditions is Black Power.

Black Power, not necessarily limited only to those of African origin, calls for an immediate and equitable (as opposed to a "more equitable") redistribution of resources: diversification of agricultural production coupled with land reform programs; localization and integration of the regional bauxite-aluminum, oil-petro-chemical and natural gas industries; localization and racial integration of the island tourist facilities; reclamation of land developments now controlled by North Atlantic real estate operators; establishment of regional insurance companies, banking systems, and transport services; and development of a pan-Caribbean culture that will reflect the image of the region's population rather than the identity imposed upon them by consumer-oriented, North American-controlled mass media.

## The Region

The Commonwealth Caribbean consists of seventeen territorial units. Fifteen of these are islands or groups of islands. Two are mainland states. Together, these territories encompass a total land-mass of 105,325 square miles and a population of five million people. British Honduras (Belize) on the Central American mainland marks the western outpost of the region. Then, east into the Caribbean Sea, a cluster of islands comprise the central grouping of the English-speaking states: the Bahamas, the Turks and Caicos Islands, the Cayman Islands, and Jamaica. Then, again a thousand miles east, a chain of nine island states—flanked by Anguilla in the north and Trinidad in the south—arc toward the South American mainland and the Republic of Guyana, the southern outpost of the Commonwealth Caribbean. As a geographical unit then, the region forms a vital land-line between the two American continents, a link that gives to the area a preeminent economic and strategic value.

The term, Commonwealth Caribbean, has recently been adopted as a more appropriate, post-colonial name for the region, otherwise known as the West Indies or English-speaking Caribbean. Politicians and social scientists consider the term, West Indies, a colonial expression. Britain called its colonial territories in the Malay Archipelago East Indies and its possessions in the Caribbean West Indies. The inhabitants of the Commonwealth Caribbean are still called "West Indians," however.

In terms of size, apart from the two mainland states (Guyana with 83,000 square miles and Belize with 8,000 square miles), the island components of the Commonwealth Caribbean are diminutive. Jamaica, for example, is the largest of the island territories but measures only 4,411 square miles. Trinidad is half that size (1,980 square miles). And Anguilla, the smallest of the island states, is only 16 miles long and 2.5 miles wide.

The constitutional status of the region's states varies from full independence to colonial dependency. Twelve of the seventeen territories are internally self-governing states: four of the twelve are fully independent and have full membership in the United Nations (Guyana, Trinidad-Tobago, Barbados, and Jamaica); six others are associated states and are internally self-governing but dependent upon Great Britain for foreign affairs and defense (Antigua, St. Kitts-Nevis, Dominica, St. Lucia, St. Vincent, and Grenada). Two others, Belize and the Bahamas, are internally self-governing, but will soon become fully independent. Four other territories, all very small, are still colonies (Cayman Islands, Turks and Caicos Islands, British Virgin Islands, and Montserrat). Finally, there is tiny Anguilla, whose status is complicated as a result of its secession from the federated state of St. Kitts-Nevis-Anguilla in 1967. In March 1969, following a British invasion of 300 paratroopers and 60 metropolitan police, Anguillans expressed their desire to have associated statehood with Great Britain, but if forced to return to association with St. Kitts-Nevis, the islanders would proclaim once again their complete independence as a republic.

The racial composition of these seventeen territories is extremely heterogeneous. The region incorporates Mayan Indians, Carib Indians, Amerindians, East Indians, Chinese, Syrians, Europeans, and Africans. Although there has been a great deal of miscegenation, particularly in Trinidad and Guyana, the predominant racial group of the region is African. These people, descendants of the eleven million men, women, and children brought to the Americas in the late seventeenth and early eighteenth centuries, today total roughly 77 percent of the region's population. As a result, the Commonwealth Caribbean is, as West Indian economist Lloyd Best says, "A House with an African Personality."

## Historical Patterns

Commonwealth Caribbean history throughout has been a story of some form of exploitation. Essentially, the theme has been a mix of white-controlled capital and cheap black labor brought together for the benefit of metropolitan interests. This history of exploitation breaks down, roughly, into three periods: first, two hundred years of colonization (1623–1834) during which the London-based merchants, a colonial plantocracy, and slaves serviced the industrial revolution of Great Britain; second, one hundred years of Crown Colony rule (1835–1940) when the post-emancipation West Indians suffered under the harsh conditions of tenant-labor and laissez-faire; and third, the contemporary period (1944–present) when the development of trade union movements and universal suffrage resulted in constitutional advancement without any concomitant change in the traditional white-capital, black-labor mix that still operates for the almost exclusive benefit of the North Atlantic economies.

### COLONIALISM

The British colonialists first came to the Caribbean three hundred years ago, when, in 1623, Scottish, Irish, and English deportees migrated to St. Kitts, Antigua, Barbados, and Jamaica. In these islands, they first cultivated tobacco without great success. Sugar proved to be more suitable, attracting higher prices on the London market. In order to secure markets and profits, however, a large supply of cheap labor was required. For this reason, patterned after the Portuguese, the British colonialists began importing slaves from Africa. The first company chartered by the British Crown, the Royal African Company, began trading an average of 3,000 slaves annually in 1663. By 1791, there were over 40 companies shipping slaves from Africa to the Caribbean, exchanging them for sugar and bartering the sugar in London brokerage houses.

Slave labor alone was not enough, however, to ensure a high rate of profit return for the island planters. Competition from other colonies, particularly from India, cut into the West Indian profit margin—so much so that the planters sought protection in the form of tariffs from the British government. In time, loans were also required to expand the acreage planted in sugar. For both of these needs—increases in tariffs and capital—the West Indian planters sought out London merchants who could act as lobbyists and financiers. By performing both these functions, the London investors and merchants inevitably assumed control of the colonial sugar industry, including eventually all financing, shipping, and marketing. In short, the focus of economic power gradually shifted from the Caribbean colonies to the brokerage houses of London.

The dynamics of protectionism and the mercantilist system rendered the West Indies totally dependent upon metropolitan interests, a dependency that has established the adverse economic patterns which persist, in more subtle forms, until today. First, intra-island and intra-regional commercial exchange was, in effect, prohibited because the only lines of trade allowed to develop were those between the individual plantations and the mother country. Second, as a result of metropolitan interests and balkanization, only a single-crop economy was encouraged—and diversification discouraged—since industrial goods and other commodities were imported from, and were a source of profits to, the mother country. Third, the plantations produced sugar in a raw, *muscavado* form only, further processing being reserved for metropolitan industries. Fourth, capital was not accumulated in the Caribbean, but rather in London where the merchants or absentee-owners were compensated for their investments. Nor was this capital reinvested in the colonies but in metropolitan industrial developments. Fifth, as a result of protectionism and slavery, the island economies became increasingly inflexible. Little or no structural transformation or innovation occurred within the sugar industry since, if markets expanded, more slaves were imported and more crops cultivated. If markets contracted, rationing for the slaves and other devices were used to cut costs and overhead.

LAISSEZ-FAIRE AND CROWN COLONY RULE

What was then called the Golden Age of Sugar ended by the middle of the nineteenth century when the British Parliament abolished slavery, emancipated the slaves in the colonies, and legislated against the protective tariffs granted the British colonies in the Caribbean. Slavery was abolished in 1804, and the emancipation of all slaves was legislated by Parliament in 1832. (Mercantilism became inoperative as a result of the Sugar Duties Act of 1846.) Such parliamentary action was not, however, the result of any humanitarian sentiment in Great Britain. On the contrary, British manufacturers, labor unions, and politicians lobbied for the development of free trade and free labor because they were convinced that protectionism and slavery prevented the expansion of Britain's markets and trade with other European powers. Economists such as Adam Smith, David Ricardo, and others from the Manchester school argued persuasively that the free trade of laissez-faire would assist England's industrial development, that expanded markets would be good for manufacturer and laborer alike. In the colonies, however, changes brought about by laissez-faire left the island economies languishing. For the post-emancipation West Indian population, there was little difference between the servile conditions of slavery and the oppressive treadmill of tenant labor that persisted after 1846, a system in which the black population remained on the plantations and worked in payment for estate-owned housing and commodities bought in estate-controlled shops.

In terms of political rights, the black West Indian was no better off than he had been in the pre-abolition society, since property qualifications and other obstacles kept him disenfranchised and subject to Crown Colony rule. This period, lasting a hundred years (1836–1940), was, officially, a time of preparation toward the day when, sufficiently groomed, the people of the Caribbean would be able to assume the responsibilities of self-government. Until that time, the Colonial Office viewed itself as the main instrument for instructing the people in parliamentary democracy, and as "arbiter" between the interests of the old plantocracy and the needs of the newly emancipated population.

In reality, however, the doctrine of imperial trusteeship, first developed by the parliamentarian Edmund Burke, and its institutional expression, Crown Colony rule, masked a British rejection of black West Indian franchisement, a fear of the idea of black rule and a consequent collapse of the socioeconomic status quo. During the 1840s, in fact, a major debate among intellectuals of the day was the "Colonial Question." Many of Britain's leading thinkers argued for retention of the Caribbean colonies. Thomas Carlyle, in his *Occasional Discourse on the Nigger Question,* argued for a return to slavery. Anthony Trollope, the novelist, ridiculed the notion that West Indian blacks could govern themselves. And James Froude, then professor of modern history at Oxford University, taught that black rule in the Caribbean would be a disaster: "An English Governor would be found presiding over a black council, obliged to read speeches written for him by a black Prime Minister . . . No English gentleman could consent to occupy so absurd a position."

CONSTITUTIONAL INDEPENDENCE

Following a century of Crown Colony rule, even the Colonial Office recognized that the West Indian territories could not remain colonies forever. This was recognized, when, in 1934, the price of sugar fell to five shillings a hundredweight and massive unemployment, food shortages, and discontent spread throughout the Caribbean. Then from 1936 to 1938, in St. Kitts, Trinidad, Jamaica, and other islands, a wave of popular unrest, demonstrations, riots, and strikes showed that the breaking point had finally been reached.

As discontent spread, West Indians in every state from lower and middle classes alike arose to organize these spontaneous uprisings. Whoever had enough charisma, courage, or ability, who could reach the pulse of the people's nationalism, became hero for the crowds. Men such as Grantley Adams in Barbados or Alexander Bustamante in Jamaica began channeling that nationalism and energy, first by organizing trade union movements (over a seven-year period more than 60 trade unions were formed), then by founding political parties that eventually formed governments. For it is one of the most persistent themes in Caribbean politics that the men who, in the late 1930s, filtered through the crowded streets, emerged from the crowds and organized the people, were also those who subsequently led the movement for constitutional independence and (with one or two exceptions) have dominated the politics of the Commonwealth Caribbean states ever since.

With the significant exception of Dr. Eric Williams in Trinidad, the majority of Commonwealth Caribbean statesmen today have arisen through the trade union movements: Hugh Shearer in Jamaica; Forbes Burnham in Guyana; Erroll Barrow in Barbados; Eric Gairy in Grenada; John Compton in St. Lucia; Vere Bird in Antigua; Robert Bradshaw in St. Kitts; and Lyndon O. Pindling in the Bahamas. In many instances, the opposition party is also headed by a trade union leader.

As a consequence of the spontaneous actions of the West Indian population and the subsequent development of trade unionism in the region, the British Government, after the Second World War, initiated a series of study groups, royal commissions and constitutional conferences directed toward establishing a form of self-government suitable for the Caribbean colonies. Discussions held over a fourteen-year period (1944–58) finally resulted in what was intended to be the principal mechanism for regional independence—The West Indies federation.

This federation, composed of ten colonial territories, incorporated the major part of the West Indian population. Officially inaugurated in April 1958, ten territories formed a political union governed by a federal parliament, ministers elected by the regions' four million inhabitants, and an administrative superstructure intended to co-ordinate the economic development of the Commonwealth Caribbean. However, after four years, because of lack of support from the masses of the region and other personal, geographical, and administrative difficulties, the federal experiment collapsed. The major event in this regard was the 1961 decision of the Jamaican people to withdraw from the federal union, leaving Trinidad and the other eight island states of the eastern Caribbean to carry on alone. At this point, Trinidad's Prime Minister Williams decided to abandon the union as well, expressing his conclusions regarding the fate of the federation in a single pithy remark: "Ten minus one leaves zero."

With the collapse of the West Indian federation in 1961, Britain was obliged to grant each of the larger territories its individual independence. Jamaica, the first West Indian state to achieve independent status, became sovereign in 1962. Trinidad followed shortly in the same year. By 1966, both Barbados and Guyana had become fully independent and members of the United Nations. For the remaining territories, a semi-independent status (associated statehood) was established, in which the islands became internally self-governing but remained dependent upon Britain for foreign affairs and defense. Written into each of the constitutions of the associated states, however, is the proviso that, at any time, following a referendum and six months notice, that state may ask for and be granted, unilaterally, full independence.

Yet constitutional independence has not altered in any significant way the economic dependency of the Commonwealth Caribbean. Oppressive material poverty and external control of the region's resources persist. And the political leadership that governs has been unwilling or unable to do much about it. On the contrary, what development policies have been undertaken by the governments of the Commonwealth Caribbean have only reinforced such conditions.

### Contemporary Society

The acquisition of constitutional independence in the past decade has brought self-government to the majority of the region's populations. Each state has its election every five years, has its house of assembly or parliament, its prime minister or premier, representatives, opposition party, flag, and national song.

Nevertheless, political independence has not greatly affected the traditional colonial class structures that have persisted since the days of slavery. In spite of the election of black politicians in every Commonwealth Caribbean state, expatriates or West Indians of European origin still exercise almost total control over the levers of economic power. The structure of the societies in the Commonwealth Caribbean states clearly reflects this fact.

At the top are the expatriate managers of the economies, those who own and control the major commercial and industrial components of the region: the managers of the Tate and Lyle sugar estates; the managers of Geest's banana industry; the directors of Kaiser, Alcoa, and Reynolds bauxite operations; the managing personnel of the various expatriate-owned hotels, night clubs, and tourist facilities; the hundreds of bank managers for Barclays, Nova Scotia, Royal Bank of Canada, and Chase Manhattan.

Then there are the local West Indian elites; very few and principally white, they share in, and often represent locally, the interests of the expatriate investors. Perhaps the most important man in this regard, the classic example, is Sir Neville Ashenheim in Jamaica. Sir Neville is the owner or controller of no less than 45 different corporations or businesses, including four insurance companies, six development companies, one bank and two public service corporations. In addition to his business interests, Sir Neville also is minister of state in the Ministry of Finance and Planning, leader of government business in the Senate and former Jamaican ambassador to the United States. Then there are the other Ashenheims in Jamaica, and the Matalon and Issa families, who together control over 75 companies, hotels, and development projects. The pattern is repeated throughout the region.

Next are the middle-class professionals and technocrats, primarily of mixed racial origins and employed in middle management positions within the business sector or as civil servants. This class is very small, overworked and caught in the undesirable position of knowing what the majority of the population must endure below while acquiring a reasonable share of the benefits, goods, and services that come from above. As teachers, doctors, lawyers, and technicians, these West Indians represent the intellectual elite of the regional society and from among them most often comes the leadership of the movement for radical change.

Then there are the 20–25,000 industrial, mining, and petroleum workers that are employed by the multinational corporations such as Kaiser Aluminum in Jamaica, Texaco Oil in Trinidad, and Reynolds Metal in Guyana. These workers, totalling only two percent of the entire regional labor force, form what one trade union leader called an "aristocracy of labor," a highly skilled and well-paid work force that receives wage and fringe benefits that are about equivalent to those obtained by the average European worker. Usually, the company provides these men and their families with housing, free medical care, insurance programs, and recreational facilities, which, as a result, set them apart from the mass of ordinary West Indian workers.

There is, then, the remaining 98 percent of the regional labor force which breaks down as follows: the non-elite, yet fully employed workers numbering approximately 515,000, or 28 percent of the total labor force; the under-employed workers, numbering 900,000 and representing 50 percent of the labor force; and, finally, the unemployed that number at least 350,000 and represent 20 percent of the overall labor force of the region.

These West Indians and their dependents are almost entirely of African or East Indian origin and account for 90 percent of the total population of the Commonwealth Caribbean. Yet the physical conditions of their lives reveal a level of material poverty that is at the core of the Black Power movement.

Apart from the elite industrial workers, the West Indian fortunate enough to find a full-time job will earn as little as $7–11 per week in the smaller states (in Grenada, average wages are 16 cents an hour, $1.28 per day and $7.78 per week), or $10–14 per week in the larger states. For the under-employed worker, usually a part-time agricultural worker who works only six to seven months of the year, the wage level is an average of $12 per week.

The per capita income of the region ($145 in the small states, $235 in the larger) does not project the actual inequitable distribution of land, wealth, and other resources that is standard for the area. In Trinidad, for example, Trinidadians of European origin earn an average income of $500 per month, when Afro-Trinidadians earn an average wage of only $104 a month and those of East Indian origin, $77 per month. Again, in Jamaica, a recent study completed by the University of the West Indies shows that 5 percent of Jamaica's families accumulate 30 percent of the national goods and services, while 60 percent of the families must do with only 19 percent of the country's resources. In Barbados, fifteen large sugar estates own the entire central portion of an island where the density of the population (1,400 per square mile) is one of the highest in the world. In many of the small islands the same is true, so that, for example in St. Kitts, the black population, cramped for space and tightly housed, is forced to occupy the land that is least productive, in this case the outer edges of the island's shore.

Housing conditions for the black West Indian are very bad. The rate of construction has not kept pace with the growth of the population, so that in wooden, two-room homes, as many as nine to twelve inhabitants share the space. Piped water and sewage systems are a luxury, particularly in the villages of the region, where, as in St. Lucia, water is carried by buckets from central taps in the streets into the houses. In St. Vincent, not even the capital, Kingstown, has a sewage system; and in the rural areas, Vincentians lack even rudimentary facilities.

The vividness of a West Indian poet's description of these villages is represented in Ian McDonald's *The Weather in Shanty Town*:

No poets' words for shanty town: the weather kills and cankers every day.
The black storm in the morning shakes through shanty town,
The wind is like a flood amid the tilting huts.
Women stuff the cracked walls full with rags against the pour of rain.
Their children play in drowning pools, laughing in the sudden mud.
The black rain and the flail of storm is horrible:
The sodden damp is stinking, the cess pits overflow, no dryness anywhere.

The water pearls on black tin walls in sweating dews of filth.
The wet air swims like slime in every space and lung.
The rain is piss in shanty town, it brings no grace of silver.
Another day the avid sun hammers the hard earth gold.
Flies blacken the silver eyes of dead pigs in the dumping grounds.
Dust stuffs the bright air streaming from the whole sky.
It is hot as ovens, hot as engines, hot as deserts.
Black vultures land with dusty wings to browse on heated filth;
The children blaze with joy and race to catch them on the carrion grounds.
The heat simmers, the sun sings in the air, torpor everywhere.
The scums of old rain crack like scabs on beggars' sores.
The brass of sunlight poisons shanty town, the hot air fumes with shame.
The smell rises in a shimmering fog, a smell of death and guts.

The educational facilities for the region's 2.8 million children are as inadequate as their housing. The schools are overcrowded with three to five hundred students to a one-room building. There are not enough trained teachers, and often the village teenagers are recruited to instruct. More often, however, they act as disciplinarians rather than as teachers.

The educational system itself is antiquated. Though there is a literacy rate of 85 percent throughout the region, schooling is more a training process than a learning process since the children are obliged to memorize and learn by rote. Further, the content of the courses is oriented almost entirely to Europe rather than the Caribbean and the students end up knowing the details of Nelson's victory over the French at Trafalgar without the slightest awareness of the island peoples living in the island states around them.

Although the West Indian is usually vital and fit, the extreme poverty of the population and the poor quality of the medical facilities result in malnutrition and worm diseases. For example, one of the most common sights in the Caribbean is a child with a swollen stomach, standing listlessly by the side of an unpaved village street. Most often, the cause is either malnutrition (protein intake in the Caribbean averages 39 grams per day, one half that required for a normally active person), or worms (a most common worm disease, schistosomiasis, has infected at least 80 percent of the children in St. Lucia).

Health services in a recent study completed in St. Vincent and Jamaica are described as "primitive," with government expenditures averaging only five dollars per person annually. Hospitals are overcrowded—there are reports of three persons to a single bed in St. Vincent—antiquated, and obliged to perform curative to the exclusion of preventive methods of medical treatment.

Yet worse than the material poverty of the region is the state of mind of its inhabitants. The effects of three hundred years of colonization and its continuation in other forms today have conditioned large sectors of the population to believe that there is no other way to live, that the objective of each day is to endure until the next, to scrape together enough to survive. And to survive, the villager of the Caribbean has conditioned himself to be submissive—at least on the surface —so as not to incur the displeasure of the manager of the hotel, the white tourists on the beach, or the proprietor of the local industry. As a result, particularly among the older men of the region, there is an apathy bordering on despair, a lack of energy that the elites of the Caribbean attribute to racial or cultural characteristics rather than to the black man's own realization that what work there is to be done each day does not benefit "we," but only "they."

## From the Bottom Looking Up

From the viewpoint of 90 percent of the Commonwealth Caribbean's population, that is, from the impoverished bottom looking up, what is immediately apparent is the amount of wealth and economic power, largely expatriate-owned, concentrated at the top.

*Sugar:* This industry, traditionally the largest employer of the region, is so structured that only a few British-owned firms control over 60 percent of the region's cultivated acreage and over 85 percent of the production process. One of the major producers in the region is Bookers which owns eleven of Guyana's thirteen sugar estates. The other two are owned by Jessell Securities Ltd., a London-based investment firm that also owns a Guyanese rum distillery, an investment company, and a development corporation. Another major sugar producer is Tate and Lyle of Great Britain. Tate and Lyle has full or controlling interests in the largest sugar estates operating in Trinidad, Jamaica, and British Honduras.

*Bananas:* The second agricultural industry in the region, bananas, is also expatriate-controlled. Elders and Fyffes, a subsidiary of United Fruit, has effective control of the shipping and marketing of Jamaica's annual banana production. Geest Industries Ltd., also a British firm, owns the largest estates, as well as the shipping and marketing facilities of the entire banana production of Barbados, Dominica, St. Lucia, St. Vincent, and Grenada.

*Bauxite:* The Caribbean bauxite industry, providing 80 percent of the basic raw materials for the North American aluminum industry, is owned by five multi-national corporations headquartered in North America: Kaiser, Alcoa, Reynolds, and Anaconda in the United States, and Alcan in Canada. These five companies together mine over fourteen million long tons of bauxite from Jamaica and Guyana each year and account for over 50 percent of their annual export earnings.

*Oil, petro-chemicals and natural gas:* These industries, located primarily in Trinidad, are entirely American-owned. Texaco, which operates the fifth largest oil refinery in the world in Trinidad, processes together with Shell Oil's refinery an average of 157 million barrels each year. This oil represents 25 percent of Trinidad's gross national product and 80 percent of the country's total exports. Trinidad's petro-chemical industry, centered at Federation Chemical in San Francisco, is owned by W. R. Grace and Co. of New York. The nation's newly discovered natural gas deposits (now producing 500 million cubic feet per day and expanding rapidly) are already bargained away to Pan American Oil, a subsidiary of Standard Oil of Indiana.

*Tourism:* Reflecting the patterns of the other major industries, the Commonwealth Caribbean's tourist facilities are also foreign-controlled. For the smaller island states, dependent almost exclusively on their tourist industries, the domination of expatriate-owned hotels is almost complete. In St. Lucia, for example, eleven of the island's fifteen hotels are owned by North Atlantic interests. Over 50 percent of the Jamaican tourist industry is in foreign hands—the other half controlled by a small Jamaican elite. In the Bahamas, the situation is even worse, since its tourist facilities are simply an appendage to Miami and, in many instances, quietly controlled by another American phenomenon, the Cosa Nostra crime syndicate.

*Land development:* Paralleling the regional tourist industry, hundreds of North Americans have capitalized on the Caribbean's sun and sea by buying up almost every piece of beach land available. At last count, there were at least 300 different real estate schemes through which North Americans could obtain Caribbean property totalling 100,000 acres of prime beach land. The profiteering is on a large scale, and in a short period, roughly 250,000 North American buyers will have rezoned this land and built their winter homes on it.

*Manufacturing:* Throughout the past decade, employing an "open strategy" of industrial development—most often called the Puerto Rican model of industrialization—the Commonwealth Caribbean has received approximately $300 million of direct U.S. investment from more than 500 American corporations. These companies, provided with regionally sponsored incentives, have been attracted by the same conditions that were available in Puerto Rico during the 1950s: monopoly rights, freedom from fiscal controls, tax-free holidays, protective tariffs, low wages, and even government assistance in locating or building factories.

In brief, the Puerto Rican model as it was promoted by its earliest advocates such as the West Indian economist Sir Arthur Lewis aimed at opening up the Caribbean economy to metropolitan investors for three reasons: first, to create 420,000 jobs for the unemployed work force; second, to shift the burden of employment away from the traditional agricultural, mining, or public service sectors of the economy; and third, to promote a local entrepreneurship that Sir Arthur Lewis argued would develop because "the local people would have learnt the job, built up their own savings, and in one or two generations, go right in."

## PROBLEMS REINFORCED

As a direct result of this expatriate (increasingly North American) grip on the regional economy, the traditional colonial relationship—and the consequent material and psychological underdevelopment—has not been altered at all, but rather reinforced. As has been the case for three hundred years, the Commonwealth Caribbean is still dependent upon and exploited by North Atlantic metropoles.

The foreign sugar interests have maintained a traditional control of the best agricultural lands throughout the region so that no Caribbean government has been able to carry out badly needed land reform or crop diversification programs. Instead, the rural population has been confined to small one-or-two-acre plots of land while the region continues to import almost its entire food supply.

Because two privately-owned, foreign companies dominate the regional banana industry, growers in Jamaica and the Eastern Caribbean states are continually vulnerable to the damaging effects of price-cutting whenever one or the other company attempts to take a greater share of the British market. So as a result, not only are returns to the growers lower than they otherwise might be, but expatriate monopoly of the industry has prevented the Commonwealth Caribbean states from establishing a regional shipping-marketing operation that would increase employment and profits substantially.

The multinational corporate control of Caribbean bauxite results in a loss of profits, employment, and structural development for the regional industry as a whole. The vertical (corporate) rather than horizontal (regional) integration of this industry means that vital economic decisions affecting the uses and processing of bauxite are made in the interests of the companies rather than the host countries where the bauxite is located. The processing of bauxite into aluminum, for example, is so structured that for every four long tons of dried bauxite shipped out of the Caribbean, $893 flow to the United States with it. Since the various stages of processing bauxite into aluminum sheeting are completed outside the host country, the losses incurred are evaluated in stages. For example, one ton of prefabricated aluminum has seventeen times the value of its equivalent in dried bauxite. Thus, four long tons of dried bauxite valued at $25 reduces into two short tons of alumina valued at $105. This alumina smelted into one ton of aluminum increases in value to $382, and semi-fabricated into one ton of aluminum sheeting will have a final value of $918. In terms of employment, Jamaica's bauxite industry now employs only 8,000 workers since the mining and drying process is capital rather than labor intensive. Were the entire process completed in the Caribbean, an additional 42,000 jobs would be available. Thus the potential of the industry is grossly under-utilized in terms of the interests of the Commonwealth Caribbean states.

Tourism, so highly encouraged by a number of international agencies, metropolitan governments and West Indian politicians, has contributed almost nothing to the economic development of the Caribbean. Hotels are expatriate-owned, so that profits from the tourist industry do not remain in the region but are repatriated to North America. A steady, outward flow of tourist dollars is also quickened because the regional states must import most of the food and other commodities consumed by the visitors. Even return on transportation is limited since most of the profits are also returned to North American investors. (A recent study of Caribbean tourism completed by Zinder Associates in Washington finds that for every $1 spent in the Commonwealth Caribbean states, $.77 returns in some form to the metropolitan centers.) In Barbados and St. Kitts, where sugar is still being produced in the interior flatlands of the island, the islanders must make the best of a narrow strip lying between the tourist-dominated shore and the estate-owned interior. Tourism has also resulted in an inflation in the cost of living for the people of the region. Land prices have soared. And the beaches have become playgrounds for whites only, while the indigenous population has been obliged to move to cheaper terrain, into the interior and hillsides away from the shore.

The loss of the ownership of the land by the islanders has been the most obvious consequence of land development in the Caribbean. Hundreds of foreign real estate developers have made fortunes by buying up most of the land available and then selling it to eager North Americans looking for a tropical paradise. Even worse than tourism, which provides some jobs and a trickle of foreign exchange, these retirement homes and land schemes add little but luxury white ghettos to the regional landscape.

With regard to the manufacturing sector, the hopes projected for the Puerto Rican model, as applied to the Commonwealth Caribbean, have been in vain. The strategy has been a failure. Its primary aim of employment-creation has left 350,000 West Indians unemployed. (A slowdown in emigration, rise in population, underestimates of the costs of job promotion through incentives, and the consequent capital rather than labor intensive character of North American investment patterns have all contributed to the ineffectiveness of the model.) As a result, the burden of employment still rests with the traditional, primarily agricultural sector of the economy where the majority of laborers are underemployed. Nor, of course, have many West Indians, least of all black West Indians, "learned the tricks of the trade and set up business for themselves."

Meanwhile, all the negative aspects of the Puerto Rican model have appeared. Although per capita income has increased in the past decade, so has income inequality. There has been no attempt to distribute the resources of the region more equitably. Metropolitan consumption patterns have been imposed on the region. A balkanization and reinforcement of the traditional metropolitan control of the regional economy has resulted; and in Lloyd Best's phrase, a "perpetuation of the house-slave mentality" has permitted the dynamics of change in the manufacturing sector to remain with the metropolises, as local leaders busy themselves trying to create the "welcoming society."

## The Role of Aid

Concomitant with the expansion of American corporate investment in the Caribbean, a significant increase in United States development loans, technical assistance, and other related projects has occurred. These assistance programs have been channeled almost exclusively through the Agency for International Development (AID)—an arm of the United States State Department. For fiscal years 1970–71, for example, AID provided the Commonwealth Caribbean with loans and other assistance programs totalling $24.7 million.

The impact of these AID programs is significant—not, however, for their positive value, but for the negative effect they have had on the Caribbean economies. For essentially, the result of AID programs in the past has been to make the need for more aid inevitable; that is, instead of assisting the Commonwealth Caribbean states toward greater economic development and independence, the AID programs have in effect increased regional dependency upon the United States. Moreover, it has not been the Caribbean peoples who have chiefly benefited from the millions of dollars AID has channeled into the Caribbean, but the American corporations that have been provided investment assistance.

Specifically, AID funds are designed to perform one of three basic functions: to assist the underdeveloped country to modernize infrastructure and administrative facilities so as to be more receptive to, and provide inducements for, United States investment; to assist the United States investor in gaining access to the recipient economy by locating, evaluating, underwriting, and insuring a given capital investment; and third, to assist the host government in stabilizing the political climate.

MODERNIZATION

To modernize regional infrastructure, the Commonwealth Caribbean has received $55 million from AID since 1963. Guyana, for political reasons, has obtained by far the greater share. As a result, $37.7 million has been authorized to build the Atkinsen-MacKenzie highway, which connects the North American bauxite mines with the capital, Georgetown, and the sea to the north. AID funds have also helped to modernize Guyana's airport, water systems, agricultural facilities, and other highways throughout the country. For American investors, however, the future is in the underdeveloped interior; so as a result, $8.5 million has been authorized to "lay the base for economic and political development of the sparsely populated interior, to relieve congestion on the coastland and possibly reduce unemployment." In addition to infrastructure, AID is also concentrating on administration, particularly within the public services. Consequently, AID funds have been channeled to the Guyanese government "to make needed improvements in the administration of development programs, particularly in such areas as tax collection."

In the eastern Caribbean, AID loans totalling $10 million have been granted to assist regional tourist development and economic integration in other areas. This will provide North American developers and investors with access to a better organized tourist industry and, with economic integration, a larger market for United States products. Another AID-funded project is a study, now underway, to "provide the island governments with a blueprint for regional economic planning, including the identification of priority projects for external financing and AID is prepared to assist in developing investment proposals within the regional priorities."

In Jamaica, AID is also interested in helping the government there to "reorganize and improve the income tax administration in order to improve tax yields and more equitable burden sharing." A fulltime AID-funded consultant and $106,000 has been authorized for this project.

Besides assisting the United States investor with a more developed infrastructure, AID loans have directly financed millions of dollars of American export commodities. This is a consequence of loan conditions that force borrowing governments of the region to buy goods produced in the United States. Since 1964, this tied aid has been even more advantageous to the American exporter since "additionality" has been part of the AID contract. Thus, not only is the recipient of an AID loan obliged to buy United States goods with that money, but he is given a selected list of products that tend to be poor international competitors and therefore in low demand. In this way, even the noncompetitive American exports benefit from AID programs.

ACCESS

AID's Office of Private Resources has several programs that assist United States investors in their development of the Caribbean. As a start, "to induce entrepreneurial interest in priority areas," there is the pre-investment assistance program. Through this program, AID will reimburse a given company for half of the cost of a survey (feasibility study) if, after surveying a potential investment, the company decides not to invest. As a result, much of the risk of investing in underdeveloped countries is eliminated. And if, after taking the survey the company does not invest, AID will make the report available to other potential United States investors.

If, on the other hand, the feasibility study indicates that an investment is profitable, AID will provide 75 percent of the loan and equity guaranty. Thus, if the United States firm can arrange to have the other 25 percent underwritten by the host country, something many Caribbean governments would do, the company's loans will be fully covered.

Then, through a political risk insurance program, AID will insure the investor against losses "arising from inconvertibility, expropriation, war, revolution or insurrection." In the Caribbean, this program has provided $440 million of risk insurance to approximately 40 companies and large corporations (bauxite and petrochemicals among them) since its inception. Currently, the entire program has outstanding coverages totalling $7.3 billion, worldwide.

STABILIZATION

Once located, underwritten and insured, the American investor can be sure that AID will make every effort to see that the company will operate within a stable political climate. For this service, AID relies primarily on its "Public Safety" programs.

Public Safety, begun in 1962, is "coordinated in the field by the country team (the American embassy) and in Washington by an interagency program review," according to AID's official report to Congress. The point of the program is to develop the local police forces so that they are able first "to perform their regular duties more efficiently"; second, to acquire "investigative skills for detecting criminal or subversive individuals and neutralizing their activities"; and third, "to control militant activities ranging from demonstrations, disorders or riots through small-scale guerrilla operations."

The policy that underlies Public Safety is perhaps best described by former AID Administrator David Bell:

> Maintenance of law and order including internal security is one of the fundamental responsibilities of police . . . Successful discharge of this responsibility is imperative if a nation is to establish and maintain the environment of stability and security so essential to economic, social, and political progress, and to attain the goal of free, stable, independent and self-reliant government. Clearly, this progress and this goal will not be attainable if law and order is replaced by disorder and violence. Communist subversion, terrorism, and insurgency typically strive to break down law and order and internal security.

In the Caribbean, Public Safety is represented by three technicians supported in a program that runs to $1.7 million. Guyana, to combat the influence of the Marxist-oriented Peoples' Progressive Party, has received special attention from AID: a total of $1.25 million has been authorized for training Guyanese policemen (32 have been to Washington's International Police Academy for their course work), for the purchase of counterinsurgency equipment, and for the support of Public Safety personnel in the area. Jamaica's program has been less costly. During the past two years, only $514,000 has been spent training 34 Jamaican policemen at the Academy.

## Labor as the Base of the Triangle

American corporations and AID programs, however, represent only two sides of a triangular penetration of the Commonwealth Caribbean economy. The third side, without which the ease of this process would be severely threatened, is the organized "Americanization" of the Caribbean trade union movement's role in Caribbean politics. With the sole exception of Trinidad, most major political parties are rooted in a labor union and the vast majority of premiers, prime ministers, and even leaders of the opposition are themselves trade unionists. Thus, the axiom holds that the politics or ideology of the trade union movement will affect the policies of the regional governments and that the more receptive Caribbean labor is to the presence of American investment and management patterns, the more so will be the regional politicians.

In this regard, the most effective programs designed to Americanize or, in the more subtle parlance of its enthusiasts, "to strengthen and develop a free trade union movement in Latin America and the Caribbean" are those implemented by the Washington-based American Institute for Free Labor Development (AIFLD).

Founded in 1961 by President Kennedy and George Meany, and since then a channel for approximately $100 million in AID, American Federation of Labor, and corporate funds, the AIFLD has become, as Senator J. William Fulbright has said, "the primary, if not exclusive, instrument for implementing U.S. labor policy in Latin America"—a recognition justly deserved.

The men and money behind AIFLD are an ironic combination of the United States government, the AFL-CIO, and United States corporations. Once reportedly funded by the Central Intelligence Agency, AIFLD now receives 90 percent of its grants from AID. George Meany's International Affairs Directorate pumps 20 percent of its budget into AIFLD in the form of loans. Over 70 American companies have also contributed. The AIFLD's chairman of the board is Peter Grace, president of W. R. Grace and Company, a major United States investment group in Latin America. AIFLD explains this unique blend as a "reflection of the true pluralism and consensus of American society."

Since its inception, AIFLD's goal of "strengthening and developing free trade unionism" has been partly accomplished by training 148,515 local trade unionists in regional seminars held throughout Latin America and the Caribbean. From this group, 1,000 men have taken an advanced course in trade unionism at the Institute's Front Royal school near Washington.

In the Caribbean alone, 5,000 trade union leaders have participated in these AIFLD-sponsored seminars held in Jamaica, Guyana, and Trinidad; and a core group of 75 trade unionists, including the current leadership of the Caribbean Congress of Labor, have attended the labor college at Front Royal and been supported for a year on their return to the Caribbean.

In the field of operations, the AIFLD's Serafino Romualdi and Arnold Zander of the Public Services International (one of seventeen international trade secretariats [ITS] linking United States and third world trade unions) were reportedly responsible in 1963 for channeling CIA funds and personnel into a strike committee composed of anti-government elements attempting to overthrow the popularly-elected government of Cheddi Jagan, the PPP leader, in Guyana. The result in the end was a series of race riots and a general strike lasting 80 days that left Guyana a racially divided nation, pitting blacks against East Indians.

In Jamaica, another ITS (the International Metalworkers Federation) gave $7,200 for a strike fund set up by the National Workers' Union (NWU) in June of 1968. The NWU is the union base of the opposition party, the People's National Party, which, at the time of the strike, was engaged in a battle for control of bargaining rights critical to its political future. NWU officials have received other benefits from American labor: travel grants, training programs, and loans, the latest for use in constructing a new union headquarters ($10,000).

More recent are the subcontracts AIFLD has allocated to at least eight American ITS affiliates. These subcontracts (AID funds that AIFLD contracts out), totalling over a million dollars annually, are used by the American trade union affiliate to operate programs in the Caribbean. In some cases, an American affiliate, such as the International Federation of Petroleum and Chemical Workers (IFPCW), has attempted to discredit the local trade union leadership. The following request for funds was made by the IFPCW's General Secretary, Lloyd Haskins, in May 1968:

> In the Caribbean, most of our activities have been concentrated in Trinidad. The Oilfield Workers Trade Union is our largest affiliate in this area. During the past few years, its leadership has come under increasing com-

munist leadership, if not under the direction of communist leaders . . . We have a full-time office established in Trinidad and its purpose is to preserve the OWTU for the democratic trade union movement . . . During the next few months, an election will be held in this union which could well determine the course which it will take in the future. Its present leadership is being challenged by a group of leaders who are dedicated to the free trade movement . . . The petroleum industry is one of the most vital industries in the Caribbean and Central America. Many new refineries have been built in this area and they are the target for trade union activity for the organization.

Presumably, Haskins was referring to the Oilfield Workers' President General, George Weekes, who has long opposed United States control of Trinidad's oil industry.

The following year, this assessment of the IFPWC program in Trinidad was sent by the ITS to AIFLD and AID:

The IFPCW program in this area continued to make steady progress to diminish the effectiveness of the communist element among the leaders of the largest IFPCW affiliate in the Caribbean, the Oilfield Workers' Trade Union in Trinidad.

## Black Power

The Caribbean is a beautiful "house with an African personality"; but its wealth and beauty have been the privilege and property of Europeans or North Americans for over three hundred years. And all the while, the Afro-Caribbean character of the region has been continuously exploited or oppressed. It seems inescapable that this contradiction, dehumanizing both for the oppressor and the oppressed, will have to be radically changed, one way or another.

So it is that Black Power has come to the Caribbean, or rather, surfaced in the Caribbean. For the idea of Black Power has been indigenous to the region for 50 years—primarily because of the legacy of two men: Jamaica's black nationalist, Marcus Garvey, and Trinidad's pan-Caribbean populist, C. L. R. James. Together, these two represent the source of Commonwealth Caribbean radicalism; and their achievements, acknowledged or not, persist today in the substance of the movement. During the 1920s, Garvey stressed racial pride, the dignity of blackness, and attempted to organize black nationalist groups in Jamaica and the United States. In the 1950s, James tried to mobilize a pan-Caribbean nationalism based on full economic and political participation of the West Indian masses. Both men encountered hostility in their respective islands and both subsequently chose exile.

ORIGIN AND DEVELOPMENT

The contemporary Black Power movement began in Guyana during the early 1960s, where a group of Guyanese intellectuals, motivated in part by metropolitan attempts to overthrow the government of Cheddi Jagan, gathered to form the New World Group. Within a short period, their discussions appeared in the Group's journal, the *New World Fortnightly*. Circulated throughout the Caribbean, the *Fortnightly* eventually sparked the development of similar groups in Jamaica, Trinidad, Barbados, and the smaller islands. Then, together with the Guyanese group, "associates" from other Caribbean states fused and started publication of another journal, the *New World Quarterly*, containing contributions from various groups and written from a pan-Caribbean perspective.

In the *Quarterly*, the Group's economists, such as Maurice Odle and Clive Thomas in Guyana, Lloyd Best in Trinidad, or George Beckford and Norman Girvan in Jamaica, presented critical work on all aspects of the Commonwealth Caribbean economy: for example, plantation economies, the mechanics of the Puerto Rican model of industrialization, and the structure of foreign control of the contemporary economy. Political scientists within the Group—James Millette in Trinidad or Trevore Monroe in Jamaica—focused on neo-colonialism and demonstrated how current Caribbean politicians had failed to alter the political impotency of the post-independence society. Historians such as Elsa Goviea, Woodville Marchall, and Douglas Hall reinterpreted Caribbean history from the black West Indian's perspective; and sociologists such as Orlando Patterson probed the devastating heritage of colonial culture and slavery.

Then, as the Group's work expanded, its analysis deepened and inevitably proposals for change were presented, always from a regional perspective. For example, Clive Thomas' examination of the Caribbean sugar industry eventually provided the Group with an alternative to the present under-utilization of human and natural resources. Thomas argued that only through diversification (and localization) would there be a halt in the financial drain of repatriated profits, the cost of importing foodstuffs that otherwise might be grown on lands not controlled by Bookers and Tate and Lyle, or an end to the dehumanization of thousands of sugar workers obliged to support themselves and their dependents on $10–12 a week.

As soon as the issue of diversification is raised, the plantation boys throw their hands in the air and shout the question, why use our lands for this if there is other idle land in the community. Put in this way their question raises an even more profound and disturbing issue. How can a poor, land-hungry island economy really have "idle land"? And if this land is idle what are the institutional restraints which prevent it from going into production? My answer in brief is the plantation system and any programme of land tenure reform in the country must be based on the elimination of these private latifundias and latifundistas. It is the plantation system which contributes to the fact that 0.7% of the farms of Jamaica occupy 56% of the total acreage while 71% of the farms occupy 12% of the total acreage.

George Beckford's work on the Caribbean banana industry stressed the need for radical alternatives. He advocated the rationalization of land patterns used to grow bananas and a reorganization of regional shipping and marketing operations.

Bananas for export are produced more or less indiscriminately in various parts of Jamaica because the industry was grafted on to an infrastructure designed for sugar production and developed by numerous small-holders who had limited access to suitable lands . . . What is implied is that . . . substantial economies could be derived from shifts in the location of production . . . such shifts would have several major effects. First, the elimination of marginal producing areas would lower the over-all average cost of banana production. Second, concentration of production would . . . facilitate disease control and improvements in technology. Third, the costs of purchasing and transporting fruit to ports would be considerably reduced. Fourth, administration of the industry would be less unwieldy . . . And fifth, production of foodstuffs for the home market could be increased if, as appears, land withdrawn from bananas is suitable for this purpose.

Then, the most obvious way of doing our own shipping and marketing would be to expand the Jamaica Banana Producers Association into a National Line capable of handling the entire trade. One difficulty would be the high cost of new ships. But when one considers that some 75% of current marketing costs consists of freight and commission to marketing agents, it would seem that investments of this type would pay high returns in terms of national income creation. Another solution could be to secure access to supplies from other West Indian islands. One way would be to expand the company with share capital subscriptions by Windward Island growers and partly with capital subscribed by all West Indian governments to transform the company into the West Indian Banana Growers Association. This would be the nucleus of a regional shipping line which would handle more and more of our trade with the rest of the world.

As for the Caribbean bauxite industry, the New World Group argued that under existing organizational and financial arrangements, the potential of the industry had not been fully exploited. The analysis of one of the *New World Quarterly's* editors, Norman Girvan, shows that relative to its potential, "the bauxite industry's contribution to economic development has been low." Girvan insisted that there was a need to rationalize the operational structure of the industry in four ways: first, in terms of the financial arrangements, specifically tax agreements made with foreign companies; second, in respect to Caribbean participation in the various stages of aluminum processing; third, regarding depletion problems; and fourth, the manner in which the Caribbean could profit rather than lose from any technological advances made within the industry.

The matter of taxes is a complex problem, but there is evidence that the American aluminum industry has been undervaluing the bauxite they have been mining in Jamaica, and as a result, United States companies have been paying less tax. Specifically, the local American plants have been fixing one price on bauxite for the benefit of the Jamaican government and another, much higher, for the United States Internal Revenue Service. Figures available suggest that the American aluminum industry or the United States government owes Jamaica $50 million as a result. (This problem was explained to envoy Nelson Rockefeller when he visited Jamaica as part of his Latin American tour. He was asked if he could arrange to do something about it.)

The problem is a difficult one since bauxite is transferred from one branch to another of the same international company. Thus, the producer cannot be taxed in the normal manner of deducting cost from income. An accounting procedure called "transfer pricing" must therefore be used to determine value. As Girvan pointed out, the Jamaican government at first "naively accepted the Corporation's evaluations with the result that while the average price of U.S. aluminum rose by 20% and the value of domestic bauxite by 80% the price set on imports . . . hardly changed at all."

The issue of participation in all stages of aluminum processing involves the question of how the Caribbean can share in the increased value of bauxite as it moves from red dust to metal ready for fabrication. As indicated above, the value of the finished aluminum is seventeen times that of the unprocessed bauxite. To date, Jamaica has secured only a very low share of the profits, a consequence of the industry's foreign ownership.

Girvan's concern over the inevitability of bauxite depletion is tied to these problems. Since the location of aluminum processing is outside Jamaica, the government has had to encourage the mining of as much ore as possible for maximizing revenue from taxes. As a result, as Girvan figures, "current levels of output with currently known reserves indicate that Jamaica's deposits will be exhausted in 55 years." If output increases, the reserves will be fully depleted within 24 years. This, however, does not seem to be a problem for the multinational corporation, for:

> When reserves come near exhaustion Kaiser will shift output to Australia and Reynolds will probably shift emphasis to Guyana. Alcoa and Alcan will probably shift to alumina production in Australia as well. Thus by the end of the present century, the Caribbean could be faced with the prospect of secular stagnation of its mineral industry and the retrospect of insufficient exploitation of its potential during its existence.

The fourth point Girvan emphasizes is that any technological innovations produced in the bauxite-alumina-aluminum industry are in the interests of the foreign companies rather than local needs of the

Caribbean. Research, for example, on the commercial production of aluminum from clay is certainly in the interest of companies head-quartered in the United States where bauxite reserves are almost depleted. Jamaica would hardly benefit from this type of research, however. Another example is the seeming lack of interest on the part of the North American companies in researching cheaper forms of electricity since in Canada and in the United States these companies already have sufficient power to operate their aluminum smelters. On the other hand, such a breakthrough is just the sort of innovation Jamaica needs.

Thus, Jamaica and the other bauxite producers of the Caribbean are totally dependent upon the needs of the foreign corporations now engaged in mining operations within the region. And while the needs of the corporations, profitability and growth, may appear to benefit the states in which they are operating, the reality of the situation is quite different. The profits generated from bauxite are intra-corporate rather than intra-national or regional.

Girvan's proposals mean a change in this pattern. He suggests a regional bauxite-alumina-aluminum industry would make use of the resources of the Caribbean in the interests of the member states. A necessary accompaniment to such a rationalization of the area's resources would be a change in the industry's organization. For "even if the suggested production plans were possible under foreign ownership the accrual of profits abroad would remain a major cost." More important for Girvan is the fact that such a reorganization of the industry is "fundamentally prohibited by the structure of the international corporations, whose framework diverges basically from that of the region . . . Organizational rationalization will require that the agencies of resource allocation be the public authorities of the region."

How this is to be accomplished in the face of capital shortage, limited technical personnel, maneuverability, and independent markets is yet a subject for debate. The fact that such "reorganization" is necessary is not. Girvan proposes that a "phasing out" of the international companies and a "phasing in" of the regional network be accomplished through a regional shareholding plan under the direction of a regional development program. Acquiring surplus, reorientating technical and educational programs, and developing market contacts with East and West Europe, Asia and Africa represent portions of the comprehensive plan suggested.

Meanwhile, the Group in Trinidad, particularly economist Lloyd Best, outlined a program "to deal with petroleum and the banks." To begin, Best points out that a reorganization of the economy (that is, the placing of economic control of the economy in the hands of the population) "demands two major acts of policy": first, a settlement with oil and the banks; the second, an emancipation of local enterprise.

The biggest single problem here is that the petroleum and sugar industries are in the hands of foreign companies and that these companies have interests which are in conflict with those of the nation. We have to resolve this conflict once and for all by localizing these companies and fitting them into the framework of national planning. We have to make it clear that we are intending to break up the huge international corporations. We are not alone in this; other countries are thinking the same way too.

For Best, the objective would be a national oil company as soon as possible. Toward this end, several steps would be taken immediately:

A separation of Texaco (Trinidad) from Texaco (International); shares in Texaco Trinidad must be traded on the local market and made available to the unions, the central government, the local authorities and the public at large. A schedule of jobs which must be held by nationals within a specified period. The accounting practices of the companies must conform to national specifications. All advertising, banking and insurance service must be locally procured.

Then there are the banks and insurance companies. Best insists that these foreign organizations bring nothing to Trinidad that the nation cannot provide for itself. In fact, he shows that they often "stand in the way of rational management of the local monetary system." They would also be localized immediately. The same would hold true for all advertising and the media. This would save the country from a constant stream of American-oriented programming—everything from hair oils to Garner Ted Armstrong's moralizing.

### TACTICS

By the fall of 1968, because of the New World Group's work, the intellectual basis for radical change had been presented. But the practical problem still remained: how to actualize the programs given the political context of the Caribbean as it is today. This became a matter of tactics. And it was at this point that the concept of Black Power was introduced into the Caribbean.

In this respect, the most important figure was Walter Rodney, a 27-year-old Guyanese historian, who had returned to the Caribbean from Africa where he had been researching and lecturing in African history. Posted as a resident lecturer at the University of the West Indies (UWI) in Jamaica, Rodney soon gained the respect of his students and associates for his understanding and ability to communicate the history of the African peoples—both in Africa and the Americas. Essential to this history, Rodney explained, was an understanding of Black Power; and it was in this context, in speaking to groups on or off the UWI campus, that Rodney first introduced the term Black Power into the Caribbean.

Lecturing often and well about Black Power, Rodney's greatest assets, his simplicity and clarity, enabled him to communicate with the university community and villagers alike. And it was this ability to communicate from university to village that made the young historian so effective. Black Power, then, became the focus for the first serious contact between the radicalism of the campus and the potential radicalism in the villages. And Walter Rodney was the vital link.

For Rodney, Black Power in the Caribbean meant three essential and closely related things:

> First, a break with imperialism which is historically white racist. Second, the assumption of power by the black masses in the islands. Third, the cultural reconstruction of the society in the image of the blacks.

In response to questions about the definition of "black," Rodney offered a militant yet tolerant explanation:

> I shall anticipate certain questions on who are the blacks in the West Indies since they are in fact questions which have been posed to me elsewhere. I maintain that it is the white world which has defined who are blacks—if you are not white then you are black. However, it is obvious that the West Indian situation is complicated by factors such as the variety of racial types and racial mixtures and by the process of class formation. We have, therefore, to note not simply what the white world says but also how individuals perceive each other. Nevertheless, we can talk of the mass of the West Indian population as being black—either African or Indian. There seems to have been some doubts on the last point, and some fear that Black Power is aimed against the Indian. This would be a flagrant denial of both the historical experience of the West Indies and the reality of the contemporary scene. It seems to me, therefore, that it is not for the Black Power movement to determine the position of the browns, reds and so-called West Indian whites—the movement can only keep the door open and leave it to those groups to make their choice.

And in defining the second half of the concept, "power," Rodney stated the simple proposition: "The Caribbean is predominately a black nation, and as such the blacks have a right to power commensurate with their own numbers."

> This is a black society where Africans preponderate. Apart from the mulatto mixture all other groups are numerically insignificant and yet the society seeks to give them equal weight and indeed more weight than the Africans. When we go to Britain we don't expect to take over all of the British real estate business, all their cinemas and most of their commerce as the European, Chinese and Syrian have done here. All we ask for is some work and shelter, and we can't even get that. Black Power must proclaim that Jamaica is a black society—we should fly Garvey's Black Star banner and we will treat all other groups in the society on that understanding—they can have the basic right of all individuals but

no privileges to exploit Africans as has been the pattern during slavery and ever since.

Walter Rodney's ability to communicate greatly imperiled the political power of the Jamaican government. So much so that in mid-October 1968, as the young lecturer returned from a black writers' conference held in Canada, Jamaica's police were dispatched to the airport with deportation orders. With no official reason ever given, Walter Rodney was banned from Jamaica.

Rodney's appearance, however, marked the beginnings of a tactical shift on the part of the Caribbean radical movement. For prior to Rodney's efforts, the movement had centered only within an intellectual community. It had little impact on the mass of West Indians. After Rodney's departure (since his expulsion, he has returned to Africa), the movement recognized the need to communicate more directly with the people, "to ground with the people" in Rodney's words. So out of this need arose numerous groups and publications directed toward the West Indian masses: for example, *Moko* and *Tapia* in Trinidad; *Ratoon* in Guyana; the *Forum* in St. Lucia; and *Abeng* in Jamaica.

The *Abeng* movement in Jamaica serves as a good example since it was a direct response to the Rodney affair. A small four-page newspaper, *Abeng* first appeared February 1, 1969. It stopped publishing ten months later. Yet for the time it existed, *Abeng* represented, and gave expression to, the most radical politics Jamaica has produced. In some ways, the publication was disjointed and contradictory, but still it accomplished what no other radical organization had been able to do. It communicated with the Jamaican people.

*Abeng* derived its name from the horn early revolutionaries once used to call one another. The name was appropriate. The columns were used to exchange views between the people within the university and the Jamaicans who lived in the slums of Kingston or in rural villages. If an article or statement came to the editors from a small village in Manchester, the piece would be printed as it was, without editing. The language of the paper was the language of the people. And on Thursday evenings when the four-page weekly would come from the press, dozens of vendors circulated the paper by car throughout the countryside. As the months went by, these vendors began to notice that the villagers would be standing by the roadside, waiting for their weekly supply. Often a vendor would be handed a little note with questions on it about some point made in the paper the week before. The vendors would stop and explain, then be invited to come back and speak to the people of the village at some later date.

*Abeng* had no "set line," however. It was composed of many different types of people with different ideological perspectives. On the masthead, for example, was a quotation from Marcus Garvey, while the newspaper's analysis of Jamaican society was a blend of Marxism, Caribbean nationalism, and black nationalism adapted to the uniqueness of Caribbean conditions. More than anything else, however, *Abeng* was agitational. It moved people. *Abeng* carried pictures of police beatings, stories about discrimination in the tourist hotels of the north shore, and in language the people could understand, analysis of the economic conditions of the country. There were features about Marcus Garvey, his thought and vision; historical articles about past Jamaican revolutionaries; and news about the black struggle in the United States and in Africa. But all the while, *Abeng* focused its criticism on the Jamaican government, attacked it for corruption, inefficiency, and inability to deal with the conditions oppressing the Jamaican people.

Meanwhile in Trinidad, St. Lucia, Belize, and Guyana, the same type of little newspaper has appeared. Some have been less effective than others, but all have had an impact on the politics of their respective countries. In Guyana, for example, it was the *Ratoon* group that invited Stokely Carmichael for a visit in May 1970, a visit that has since sparked controversy within Guyana and throughout the Commonwealth Caribbean states. For Carmichael's visit, *Ratoon* had the support of the two major political parties, Prime Minister Forbes Burnham's People's National Congress and Dr. Cheddi Jagan's People's Progressive Party. During his week-long stay, Carmichael's concepts about what direction the movement in the Caribbean should take provoked great controversy about tactics for revolutionary change. In Trinidad, *Moko* and *Tapia* provided some of the political activism that led to what became Trinidad's February Revolution.

THE FEBRUARY REVOLUTION

The most significant show of radical power to date has been in Trinidad where, for eight weeks (February 26–April 22, 1970), a small, activist organization called the National Joint Action Committee (NJAC) led a mass movement of thousands that nearly brought the first successful Black Power revolution to the Caribbean. Starting with only a nine-man demonstration on the afternoon of February 26, NJAC's leadership was able to mobilize ten thousand followers within a week, and ten times that number within six weeks.

Led by Geddes Granger, a recent graduate of the University of the West Indies, NJAC called for an end to economic colonialism and attacked the white power structure that controls the Caribbean:

> Our movement is working towards the day when each black person will be able to get a fair deal, be he of African or East Indian descent, will be able to feel that he has a stake in the future of our society. We are therefore against the present system in Trinidad which can only result in the perpetuation of the status-quo. In Trinidad we have a black Gov-

ernment which is not working in the interest of the people, for they strive to perpetuate a system of capitalism, a system which serves to provide huge profits for the foreign firms like the Royal Bank of Canada, Alcan, or Texaco Trinidad. We cannot and indeed will not allow our black people to be further dehumanized. And I say to you, there must be change.

For eight weeks, demonstrations numbering eight to twenty thousand Trinidadians kept the country in a perpetual state of protest. Granger with his arms uplifted pleaded with the crowds to rise up and rid Trinidad of its white oppressors. Meanwhile, the local press and government agreed that there was need for change, that the black population had been short-changed, but that violence and revolution were not the answers. Yet Granger kept marching—and with him the population. The middle class, threatened as they have never been, began to panic and packed their bags to leave for "vacation" in Barbados—a haven for the middle-class whites of the Caribbean.

Finally, by the second week of April, the movement was ready to peak. Granger's NJAC, university students, East Indians, thousands of unemployed blacks and even labor (led by George Weekes' Oilfield Workers Trade Union) appeared to be ready to ask the government to resign. A mass rally and general strike was called for April 22 to spearhead the movement's demands.

On the night of April 20, however, Prime Minister Williams declared a state of emergency, imposed martial law on the country, and had most of the rebel leaders in prison by the next morning. In spite of the government's action, half of Trinidad's Army rebelled as they were issued arms by their officers, seized the main arsenal and held it for four days before surrendering to loyalist troops and police equipped with $80,000 worth of arms and ammunition provided by the United States government. Today, over a hundred soldiers and civilian militants are in prison, awaiting trials for sedition or treason.

Meanwhile, as the tribunals and trials began in Trinidad, other Commonwealth Caribbean states have also taken action against the region's activists. The government of Barbados has banned all Black Power spokesmen from the state and introduced a Public Order Act preventing Bajans from speaking publicly about Black Power. In Grenada, Premier Eric Gairy has doubled the island's police force and over the radio explained that Grenada did not need Black Power as in the United States since in the Caribbean "power is already in the hands of black people." In St. Vincent, scores of names are on the island's "undesirable aliens" list, names that are associated with the movement in the Caribbean. In Belize, two Black Power advocates, members of the United Black Association for Development, were charged with seditious conspiracy after their newspaper, *Amandala*, published demands for an end to economic colonialism. In St. Lucia, the *Forum* has been prevented from going into the villages of the island to talk to the people about Black Power. In Dominica, similar actions have been taken by government, and in Jamaica, the writings of black leaders such as Malcolm X, Eldridge Cleaver, and Bobby Seale have been confiscated. It was getting to the point when, as C. L. R. James has recently said, "even the writings of Dr. Eric Williams will have to be banned in the Caribbean."

Nevertheless, in spite of the pressure from regional governments, the Commonwealth Caribbean radicals have continued to organize. And as in the past, when different conditions required changes in tactics, so now the Caribbean militants (ranging from Marxists to black nationalists) recognize that present circumstances dictate new strategy. So the shift from pure analysis to mass actions to marches and demonstrations has become a foundation for the more serious work of organizing at community or village level, work that is certainly less dramatic and less obvious, but in the end far more likely to bring effective action.

In Guyana, various groups are highly active, particularly after Stokely Carmichael's visit. If nothing else, Carmichael's presence in Guyana provoked a wide-ranging debate over the tactics to be employed by the Caribbean movement. In Trinidad, the few activists who are not in prison continue to organize. Lloyd Best's *Tapia* Group is still intact, concentrating on community action programs at village level. A former Best associate in the New World Group, James Millette, has chosen a different route and formed a political party (United National Independent Party) to challenge Prime Minister Williams. Then, there are those who have gone underground, some to work with the rural population, others with labor.

In the smaller states, there are also young activists—many returned from universities in North America—developing strong radical movements. These young blacks have experienced racism in North America, actively participated in the struggle of North American blacks, both in the United States and Canada, and are determined to implement the programs (earlier offered) by such groups as the New World.

Before long these movements must begin to surface throughout the Caribbean, creating new "February Revolutions." The economic structure of the Commonwealth Caribbean, the racism intrinsic to that structure, and the inability of the current political leadership to enact the necessary changes must, in time, result in greater confrontation. In all probability, it will be violent confrontation, basically because the Black Power movement will be responding to state violence, to pressures from the police, and to the American presence. The probability is that it will be a racial confrontation as well, simply because the economic lines have been drawn that way.

Juan de Onis

# The Hispanic Caribbean

## The Dominican Republic—
## Insular Nationalism and Economic Dependence

The Dominican Republic is an important fragment of a cultural archipelago that can be called the Hispanic Caribbean. This tenuous grouping includes the islands of Cuba, Puerto Rico and Hispaniola, of which the Spanish-speaking eastern half is the Dominican Republic (Haiti is the western region), and certain portions of mainland countries bordering on the Caribbean, particularly coastal Venezuela, Panama, and eastern Honduras.

The fifteen-to-twenty million people who live within the perimeter of the Hispanic Caribbean share a combination of cultural and historical affinities that give them a dimension of common origin and related evolution. These affinities include long centuries of Spanish colonization, assimilation on a major scale of imported African slaves into mulatto societies, and an experience of national independence that was overtaken by economic subordination to the United States. There is, as well, the pervasive influence in the area of a uniform habitat contributing to similar economic activities and social traditions, and a significant interchange of persons and ideas.

These factors have contributed to similarities in the appearance, manners, and attitudes of the people in these countries that are readily apparent to any visitor. Dress, food, music, sports, family relations, religious practices, political style, and highly developed social com-

---

JUAN DE ONIS *covers the Caribbean for* The New York Times. *He has won the Maria Moors Cabot award for excellence in reporting Latin American affairs. Mr. de Onis is the author of* The America of José Martí *and co-author of* The Alliance That Lost Its Way, *a study of the Alliance for Progress.*

munication are so much alike that one can almost speak of a common regional identity. It is easy to form an impression of the Hispanic Caribbean as a region which once was an organic whole, but was later broken into geographic and political pieces. One may be led to think that the causes of this disintegration can be overcome by the unifying impulses generated within the region.

A study of the Dominican Republic and its relations with other Spanish-speaking countries of the Caribbean suggests that this impression, despite appearances, is misleading. Making due allowance for all the kindred factors in the region, the absence of interlocking political structures and the primitive level of economic complementation among the countries involved preclude seriously considering the Hispanic Caribbean as a functional regional community. Indeed, there appear to be no greater set of misfits for integration in Latin America than the components of the Hispanic Caribbean because of their ingrained insular nationalist attitudes, special forms of economic dependence on the United States, and internal political conflicts.

This poses in the long run a limitation on the possibilities of these small countries achieving national goals of development through an expanded and more self-reliant form of economic and political association. It would seem that only a compelling opportunity for broader association introduced from outside the region, with the acquiescence and cooperation of the United States, can break the isolation that impedes integration.

### An Ill-Starred Land

The historical evolution of the Dominican Republic, the center of the Spanish Caribbean, is marked by economic disasters and political interventions that have blunted at fateful moments the country's potential for national development. Probably no other Latin American country has undergone so many near catastrophes in its past. The Dominican Republic is a child of grief and turmoil from its colonial days down through its troubled years of independence that climaxed in the crisis of a civil war in 1965.

The Spanish occupation of the New World began in organized fashion on Hispaniola with the establishment by Columbus of the permanent settlement of Santo Domingo in 1496 at the mouth of the Ozama River on the southeastern coast of the island. After a brief flurry of gold mining, Santo Domingo became the jumping off point for the occupation of Cuba, from which the fast-moving colonial enterprise advanced to the American mainland and the fabulous riches of Mexico and Peru. But, soon, Cuba supplanted Santo Domingo as the staging area for expeditions and as a strategic naval base to protect galleons moving through the Caribbean to Spain. Following a short-lived success with the first sugar plantations worked by African slaves in the

Caribbean, Santo Domingo declined into a colonial backwater. This was the first of the many colonial cycles of boom-and-bust in Spanish America.

Spain's imperial policies rigidly subordinated the economic development of overseas territories to metropolitan commercial bureaucratic interests. These imposed severe limitations on trade between the colonial territories and third countries, particularly France, the Netherlands, and England, and restricted the establishment of industries and professions in the colonies. No territory suffered more from these policies than Santo Domingo, for Spain lacked the resources and the political will to promote alone the colonization and development of its vast American empire.

At the beginning of the seventeenth century, Spain's shaky will to hold Hispaniola became apparent. In an extraordinary decision, King Philip III ordered the eradication of ports and cattle ranches that Spanish Creole herders and runaway slaves had established on the northern coast of Hispaniola. These rustic communities, which include present-day Montecristi and Puerto Plata, were thriving on contraband trade of cattle hides and tallow with "protestant" merchantmen who called at these ports without tribute to the Spanish crown. An armed Spanish expedition forced these populations to move to the center and southeast of the island, leaving the northern coast abandoned.

Huge numbers of cattle remained behind and multiplied in the lush grasslands. The capture of wild cattle and the trade in hides was taken over by lawless buccaneers, many of whom had connections with France. By the end of the seventeenth century, the steady weakening of Spain through wars on the continent led to the Treaty of Ryswick in 1697, through which France acquired the colony of Haiti, occupying the western two-fifths of Hispaniola, until then virtually unpopulated.

Paradoxically, the loss to France of the western portion of Hispaniola led to a new economic boom for Santo Domingo—followed by disaster.

During the eighteenth century, the burgeoning mercantile capitalism of France demonstrated in Haiti the enormous potential for tropical production of Hispaniola, which Spain had neglected. By the seventeen-eighties, about 90 percent of Haiti's fertile land was under cultivation in 8,500 slave plantations producing sugar, indigo, cotton, coffee, cacao, and other products that made the fortunes of processers, traders, shippers, and bankers in France, as well as planters in the colony. Gérard Pierre-Charles in his study of Haitian economic development, *The Haitian Economy and Its Road to Development*, observes: "If the dimensions of the colony are considered, it can be said that, in those days, there was no similar concentration of wealth anywhere else in the world."

The population of Haiti soared toward the end of the eighteenth century to 600,000 persons, of whom 500,000 were slaves. The population of Santo Domingo, on twice the territory of Haiti, probably did not exceed 130,000 persons. The derivative effects of the Haitian economic boom were not long in making themselves felt in the backward neighbor. Despite continuing Spanish restrictions, the flow of cattle, both for beef and traction animals, as well as fuel wood, lumber, and foodstuffs for the Haitian plantations activated Santo Domingo's economy, particularly in the central and northwestern regions of the Cibao. Yet, the colonial administration based in the city of Santo Domingo remained so impoverished that salaries for public officials had to be paid by periodic shipments of silver coins from the wealthy seat of colonial administration in Mexico. To such low estate had Santo Domingo fallen as an overseas territory of Spain that contemporary authors say the merchants and bureaucrats would line the waterfront like shipwrecked sailors to spy the appearance on the horizon of the dole ship from Mexico.

### BLACK REVOLUTION

Whatever glimpse of emergence from backwardness and poverty Santo Domingo may have enjoyed as a colony through its relationship with Haiti was obliterated by the political cyclone unleashed in Hispaniola by the French revolution. Whatever incipient economic and social institutions had taken hold were reduced to the level of subsistence by the revolt of the mulattos and slaves in Haiti that turned Santo Domingo into a battleground when French armies tried to use its territory for counterattack against the Haitian insurgents.

The destruction of the Haitian plantation economy by the social upheaval of the slave revolution destroyed Santo Domingo's major market. The fear of annihilation at the hands of invading Haitian troops drove tens of thousands of Dominicans into exile in Venezuela, Puerto Rico, or Cuba with what capital they could salvage.

In the period from 1808 to 1822, when most Latin American countries waged successfully their wars of independence from Spain, and emerged as free nations, Santo Domingo staggered between restoration of Spanish colonial rule and Haitian domination. The latter was finally imposed in 1822 under the rule of President Boyer of Haiti and lasted until 1844, when a nationalist movement gestated among young Dominicans of the new urban commercial and professional class declared for independence. There was almost no Haitian resistance and the Dominican Republic emerged to self-rule virtually without political, military, or administrative institutions on a national scale.

### INADEQUATE NATIONHOOD

A measure of the weakness of the national state even 25 years after independence can be seen in the report on the Dominican Republic prepared by an official United States commission, appointed by President Grant, that visited the island in 1870–71. The commission found that there was not one chartered bank, no telegraph system, and no all-weather highway linking Santo Domingo, the capital, with Santiago de los Caballeros, the country's second city in the Cibao region which produced the then major export crops of tobacco, coffee, and cacao.

The absence of a sense of national purpose or even identity was reflected also in the chaotic political and administrative life of the Dominican Republic after independence. The period was characterized by the spirit of faction and individual opportunism for personal gain in public affairs. Chronic instability reigned, with armed political bands leading revolts against precariously constituted governments. One of them, in search of external support, briefly annexed the Dominican Republic back to colonial status under Spain from 1861 to 1864, while the Civil War was underway in the United States.

## Dictatorship

The absence in the Dominican society after independence of elements that could form a ruling elite with a cohesive vision of national development has been a fundamental cause of this country's misfortunes. The root of the problem has been described in a perceptive study by Abraham F. Lowenthal, *The Dominican Republic: The Politics of Chaos,* in which he observed:

> . . . throughout its independent history the Dominican Republic has lacked a powerful oligarchy. A series of emigrations by elite families, particularly after the Spanish withdrawal in 1795 and during the Haitian occupation of 1822 to 1844, eliminated from Dominican society many who might otherwise have dominated the country's economy and politics. The few white, socially prestigious families remaining in the Dominican Republic in the late nineteenth century were not wealthy or powerful but insecure.

The weakness and insecurity in a country prone to violence in personal and political relations have led in the internal to the rise to power of "strong men" and in the external to foreign protection against social upheaval.

The Dominican Republic's first dictator after independence came in the person of Ulises Heureaux, a mulatto general, who emerged from among the competing leaders of armed bands and ruled from 1887 to 1899 with a ruthless hand. He fomented some important public works, which were long overdue, but he combined terror with corruption; and the Dominican Republic accumulated onerous debts, mainly with United States creditors. When Heureaux was assassinated in 1899, the country's finances were in deep trouble.

UNITED STATES ENTANGLEMENT

It seemed inevitable that the Dominican Republic, with the proclivities in its political circles to seek a foreign protector and source of funds, would enter into a "special relationship" with the United States when the latter began its expansion into the Caribbean as a sphere of commercial and strategic interest.

After the visit of President Grant's commission to the Dominican Republic, the United States Senate narrowly rejected a proposed treaty that a Dominican president had eagerly signed in hopes of a loan under which the United States was to acquire virtually sovereign control of the Samana peninsula at the eastern end of the island for a naval station. President Grant's enemies in the Senate argued that there was little evidence that the Dominican people had given their government a mandate for a territorial concession.

Such Congressional restraint toward United States involvement in Dominican affairs lost validity after the Spanish-American War led to the annexation of Puerto Rico and the occupation of Cuba, followed by United States actions leading to the Panama Canal treaty. With United States holders of Dominican bonds and bank creditors clamoring for overdue payments, and United States sugar interests moving into Dominican holdings, an agreement was obtained in 1906 by which our government appointed the collector of customs in Santo Domingo. A convention signed in 1907 gave the United States the right to intervene with military force to maintain public order and tax collections in the event of a breakdown of internal peace.

If the threat of United States intervention was conceived as a deterrent to political irresponsibility, it did not work. President Ramon Cáceres, who had signed the 1907 convention, established the United States dollar as the Dominican currency, and pushed through land legislation favoring United States sugar investment, was assassinated in 1911. A period of armed factional violence and administrative disorder followed until President Wilson, in the interest of humanity and United States investors, sent the United States Marines into the Dominican Republic in 1916. The occupation lasted until 1924.

Of all the effects of this eight-year occupation, the most important were a sustained expansion of American investments in sugar and the organization, under Marine Corps instructors, of a national constabulary, the *Guardia Nacional,* as the Dominican Republic's first professional, permanent military institution.

When the Marines were withdrawn, after a United States-supervised election, the main agricultural and industrial activity on the island was production of sugar for sale to the United States market. In later years, when the United States began allocating sugar imports through a quota system at preferential prices, this sugar quota became the most vital factor in Dominican foreign trade and therefore the primary link of economic dependence on the United States.

The organization of the *Guardia Nacional*, in turn, prepared the way for the most powerful "strong man" the Dominican Republic has known, Generalissimo Rafael Leonidas Trujillo Molina. As Lowenthal has observed, "by organizing a relatively effective institution in a society almost totally lacking in institutions, U.S. authorities helped make it possible for the head of the newly-established force, General Rafael Trujillo, to seize power and to retain control for over 30 years."

After Trujillo's dictatorship ended with his assassination in 1961 it became even more clear that the Dominican armed forces, by then expanded into 25,000 army, air force, and navy servicemen and 16,000 national police, were the primary stabilizing political institution in the Dominican Republic.

This assessment by the Johnson administration of the critical role of the Dominican armed forces led to the United States military intervention of 1965–66 that stemmed the tide of a populist insurrection, which included some sectors of the military. The success of the insurgents in the civil war threatened to change the character of the Dominican military from guardian and ally of propertied groups identified with American interests into the military arm of radical nationalist sectors disposed toward social revolution and changes in the status quo alignment of the Dominican Republic with the United States. The intervention, followed by a purge of military dissidents, salvaged the institutional unity of the armed forces on a militantly "anti-communist" basis acceptable to the United States. By implication, the Dominican Republic was saved by the United States intervention from becoming "another Cuba," even if this meant the establishment of a "neo-*trujillista*" regime as an outcome of the conflict.

FRUITS OF TRUJILLO'S TYRANNY

The repressive nature of the Trujillo dictatorship is too well known to require elaboration. He was a ruthless ruler in a country where political ferocity is endemic. What is of lasting significance, however, is that the political terror of the Trujillo era was an instrument by which state power, identified with Trujillo's person during his lifetime, acquired unprecedented extension and depth. Trujillo scarred a generation, but he also gave the Dominican Republic an economic structure and a level of public administration that the country had not known earlier. In a bizarrely personalistic way, Trujillo was a modernizing nationalist in the backward context in which he came to power.

The hallmark of the Trujillo dictatorship was the concentration in his relentless grasp of military, political, and economic power. He ran his small country like a private ranch for personal gain, and it is often difficult to draw a clear line between Trujillo's business interests and those of the state. It is reported by various sources that Trujillo and his immediate family amassed a fortune valued at between $250,000,000 and $400,000,000. Until the final years of his regime, the great majority of these funds were held as assets and investments in the Dominican Republic. To achieve and multiply this wealth, Trujillo had to organize the Dominican economy on a profitable basis, for he stood to gain a lion's share of any successful venture.

When Trujillo first came to power in 1930, the Dominican Republic was in financial prostration. The worldwide economic depression had driven sugar prices to ruinously low levels. The capital, Santo Domingo, had been severely damaged by a hurricane. Customs duties, the main source of public revenue, had fallen to such low levels through trade contraction that by 1932 there was insufficient government income to service the United States debt and meet the public payroll. The country had virtually no foreign credit standing.

Trujillo managed, however, to refinance the United States debt of about $20,000,000 and eventually pay it off. The Dominican treasury was managed on a sound fiscal basis, and the Dominican peso was restored as the nation's currency, convertible at par with the United States dollar. As income from sugar exports was restored by allocations to the Dominican Republic of a share of the United States preferential market, the country's imports rose and credit from foreign banks became available.

Within this sound monetary and fiscal framework, Trujillo began to build his financial empire. Some of his early operations were outright plunder, such as the private monopoly he set up for sale of salt to the Dominican market. As his capital increased, Trujillo acquired control of about 60 percent of Dominican sugar production. Either directly, or through members of his family and political associates, Trujillo became the largest cattle and rice operator. Just as he had acquired sugar mills from United States owners, he nationalized the Dominican operations of the National City Bank of New York and set up the Dominican Reserve Bank that was followed later by the Agricultural and Industrial Bank. Both these "autonomous" state institutions liberally financed imports by Trujillo firms and the creation of a string of new industries that were virtual Trujillo monopolies.

As Juan Bosch, who was elected president twenty months after the dictator's assassination, said in *Dominican Social Composition* (1970), Trujillo was "the first Dominican who rose to power with the intention of using power to make himself into an authentic bourgeois," meaning a large-scale capitalist. In so doing, Bosch said, Trujillo had personally fulfilled the role of capital concentration that normally has fallen to a class of national entrepreneurs and bankers in other developing countries.

The personalistic way in which Trujillo introduced capitalist organization to the Dominican economy of planters, merchants, artisans, and peasants had an odd but important outcome for the country's economic and political structure. After his death, and the flight from the island of his family with all the gold bars and dollars they could carry away from the Reserve Bank, all of Trujillo's industries, enterprises, and lands were confiscated as properties of the state.

The empire remained concentrated under public ownership creating a somewhat anomalous situation in a non-socialist society. It was estimated in 1962 that 51 percent of all industrial capital was held by the state, including 12 sugar mills producing 66 percent of the country's main export crop. Twenty-eight enterprises from the Trujillo complex that are controlled by the State Enterprises Corporation (CORDE) accounted for 22 percent of non-sugar industrial wages and salaries in 1966.

These sugar mills and state enterprises are the political plum in jobs, contracts, and other forms of patronage that falls to whatever political group is in power in the Dominican Republic. In a country where professional opportunities are limited and unemployment in the capital exceeds 30 percent of the potential labor force, the state enterprises are a major stake in the violent Dominican political game.

## Political Atrophy

One aspect of Trujillo's concentration of power was his organization of the Dominican Party, to which all public employees had to turn over 10 percent of their pay. The party provided a structure of federal officials, provincial governors, and municipal authorities that was the transmission belt for Trujillo's will. As such, the party was primarily another arm of the dictator's bureaucracy.

Trujillo had a pharisaic concern for legal appearances. There were a series of elections for president and other executive and legislative positions, and congress met each year to enact laws proposed by Trujillo. This was a façade because no opposition activity was tolerated.

It is important to note that Trujillo and his propagandists equated with "communism" virtually any expression of dissent with the regime, or any independent action to organize labor, students, or professional groups. For 30 years, the Dominican people were told that their island and the "Benefactor" who ruled them were the object of a conspiracy by the forces of "international communism" in the Caribbean.

Therefore, when Dominican exile groups received support from democratic governments in Costa Rica and Venezuela as well as from Cuba for several abortive attempts to overthrow Trujillo before 1961, this was presented in the official version as "the hand of communism." Not surprisingly, this propaganda had the effect on anti-Trujillo Dominican youth of making "communism" attractive. Toward the end of his regime students and young professionals began to make their way to eastern Europe and later Cuba to be trained as revolutionaries.

When Trujillo was assassinated by a group of conspirators that included disgruntled henchmen and a general the dictator had once slapped in the face, the collapse of the dictatorship found the Dominican people as unprepared for self-rule as they had been before Trujillo. The opposition had almost no political experience except conspiracy. There was no unifying anti-Trujillo party and the political compass swung wildly as in a magnetic storm between groups that were soon at each other's throats.

There were returning exiles, some of whom had conspired from abroad for decades, and submerged domestic elements, mostly in the commercial and professional sector, who had nursed their antagonism toward Trujillo in fear and silence for many years. There were the surviving assassins, Antonio Imbert Barreras and Luís Amiama Tió, whose political interest revolved around obtaining personal security against reprisal by hired killers of the Trujillo clan and preserving the wealth and property they had accumulated under Trujillo. There were ambitious young army officers, molded by Trujillo's authoritarian, anti-communist indoctrination, and young radicals, some of them trained in Marxist revolutionary methods.

In eclipse, but still in the wings, were the remnants of the Trujillo political machine and propertied individuals, businessmen, and managers who wanted security for themselves and orderly, conservative hands at the tiller of government. One of these "widows" of the fallen dictator was Joaquín Balaguer, Trujillo's last vice-president, an historian and diplomat, trained in law at the Sorbonne, who in 1958 made the following statement of loyalty to Trujillo in a letter to *The New York Times*:

> It is not secret to any Dominican that I am solely an intellectual creation of Generalissimo Trujillo and if there is any merit I have as a member of the spiritual and political family of this illustrious government it is for the fidelity which I employ in reflecting, in my modest interventions as a publicist, the thinking of the man who personifies actually the Dominican life.

Balaguer succeeded to the presidency, as head of a council of state, after Trujillo's death, but he was driven into obscure exile in New York by political riots and a military uprising in January 1962. He would return, however.

## THE DOMINICAN REVOLUTIONARY PARTY

The Trujillo era occupies a time span during which the Dominican population expanded enormously. The national census of 1920 reported a population of 895,000. Fifty years later, the census of 1970 placed the population at 4,011,500. The National Statistical Office projected a population for 1980 of 5,445,000 based on no significant change in the population growth rate, which stood at 3.6 percent a year during the nineteen-sixties.

The Dominican population distribution is strongly rural. Nearly 80 percent of Dominicans were reported to be living in rural areas, or towns of less than 5,000 people, in the 1960 census. Therefore, the impact of rapid population increase has been felt first in great pressure on available agricultural land and at a second stage in a heavy flow of unskilled, largely uneducated farm laborers and their families to the two major urban centers, Santo Domingo and Santiago de los Caballeros.

As in most developing countries, the population composition is heavily weighted toward young people. The average life expectancy of Dominicans was estimated in 1965 at 52 years, and half the population is under 18 years old. Consequently, education has been an area of growing pressure for expanded facilities. In the final decade of Trujillo's rule, investments in primary schools reduced the level of illiteracy from 59 percent to 35 percent. At the same time, this generated great pressure for secondary school and university enrollment.

These demographic factors, with the economic pressures and social dislocations that accompanied them, underlie the sudden success of the Dominican Revolutionary Party in the first free election for president held after Trujillo's death. From a skeletal political organization of "Democratic Left" intellectuals, scattered about in exile until 1960, Juan Bosch's Dominican Revolutionary Party (PRD) swept into power with 600,000 votes in the general elections of December 1962. Bosch was a writer of short stories, an informal sociologist and historian, whose main weapon in opposition to Trujillo was the pen. His political peregrinations to Venezuela, Cuba, New York, Costa Rica, and Puerto Rico established him among the Caribbean intelligentsia, but he was unlikely stuff to lead a populist movement. Yet, without experience in political command, his simple, vernacular exposition of a program of nonviolent social revolution fired the hopes for change of unemployed urban shantytown dwellers, landless peasants, reformist urban groups, such as emerging labor organizations, and moderate students. Bosch assumed the presidency in January 1963.

RIGHT-WING REACTION

Eight months after Bosch took office, the commanders of the armed forces and police overthrew the government. After a short period of pressure from the United States embassy to give the government a "civilian image," a three-man junta was installed that ultimately came down to the de facto exercise of the presidency by Donald Reid Cabral, a well-to-do automobile dealer, whose brother Roberto, a physician, had been killed by Trujillo's police for complicity in the dictator's assassination.

Eighteen months after the overthrow of Bosch, a group of younger military officers began a revolt against Reid Cabral in the name of the restoration of constitutional government. There were at the time several other plots afoot among the military against Reid Cabral. It has never been clear whether the "Constitutionalists," who included some officers that had been plotting with the PRD, were agreed on bringing Bosch back from exile, or whether they were simply agreed on displacing Reid Cabral, and with him, the senior echelon of officers then in the high command, thereby advancing to the top posts.

In any case, the disunity within the armed forces, reflecting the struggle to fill the political vacuum left by Trujillo's death, brought the Dominican Republic to the verge of civil war. Crowds of supporters of Bosch and more radical revolutionary groups poured into the streets of Santo Domingo. The "Constitutionalist" military armed them after the right-wing air force commander, Col. Elias Wessin y Wessin, sent his jet fighters on strafing and bombing runs against the presidential palace and a key radio station controlled by the insurgents. The enraged populace seized police stations. They halted Wessin's tanks from entering the city with barricades and firebombs. They formed commando forces and successfully assaulted the Ozama fortress in the city, seizing hundreds of heavy weapons.

With the issue in doubt, Wessin and his associates called for United States military intervention. President Johnson dispatched the Marines and the Eighty-second Airborne Division who divided the capital in two parts with an armed corridor and confined the "Constitutionalist" insurgents to one section of the city. The revolt was, in effect, crushed, but a long period of negotiations followed before the "Constitutionalists" and the right-wing military command agreed to allow a provisional government headed by a "neutral" to be installed for the purpose of holding an election.

As a result of this process, Balaguer, Trujillo's one-time vice-president, returned from exile in New York to be elected president in May 1966. Bosch ran second. In a technical sense, it was a free election, supervised by observers from the Organization of American States. It is also true, however, that Dominican military and police commanders in important rural areas openly supported Balaguer. Bosch, allegedly from fear of assassination, confined his campaign mainly to radio broadcasts. Many "Constitutionalist" combatants and PRD activists were killed by police and right-wing armed groups, and these in turn were targets of reprisals.

## Reconstruction

The failure of the Bosch government can be ascribed to various factors. Bosch, as well as some independent observers, claimed that opposition to his government only became virulent in military and business circles when he sought to eliminate corruption in government through which high-ranking officers and contractors had profited since Trujillo's time. It is also clear, however, that lack of political cohesion among PRD supporters and Bosch's weaknesses as an administrator undermined government action, dispersed funds, and alienated independents who favored moderate reform.

Bosch thus became vulnerable to a vicious campaign mounted by anti-communist zealots against his modest agrarian reform program and the PRD's efforts to promote cooperatives and labor unions. The military, long conditioned by anti-communist indoctrination, readily fell in with the anti-Bosch position, particularly when some United States military advisers privately sided with the Dominican commanders, despite the American embassy's support for Bosch.

The Reid Cabral government failed because of its lack of legitimacy and political support outside the business sector and because of poor political strategy in applying an austerity program that became necessary when sugar prices plummeted on the international market. Some of the stabilization measures affected the military, with whom Reid Cabral had uneasy personal relations. Beyond financial stability, the program offered little in the way of easing unemployment or containing the cost of living. Strong endorsement from the United States government could do little to prevent the collapse when the military split, opening the way to an explosion of frustrations in the capital.

Balaguer faced many of the same basic problems that beset his immediate predecessors when he assumed the presidency in 1966. In one key respect, however, he started with a vital advantage. For the first time since Trujillo, the president enjoyed relatively stable support from the armed forces. The Dominican military institution is chronically prone to personal and factional infighting, but the experience of 1965 exposed the military to the dangers of disunity. In hours of stress, the lesson has been remembered.

After four years in power, Balaguer retained the backing of the military for his reelection to a second four-year term in 1970, despite determined efforts by the PRD and a variety of right-wing political groups to open a breach between the president and the armed forces.

His Reformist party substantially reassembled many provincial elements of Trujillo's old Dominican party, and the administration was liberally studded with Balaguer appointees drawn from the former dictatorial bureaucracy. But Balaguer also attracted to his government many elements from the opposition parties, including the PRD, in a skillful display of the power of patronage. By so doing, Balaguer artfully edged his way into the middle ground of Dominican politics.

Balaguer's quiet, scholarly appearance concealed the calculating mind of a shrewd politician with no inhibitions over trading government favors for the backing of interest groups. With all the state enterprises at his command, Balaguer knew how to win the greatest political return with this powerful instrument. He personally ran the government's finances, doling out money to ministers and agencies for projects of political interest, while substantially augmenting the budget of the presidency for projects carrying his personal stamp. There was hardly a weekend when Balaguer was not touring the country to inaugurate public works, hand out land titles, or give new tenants the keys to apartments in housing projects.

This old-fashioned, personal style of patronage politics was in the paternalistic tradition of Dominican leaders. But it did not bring to bear on basic Dominican problems a modern developmental program. Balaguer did attract a $200,000,000 investment by a Canadian firm to develop a major nickel deposit, which was expected to add $25,000,000 a year to Dominican exports by the middle of the nineteen-seventies. He also arranged two major electric power and irrigation investments designed to relieve power shortages and increase land in cultivation.

In more complex areas of socioeconomic reform, Balaguer moved with a caution that indicated political hesitation about antagonizing conservative interests. This was primarily true in agrarian reform and public education. By the end of the nineteen-sixties, there were 500,000 rural workers in the Dominican countryside, and the number of rural job seekers was increasing 30,000 a year. Yet in 1968, only 1,518 farm families were settled under the agrarian reform program and in 1969 the number was less than 2,200.

In view of the high rates of rural unemployment, or sub-employment in a growing number of tiny subsistence plots, the Inter-American Committee of the Alliance for Progress said in an experts' review of the Dominican development process in 1970 that much greater funds and organizational efforts had to go into agriculture. The report said:

> Top priority in public investment should apparently be assigned to expansion of the agrarian reform process, a dynamic program for diversification of marginal lands devoted to sugar growing, implementation of projects primarily designed to habilitate potentially productive areas, improvement of the irrigation systems, construction of feeder roads, and establishment of adequate marketing systems for agricultural commodities.

In 1968, the United States Agency for International Development earmarked $12,000,000 for a program to expand and improve secondary education in the Dominican Republic, where only 2 percent of the 650,000 children in grade school attained high-school level. Two years later, the Balaguer government had not presented a plan to use the money, which required a large matching fund from the Dominican treasury.

Land invasions by peasants began to be a problem during the nineteen-sixties. Most such actions were put down ruthlessly by police. A number of extreme leftwing peasant organizers were killed in the countryside and some Roman Catholic priests working with peasants were deported.

One of the major areas of political unrest against Balaguer was in the National University of Santo Domingo and in the high schools in the capital and major provincial centers. There were many students among more than 50 political opponents of Balaguer's reelection who were killed by the police during repressive actions and street conflicts in 1970. The 1965 conflict had brought a significant radicalization of student politics, with the national university and many high schools under the student leadership of leftwing PRD youth or more radical Marxist-Leninist movements, such as the Dominican Popular Movement (MPD).

Both Col. Francisco Caamaño Deño, the military leader of the "Constitutionalist" movement, and Maximiliano Goméz, secretary-general of the MPD, who was released from prison in exchange for a kidnapped U.S. air force attaché, were in Cuba in 1970. Dominican extremists looked to them as possible leaders of new guerrilla operations, but the Dominican military, who had smashed Cuban-backed guerrilla invaders in 1959 and 1963, were even better armed and trained at the end of the decade.

### Conclusions

The Dominican Republic is a country that has been isolated and turned in upon itself by a long history of colonial neglect, conflict with neighboring Haiti, and internal political turmoil. It reached a more modern state of development under Trujillo, the dictator, who ran the country like a fiefdom.

The one important channel of external relations is with the United States. Sugar exports to the mainland preferential market are the main income of the Dominican Republic, which has one of the highest rates of export-import trade with the United States of any Latin American country.

The industrialization of the Dominican Republic under Trujillo through a program of import substitution created a high-cost manufacturing sector for a narrow market that has been primarily owned by the state since the confiscation of Trujillo's properties. This publicly-owned industrial complex is a major element of political power within the country.

The leadership of President Balaguer, while providing a sound, conservative basis for domestic and foreign private investment, was cautious and little disposed toward innovations.

For political reasons, which have a bearing on Dominican internal security, a basic conflict exists with the Cuban revolutionary regime. Moreover, the Dominican Republic has benefited greatly by increased United States sugar quotas distributed since the American market was closed to Cuba. There are no grounds, therefore, to expect Dominican support for an approximation between Cuba and the rest of the American community.

As a country well endowed with agricultural resources, the Dominican Republic developed a new area of minor exports of beef and vegetables to other Caribbean countries. This potential could be substantially developed, particularly if Dominican exports to Puerto Rico were promoted through new United States regulations.

Except for some rise in agricultural trade, however, the possibility of regional economic complementation is limited by the highly protectionist position of the Dominican Republic on industrial products. This makes it difficult to work out integration arrangements between the Dominican Republic and other Caribbean countries, as was demonstrated in an attempt by Venezuela to promote a joint investment in fertilizer production in the Dominican Republic. The investment was blocked by an existing Dominican fertilizer supplier. Puerto Rican investors ran into similar difficulties on proposed joint investments designed to use low-cost Dominican labor for intermediate products to be finished in Puerto Rico.

Changes in these positions in the Dominican Republic appear unlikely until more political confidence is established and until a more technocratic government influenced by regionally-minded Dominican entrepreneurs, aware of the limitations of their insular market, comes on the scene.

Gérard R. Latortue

# The European Lands

For centuries, the European powers—including Spain, Great Britain, France, Holland, and Denmark—dominated, unchallenged, politically, economically, socially, and culturally the entire Caribbean region. They assimilated these lands to the extent that St. Domingue was called little Spain (Hispaniola) and Barbados "little England." Good manners in Martinique meant for one to know which wine to serve with chicken, veal or shrimps, whereas in Jamaica, a real gentleman was supposed to know every detail about the British royal family, including birthdays.

In winning its independence on January 1, 1804, Haiti was the first Caribbean island to challenge the total domination of European powers in the area. Later, the Americans invaded Puerto Rico in 1898 and took over the island, and the Danish sold St. Thomas and St. Croix to the United States in 1917. Having acquired these new centers of influence, the United States Government began to show an increasing interest in the Caribbean. From Puerto Rico, St. Thomas and St. Croix, the Americans have tried over the years, with varying degrees of success, to develop economic and cultural ties with the rest of the region.

After World War II and the nationalist awakening of the colonized people of Asia and Africa, the European powers were forced by the

GÉRARD R. LATORTUE of Haiti is chairman of the Department of Economics and Business Administration at the Inter-American University of Puerto Rico, research associate at the Institute of Caribbean Studies, University of Puerto Rico, and executive director of Caribbean Research Associates (also in Puerto Rico). Author of published articles on his native land, Dr. Latortue was employed by the Haiti Ministry of Labor and Social Welfare and was professor of economics at the Law School of the University of Haiti in the early sixties.

pressure of world public opinion to rethink the colonial arrangements. France discovered the "Overseas Department" formula, tying the islands to the metropolis, while Holland showed a genuine interest in giving complete internal self government to its Caribbean lands. Britain went further and encouraged complete independence for the larger possessions (Jamaica, Trinidad and Tobago, Barbados, and Guyana) and promoted the associate-statehood status for the smaller islands granting them the right to declare unilaterally complete independence.

By the beginning of the 1970s, the European powers were losing their ascendancy in the Caribbean. Some of the territories in the region were gradually sliding into the United States zone of influence. Nevertheless, Europe continued to play an important role—if not politically, at least culturally, socially, and, to a lesser extent, economically—in Caribbean affairs. One may consider as European lands in the Caribbean region Haiti, the French overseas departments, and Surinam and the Netherland Antilles. Haiti is, of course, independent, but culturally and spiritually it is closer to France—or Africa—than to the Americas.

## Haiti

The Republic of Haiti occupies approximately 10,714 square miles in the western third of the island of Hispaniola, with the Dominican Republic occupying the remaining eastern two-thirds. The estimated population of Haiti in 1967 was 4,577,000, and the projected population for 1980 is 6,919,000. The population is overwhelmingly rural (92 percent). However, the political life of the country is concentrated primarily in the urban areas. The peasants are called upon exclusively to vote and/or pay taxes.

### SOCIAL GROUPS

There are three main social groups in Haiti: the mulattoes, the educated blacks, and the black masses.

The mulattoes represent less than one percent of the Haitian population. But they dominate the import-export trade in Haiti and, as a consequence, the economic life of the country. Since independence, because of this economic power, they have sought to control—directly or indirectly—the political life of Haiti. Often they have succeeded and at times failed. In their quest for political power they used all possible methods and tactics, including internal corruption and alliances with foreign powers.

In fact, the Haitian mulattoes have very little feeling for Haiti as a country. They do not like to be identified with what was and is known as the "Black Republic." Frequently they introduced themselves, while abroad, as Mexicans, Indians, or Latin Americans. On the whole, their contribution to Haiti's development has been rather negative. They have exploited the peasants and kept their profits in foreign banks. To maintain their privileges, they have never hesitated to compromise with the existing government. Their cooperation with President François Duvalier's dictatorial regime is a good example of how the mulattoes are the most opportunistic social group in Haiti. Economically, they are as powerful in 1970 as they were a century ago.

In 1970, the educated blacks represented almost four percent of the population. A large percentage of this group believes that to succeed is to "sell one's soul" to the mulatto oligarchy. This was certainly true until 1946. The revolution of 1946, however, gave greater opportunities to educated blacks, proud of themselves as blacks and of their African origins. During the government of President Dumarsais Estimé (1946–50), most of the "taboos" against the blacks disappeared. President Paul E. Magloire (1950–56) did continue—perhaps to a lesser extent than President Estimé—the policy of rehabilitating the blacks of Haiti.

The third social group in Haiti is composed of the black masses, representing nearly 95 percent of the Haitian population and concentrated in the rural areas. Although representing an overwhelming majority of the population, this group has been completely neglected by the "élites." The élites have monopolized educational privileges and used the national budget for their whim, travel abroad, and all other available benefits for their relatives and friends. While in power, they did very little to improve the standard of living of the masses or to provide them with education, public health facilities and irrigation programs. Only one alternative was left to the black masses: their African traditions. Two American scholars, R. Wingfield and V. J. Parenton, described this group in these terms:

> In this stratum the process of deafricanization is the least manifest. The Caucasian strain is slight and the majority of peasants approximates the pure negroid racial type. His technology has not evolved much beyond that of his African ancestors. His exclusive language is Creole. French, the official language, is a foreign tongue to him. Lack of schooling and cultural isolation leave him on the one hand with the most naive conception of the outer world and yet, in other ways, he displays remarkable ingenuity and common sense.

The social structure of the Haitian society is one of the explanations of the permanent crisis prevailing in this first black republic. Indeed, the social structure in Haiti is loaded with inequality. This in itself is a source of conflict.

POLITICAL TRENDS

When Dr. Duvalier was elected president of Haiti on September 22, 1957, he represented to a large segment of the Haitian electorate—

including students, workers, small businessmen, and intellectuals—
the man who could change the structure of Haitian politics. He was
credited with a willingness to give the masses a larger representation
in the government and to promote a realistic plan for economic development through the use of all the national resources for developmental purposes, thus putting an end to corruption.

One may argue the validity of the reasons for which Dr. Duvalier
was elected president on September 22, 1957. However, there are at
least five good reasons to justify the choice of the electorate:

1. Agronomist Louis Dejoie, candidate of the mulattoes, was completely
   out of consideration because of the interests he represented. His candi-
   dacy was a desperate move by a minority group to regain control of
   Haitian political life. He was bound to lose because, at this turning
   point in Haitian history, he represented not the "cause" of the country, but the interests and prejudices of his class.
2. Economist Clément Jumelle, although the best qualified to modernize
   Haiti's social and economic structures, had a poor chance to be elected
   because of his close association with the Magloire régime, overthrown
   months earlier.
3. Professor Daniel Fignolé, well known in Port-au-Prince and an "idol"
   of the masses of the capital, lost all chance to be elected by accepting,
   on May 26, 1957, the provisional presidency of the country. Less than
   a month later, on June 14, 1957, he was sent into exile to New York
   by a military junta.
4. The carefully planned silence of Dr. Duvalier during the electoral
   campaign (December 1956–September 1957) gave the impression that
   he would have been a puppet in the hands of the army and/or his
   closest advisers among whom there were the worst types of opportunistic politicians.
5. Finally, the vote of confidence was given Dr. Duvalier mostly by the
   middle and lower classes of the provinces as well as the peasantry. They
   voted in opposition to the bourgeoisie of the capital, traditionally
   active and powerful in politics and historically denying equal political
   and economic opportunities to the masses.

Once elected president of Haiti, Dr. Duvalier showed his real image.
He was no longer the timid country doctor whom the lower classes
admired; nor the honest former cabinet member who did not even
own a house; nor the ideologist conscious of Haitian problems who
wrote so many good articles about Haiti and its difficulties. He became,
in the words of a Haitian scholar, "an extremely opportunistic man
who was full of frustration and bitterness, and was waiting for the
occasion [being president] to give vent to his vengeance." The consequences were gradual disenchantment among the first followers of
Dr. Duvalier. After ten years of absolute rule, Dr. Duvalier had lost
the spontaneous and active support of most of the middle and lower

classes of the provinces. Then, to maintain himself in power, he decided to rely mainly on terror and corruption.

In June 1964, to the surprise of the world, Dr. Duvalier proclaimed himself president-for-life after a carefully prepared electoral farce. The Haitian electorate was asked to ratify Article 197 of a new Constitution designating him president-for-life. The results were 2,800,000 votes for and 3,234 votes against.

These were the reasons given officially at that time to justify the decision that Dr. Duvalier would exercise his functions for life:

1. He has ensured the maintenance of public peace and order.
2. He has laid the foundations for the country's progressive industrialization through a program of public works and by constructing the required economic and social infrastructure.
3. He has placed the state on a stable economic and financial footing.
4. He has undertaken and achieved the eradication of mass illiteracy.
5. He has imposed respect for the rights of the people and for national sovereignty.
6. He has developed a dignified foreign policy.
7. And he has directed his every action toward building a strong nation capable of fulfilling its destiny in full freedom and dignity.

The scholar whose only contact with Haiti is the official texts may conclude that the country is experiencing a tremendous political, economic, and social revolution under the leadership of Dr. Duvalier. But those familiar with the affairs of Latin America have learned to differentiate between official publications and reality. In the case of Haiti under Dr. Duvalier, this reality is tyranny, corruption, chaos, and misery.

However, one should not assume that the Duvalier regime is entirely negative. As is the case with most governments, Dr. Duvalier's administration has its positive aspects as well. On the positive side, one may mention the political neutralization of the army, the systematic Haitianization of the Roman Catholic clergy and, finally, the chance given some individuals from the lower classes to participate in public affairs.

The neutralization of the army was unquestionably needed. It was impossible for Haiti to tolerate much longer the army as the final judge of who was fitted for the presidency. The arrogance of a large group of military officers had to be broken and the supremacy of civilian authority reaffirmed. Instead of letting it be a "state within a state," it was imperative to bring down the army to the level of a simple "institution at the service of the state."

Unfortunately, however, the reforms undertaken by Dr. Duvalier in this area led to the formation of a large militia—known as the *Tonton-Macoutes*—whose members became as arrogant as the most arrogant of the military officers had ever been. Generally speaking, the *Tonton-Macoutes* sought to imitate the traditional army officers. The former abused the masses almost to the same extent as the latter. The only difference is that the *Tonton-Macoutes* are totally devoted to Dr. Duvalier and not a single one of them is in a position to stage a *coup d'état* against the regime.

The Haitianization of the Roman Catholic clergy was also long overdue. The interference of the French clergy in Haitian cultural, political, and social life was always in favor either of the privileged mulatto upper class or of foreign political and/or economic interests. Therefore, I believe, Dr. Duvalier deserves credit for having ridded the country of foreign Roman Catholic bishops and priests whose actions and behavior over the years were not in the best interests of the masses or of Haiti as a nation.

Furthermore, it must be recognized that Dr. Duvalier differs basically from the former presidents of Haiti in that he has let the masses participate in his government. In the past, political power in Haiti was concentrated largely in the hands of a few families, bowing to the will of the élites and the bourgeoisie. Most political rivalries were confined to a very small percentage of the population, comprising the Port-au-Prince élites and the urban élites of the largest four or five other cities.

ECONOMIC AND SOCIAL LIFE

To a large extent, Haiti is a feudal country. Some progress was made with the 1946 revolution. Efforts to modernize the political structure began with President Estimé (August 1946–May 1950) and continued to a point under President Magloire (December 1950–December 1956).

The achievements of Duvalier's rule mentioned above, are, however, outnumbered by the negative aspects of a regime dominated by an authoritarian who has submitted the country's institutions to his personal control. Consequently, chaos prevails in the economic and social sectors of his government.

Haiti is not yet part of the progressive group of developing countries conscious of the need to modernize their public administration system in order to attain economic, political, and social development. The government of Dr. Duvalier has never shown any concern for technical competence in the recruiting, selection, and training of public servants nor any sensitivity for the major economic problems faced by the nation.

After more than one-and-a-half centuries of political independence, Haiti is facing some extremely serious problems that may endanger its continued existence as a nation. Proud of its African heritage and its cultural ties with France, but virtually ignored in the Americas, Haiti —especially since 1963—has been left alone in the midst of serious crisis. The international community has shown complete indifference.

On the one hand, most of the Western Hemisphere nations, except for Venezuela and Costa Rica, maintain diplomatic ties with Haiti, but refuse to aid it because of the dictatorial and tyrannical nature of its government. Haiti has not benefited from Alliance for Progress funds nor from direct American foreign aid since 1963.

On the other hand, Haitian exiles encounter numerous problems with the immigration authorities of most Western countries—the United States, the Dominican Republic, Bahamas, Jamaica, and Canada. Haitian exiles are not accorded the same understanding and treatment given exiles from Cuba or Eastern Europe, as if they too were not fleeing their country because of tyranny. It would seem logical that either the Haitian exiles be given the same protection and consideration as exiles from other dictatorial regimes or that Dr. Duvalier's regime be given the same financial aid and technical assistance given other Latin American dictatorial and, in some cases, corrupted governments. Otherwise, Haitians remain penalized from both sides.

The Haitian government as well as the Haitian exiles are highly disturbed by the attitude of the United States government toward the Haitian crisis. Duvalier's regime first wished American financial aid. Disillusioned, it has turned to Europe—mostly France—and to Canada for technical assistance and new trade arrangements. The Canadians are responding to this new opportunity, but the Europeans are still reluctant to deal with Dr. Duvalier. The opposition to Dr. Duvalier is gradually becoming more radical, and political help is being sought in Europe, mostly in Eastern Europe. The United States government is being held partially responsible in most opposition circles for the survival of Dr. Duvalier's regime.

Whatever will be the future after Dr. Duvalier, a new Haiti seems to be emerging. This new Haiti will not necessarily be anti-American, but it will probably be neutral in world politics. However, it should not come as a surprise if Haiti, following the Chilean example, were to become the second Latin American country to elect a socialist president to direct the awesome task of modernization.

## The French Overseas Departments

On March 19, 1946, the French parliament voted unanimously to transform the colonies of Martinique, Guadeloupe, and French Guiana into overseas departments of France. This was done upon the petition of Antillean parliamentarians who represented these colonies in the Constituent Assembly after the liberation of France. The three territories were thus assimilated officially into the administrative system of metropolitan France.

To understand the consequences of this assimilation, it is indispensable to emphasize the previously prevailing political patterns under which the administrative organization of Martinique, Guadeloupe, and French Guiana were highly decentralized. Legally, two separate entities governed the colonies—the governor and the General Council (*Conseil Général*).

The governor, representing the French government, was delegated extensive powers. He embodied all the powers of a chief executive, assured law and order, and was responsible for defense and all the administrative services. Furthermore, he held the special power of promulgating laws, which normally belongs exclusively to heads of state. Laws voted by the French parliament were not extended to the colonies unless this was explicitly stipulated. The colonies were subject to the *Senatus Consulte* system of May 3, 1854, according to which the president of France legislated for the colonies by decree.

The General Council, elected by the people of the colonies, was considered a legal and political entity entirely separate from the governor. The colonies thus enjoyed, at least theoretically, fiscal autonomy. The General Council could determine the types of taxes to be levied, with the exception of customs duties over which it had no say, and the methods of their collection. In reality, of course, the governor could always step in.

The municipalities, on the other hand, had no effective power. They did not even possess the limited autonomy of the municipalities in metropolitan France.

The assimilation law modified greatly the administrative and legislative branches of the overseas departments, known as the *Départements d'Outre-Mer* (DOM).

## ADMINISTRATIVE SYSTEM

The administrative regime of the DOM became an appendix of the highly centralized administrative structure prevailing in France. They lost whatever fiscal autonomy they previously had with the exception of the *octroi de mer* (taxes on imports) and the *fonds routier* (taxes on gasoline). The immediate effect of this transformation was the atomization of local administration. While under the colonial regime all government departments were directly responsible to the governor, the departmentalization made them responsible to the appropriate ministries in Paris. Since 1960, however, a decree enacted in Paris placed the administrative system of the DOM directly under a *Secretariat d'État* (Ministry) of the overseas departments. The administrative set-up of the DOM is composed of three separate entities: the prefecture, the General Council, and the municipalities.

With assimilation, governors disappeared and, as in all the departments of metropolitan France, prefects were appointed to head the overseas departments. They are employees of the Ministry of the

Interior, but are named by the president of France with the unanimous consent of the cabinet.

In principle, the prefects of the DOM have the same powers as their counterparts in metropolitan France. However, given the peculiar situation of the DOM (great distance from France, low standards of living, etc.), the Caribbean prefects hold certain special powers. For example, they control the local armed forces and can declare martial law on their own initiative provided they immediately inform the central government. Finally, in their relation with foreign consulates, the prefects perform certain diplomatic functions.

The extensive powers given the overseas prefects have not escaped the criticism of the opposition parties as well as of some independent scholars. In many respects, the institution of the DOM prefecture is a virtual copy of the previous colonial governorship. Recently, the prefect of one of the DOM confessed that his office was nothing but a "mail box," implying that all the important decisions are made in Paris.

THE GENERAL COUNCIL

The members of the General Council are elected by direct suffrage. Their role has lessened considerably under departmentalization as compared to the period before the Fifth Republic (1958). In principle, the General Council concerns itself only with administrative activities. It has definite jurisdiction over departmental property, planning all the projects to be carried out with departmental funds, directing social welfare services, and passing on all matters of departmental interest brought before it through a prefect's proposal or the initiative of one of its members. The General Council also approves the departmental budget which is prepared by the prefect.

The decisions of the General Council are compulsory within ten days of the end of the session unless the prefect requests their annulment. He can do so on the grounds of excessive exercise of power or the violation of a law or regulation of public administration. The prefect's objections must be made known to the president of the General Council. If there is no repeal within six weeks from the notification date, the decisions of the Council become binding.

The General Council has always rebelled against these excessively restrictive laws, designed to exclude it from any participation in the political life of the overseas departments. Whenever the occasion has arisen, the Council has not failed to voice its opinion on matters of local interest.

Since 1960, the General Council has functioned, at least in legal theory, as an actual legislative assembly. The prefect presents to it annually a detailed report on the political, economic, and social situation of the department and the condition of the various public services.

The prefect also discusses in his reports his plans for the next year, the main points of his program, and the most urgent problems to be solved.

The Council holds certain rights to supervise the prefect's conduct. This system is excellent, but it can be distorted by the fact that most of the Council's members are also mayors, administering their municipalities under the financial tutelage of the prefect. From this situation a "give-and-take" relationship may develop. The prefect may be careful in carrying out his fiscal powers toward the mayors so that they would uphold his actions in the General Council.

MUNICIPALITIES

While the municipalities had no real powers under the colonial regime, the departmentalization raised them to the level of autonomy of their counterparts in metropolitan France.

The municipality is the smallest French politico-administrative unit. It is administered by an elected municipal council which, in turn, elects the mayor who is assisted by a number of aides. According to the 1962 census, there were 34 municipalities in Guadeloupe, 34 in Martinique, and 37,962 in metropolitan France.

The mayor is elected by the municipal council by absolute majority or, after a third ballot, by simple majority. He has the responsibility for preparing the budget, regulating local commerce, and implementing in general the decisions of the municipal council. Furthermore, the police in charge of maintaining law and order in the municipality are responsible to the mayor who is supervised by the higher administration. Administration services in Guadeloupe and Martinique are organized almost exactly like those in metropolitan France, with the exception of the special powers granted the prefect and the General Council of the DOM. From immigration services to the organization and purveying of justice and from customs to the post offices, everything in French Caribbean administration is a copy of the corresponding services in metropolitan France.

LEGISLATIVE SYSTEM

Since assimilation, all laws voted by the French parliament, comprising the National Assembly and the Senate, apply to the metropolitan departments as well as to the overseas departments—unless the law stipulates the contrary. The members of the National Assembly (deputies) are elected by direct suffrage; the senators, by indirect suffrage.

Guadeloupe, French Guiana, and Martinique are represented in the French parliament by three deputies and two senators each; which means one deputy for every 100,000 inhabitants and one senator for every 150,000. The parliamentarians from the DOM have exactly the same rights and duties as their French metropolitan colleagues.

## DEPARTMENTALIZATION VS. AUTONOMY

The French DOM constitute the only sizable West Indian territories directly governed by an European metropolitan power. This situation is not unanimously accepted by the population of these territories whose political life revolves around two main issues: departmentalization and autonomy. Those who favor the present political status (departmentalization) are called "departmentalists"; while those promoting autonomy are called "autonomists." The demand for autonomy has increased during the sixties, mostly in Martinique and Guadeloupe. In French Guiana, the political life is usually rather subdued. Former French Premier Michel Debré submitted, on June 13, 1961, a bill to the French Senate giving French Guiana a special political status—very close to internal self government—quite different from the metropolitan French departments and from the overseas departments of Martinique and Guadeloupe. But no decision had been made by the Senate on this particular matter by 1970.

Who are the autonomists? Among those who demand autonomy are the communists, an overwhelming majority of non-communist liberals, and some youth organizations.

The communist parties of Guadeloupe and Martinique are the leading political parties, insistently demanding autonomy for the DOM. Only a very small group of communists in Guadeloupe have disassociated themselves from the party's official policy by openly clamoring for independence and joining the *Groupement des Organisations Nationalistes Guadeloupeennes* (GONG).

The communists demand autonomy which would return to the people of the Caribbean departments the administration of their own affairs and assure that the territories' legitimate and permanent interests could be fulfilled. The communist program embodies agrarian reform, nationalization of big sugar and banana concerns, diversification of agriculture, manpower planning, technical and financial assistance to local craftsmen, reduction of the powers of big private monopolies in trade and transportation, and closer ties with the neighboring Caribbean countries. The communist parties on both islands are fairly strong and can command about 45 percent of the vote.

Besides the communists, other political groups also believe that a change in the political status of the DOM is mandatory if the economic and social problems besetting these islands are to be adequately faced. Among them, the most prestigious and popular is the Progressive Party of Martinique (*Parti Progressiste de la Martinique,* PPM). The PPM is the party of Aimé Césaire, a deputy and mayor of Fort-de-France, and an internationally known writer and poet. The PPM favors administrative autonomy under which the islands could conduct their own local affairs within the French constitutional framework.

This autonomy is reminiscent of the political status that Toussaint Louverture wanted for St. Domingue in his constitution of 1801, which Napoleon rejected.

Two political parties strongly oppose the demands for autonomy. They are the Union for the Defense of the Republic (*Union pour la Défense de la République*, UDR) and the Socialist Party.

Many objections have been raised against autonomy, but the most delicate and most embarassing deal with the economic consequences. Victor Sablé, a deputy from Martinique, wrote to this effect:

> Could Guadeloupe and Martinique, left to their own resources, secure the financing of the social reforms after their liberation? Would industrial output, agricultural resources, general trade revenue, taxation possibilities, everything, in short, that constitutes the islands' economic potential, assure an autonomous budget at a par with the expenses considered indispensable for French citizens?

This argument carries some weight because the populations of the DOM systematically avoid taking any risks that could sacrifice the standards of living achieved under departmentalization. This standard of living is due mostly to the transfer payments from the French budget and not to any real production in the territories. Consequently, it is a very artificial system. But the people of the DOM have become accustomed to it and spoiled by it. Nonetheless, one must recognize that important as they may be in considering the decolonization process, economic factors are sometimes neither the most significant nor the most decisive. Psychological factors often come first.

POSITION OF THE FRENCH GOVERNMENT

The succeeding French governments have generally practiced a policy of indifference toward the DOM. To them, the problem of decolonization in the French Caribbean had been solved through assimilation. But the chances for Guadeloupe and Martinique to be granted autonomous self-government looked better in 1970 than in the past. This was partially due to the relatively successful experience of the British West Indies after either independence or attaining associate-statehood status. Other reasons can be listed:

1. If the Caribbean Free Trade Association (CARIFTA) is successful, a growing number of people in the DOM (departmentalists as well as autonomists) will seek more cooperation with the neighboring islands and will realize the necessity of diversifying the present trade patterns, instead of depending exclusively on metropolitan France for all goods and services.
2. When agricultural products are fully integrated in the European Economic Community (EEC), France will find it difficult to continue subsidizing agriculture and its by-products in Guadeloupe and Martinique.

As a consequence, bananas, sugar, and rum producers will be in serious trouble as their high production costs do not make them competitive on the world market. The DOM producers will then certainly have to turn to the neighboring islands (who may face the same problems because of Britain's entry into the EEC) in order to look for common solutions to common problems.

3. The fact that General deGaulle is no longer president of France will clearly help the autonomists by increasing their following in the DOM. The population of the French Caribbean islands was, in a sense, more attached to General deGaulle than the population of metropolitan France. They would never have liked to make a choice (voting for autonomy for example) that could be interpreted as a rejection of the "Liberateur," the man who freed them from the tyrannical Vichy regime.

4. "Cartierism" is a philosophy formulated by Raymond Cartier who, since 1964, has been suggesting that France should give not just autonomy but perhaps even independence to the DOM, on the grounds that the present relationship is draining resources from France that could otherwise be utilized for the benefit of metropolitan France. It will certainly continue to grow in France as the cost of living rises. Financial difficulties in France and pressures on the value of the franc will give more weight to the views of those asking for *lachage* (abandonment) of the DOM and the utilization of all French resources for the welfare of homeland Frenchmen.

5. The relatively bad experiences (among other things, racial prejudices) of lower-class French West Indians who emigrated to France seeking employment opportunities made them realize that they are, in fact, second-class French citizens. They will constitute a vast reserve of votes for the autonomists.

In summary, there are two basic facts that must be remembered regarding the French West Indies. One is the profound attachment of the people of Martinique and Guadeloupe to France and French culture. They are really "French in mind, in heart, in blood . . . ," as Victor Sablé wrote. The other is the search for national identity among a growing number of French West Indians who sincerely wish the adaptation of the political, economic, and social institutions of the DOM to their geographical, cultural, and economic realities.

Those two facts seem conflicting at first, but on closer consideration they are not necessarily mutually exclusive. There must be found a solution in which black Guadeloupeans and Martiniquans could retain French citizenship—if so they wished—without having to renounce their identity as blacks and their Caribbean identity. To be a French citizen need not mean to them the abandonment of their destiny to persons often completely insensitive to their problems and needs—and so far removed from them.

But one wonders whether the French government will have the

imagination to adjust its colonial policy to the changing times. Historically, the French flag and *gendarme* (policeman) seemed to be the only symbols of French presence after Napoleon. One hopes, at this turning point in Caribbean affairs—when most West Indian islands and territories have won full independence or internal self-government—that the French government will be able to develop a new partnership with its overseas departments following in some ways the example set by the Anglo-Saxons and the Dutch in the relations with their former colonies.

## Surinam and the Netherlands Antilles

Among the European powers, Holland has shown the greatest interest in the decolonization process in the Caribbean. The Dutch governments were always favorably predisposed toward the recognition of local peculiarities and the encouragement of participation by the natives in the administration of their local affairs and even in the formulation and execution of Dutch foreign policy.

Surinam and the Netherlands Antilles are equal partners with the metropolitan Netherlands in the Kingdom of the Netherlands. Each of the three countries within the Kingdom has its own constitution. The Charter of the Kingdom of the Netherlands, proclaimed by Queen Juliana on December 29, 1954, takes, however, precedence over the constitution of each partner. The Charter regulates the relations between the three partners and defines the matters which are the concern of the Kingdom as a whole (defense, nationality, and foreign affairs) and those which are in the competence of each partner (public health, education, monetary policy). Any amendment to the Charter must be approved by Surinam and the Netherlands Antilles.

### SURINAM

Discovered in the sixteenth century by the Spaniards, Surinam came under Dutch control in the seventeenth century. It is located on South America's north coast on the periphery of the Caribbean area. It has an area of 55,167 square miles and a mixed population of over 365,000 inhabitants. The per capita income is about $307 per year.

The interior of Surinam is the archetype of rain forest vegetation. This makes Surinam an ideal location for jungle safaris. There are safaris of a couple of days to the more accessible Bush Negro and Amerindian villages and safaris lasting several weeks to reach other tribes in the most remote areas.

The population of Surinam is so mixed that the country is called a "world in miniature." Thus, 36 percent of the population are Creoles; 33 percent Hindustanis; 16 percent Indonesians; 11 percent Bush

Negroes and Amerindians in the interior; 2 percent Chinese and 2 percent Europeans and others. Surinam is a success story of people of different races and religions living harmoniously together, an example that many countries, including the United States and some Caribbean states, might follow.

Many political parties exist in Surinam along racial and/or religious lines. This, however, does not conflict with the existence of good racial relations. The two main political parties are the Hindustani Party (VHP) and the Progressive National Party (PNP). While the VHP opposes independence, the PNP would like to see Surinam independent by 1974. Other political parties include the National Party of Surinam (NPS), which wants independence immediately, and the National Republic Party (NRP), which wishes Surinam to become a socialist republic as soon as possible along a strong nationalistic line. There is also a small Javanese party (SRI), which opposes independence.

Surinam possesses abundant natural resources, including bauxite and extensive reserves of lumber. The Surinam Aluminum Company (SURALCO) is a completely integrated enterprise of world stature. Surinam supplies 14 percent of the world's bauxite, and its total bauxite reserves are conservatively estimated at 300–400 million tons.

Eighty-five percent of Surinam is covered by tropical rain forest. This makes lumber an important source of revenue. In 1947, a reconstituted *Lands Bosbeheer* (National Forestry Administration) was organized with the main purpose of making a complete inventory of forest areas. One obstacle to the full exploitation of the vast forestry reserves is the inaccessibility of the jungle. Roads need to be constructed in order to allow economic exploitation of the forests. The forest reserves are immense. However, the National Forestry Administration is very concerned about replanting trees in order to avoid future shortages.

Surinam exports large quantities of lumber handicrafts made primarily by the Bush Negroes. They produce artistic works that have no equal in the Caribbean, except for the Haitian handicrafts.

Agriculture flourishes in Surinam. Thanks to development aid from the European Economic Community (EEC), several agricultural projects were launched, including drainage and irrigation work. The most important agricultural product is rice (total paddy production in 1967 amounted to 119,529 tons). Surinam also produces bananas (production of 35,000 tons in 1968), sugar (about 18,500 tons yearly), fruits, and vegetables. A large quantity of the agricultural output is exported to Europe, mostly to the EEC members.

Surinam has a bright future. Its close association with Holland secures developmental aid and technical assistance while the country enjoys all the attributes of sovereignty for local matters. When Surinam achieves independence, certainly before the 1980s, the country will have acquired a long tradition of political stability, racial equality, and harmonious economic development.

## THE NETHERLANDS ANTILLES

The Netherlands Antilles are comprised of six islands divided into the Windward group (Saba, St. Eustatius, and the southern part of St. Maarten) and the Leeward group (Aruba, Bonaire, and Curaçao). These two groups of islands are situated approximately 550 miles apart. The total area is 394 square miles and the population about 250,000 inhabitants.

Curaçao and Aruba are the most important islands of the Netherlands Antilles. They occupy 63 percent of the territory and their combined population represents almost 95 percent of the total population of the Netherlands Antilles.

The political situation in the Netherlands Antilles was traditionally quiet. The islands were known as a paradise for tourists looking for sun and fun. But the world awakened on May 31, 1969, to the reports that bloody riots had occurred in Curaçao the day before. From these disturbances came the incentive to analyze how and why such a "nice" population became overnight so violent and destructive.

Although it is difficult to list all the reasons behind the 1969 riots, at least two profound causes, both of economic nature, may be singled out:

(a) The job lay-offs resulting from the automation of the oil industry (Shell) made a severe impact on the native workers. Thousands of workers had lost their jobs since 1955. In the beginning, the lay-offs affected only the imported workers from neighboring islands, who were asked to leave Curaçao. By 1960, however, the native workers, too, began to be affected.

(b) With increasing automation, Shell decided early in the 1960s to concentrate its efforts exclusively on oil refining while subcontracting to other companies the cleaning, construction, and other services that it traditionally performed. The main consequence of this new policy was a considerable wage differential between Shell workers and employees of other companies working for Shell on its properties. Almost overnight, the same worker would be offered half his previous pay for exactly the same work he had been performing on the Shell properties.

Furthermore, the parties in power in the Netherlands Antilles (Democratic Party of Curaçao and *Partido Popular Arubano*) have lost contact with the masses in general and the trade unions in particular after fifteen years of unchallenged government.

Thus, since May 1969, the political situation has considerably changed in the Netherlands Antilles and Curaçao in particular. Things may never be the same again. In July 1970, for the first time in history, the Netherlands Antilles had a black governor, Benjamin Leito. The prime minister of the Netherlands Antilles, Mr. Ernesto Pretonia, elected in October 1969, was also black.

The economy of the Netherlands Antilles depends primarily upon oil and tourism. Efforts are being made, with limited success, to diversify the economy and promote the establishment of industrial enterprises and hotels. Thus, the Japanese have built a center of distribution for cars and parts in Curaçao to serve the Caribbean area and part of Central America.

Despite all the efforts made by the local government and the financial assistance of Holland, unemployment in the Netherlands Antilles still stands at over 25 percent.

The future of the Netherlands Antilles is somehow uncertain. In 1970, a Dutch parliamentary commission began searching for an alternative political status for the islands. Among the alternatives under consideration are: union with Holland (an adapted version of the Commonwealth status of Puerto Rico), link with Venezuela, membership in an eventual Caribbean federation, and independence—at least for Curaçao and Aruba.

Should this last alternative be selected, many Aruban leaders are likely to oppose an independent federation or union with Curaçao. In the event Curaçao becomes independent, they would prefer direct links with Holland or Venezuela as a better solution.

In any event, Holland seems greatly interested in reconsidering its relations with both Surinam and the Netherlands Antilles. It is from Holland that the pressure comes for Surinam independence and for a new political status for the Netherlands Antilles. It is almost certain that a final decision will be reached by 1978.

## Conclusion

In conclusion, it is clear that the twentieth century will witness the complete break-up of European empires in the Caribbean. However, new types of ties will most certainly replace the old colonial arrangements. Great Britain and the Netherlands, as Professor Thomas Mathews wrote in his *Politics and Economics in the Caribbean*, ". . . have realized that strong cultural ties cannot be enforced by pressure . . . Pressure for self-government or independence has not been met by these two powers with opposition or repression, but on the contrary, they have nudged forward the small communities on the road to autonomy." This is certainly the right direction for the European powers to follow if they want to keep the respect and the friendship of the populations of their former colonies.

Haiti remains a "European" land because in the heart of every Haitian, Paris is still the center of world civilization. His profound aspiration is to visit France, to learn French, and to develop good cultural relations with France. It may seem paradoxical that the French Overseas Departments do not show as much love for France. Political pressures and the repression applied by the French government to impose its program of assimilation are the profound causes of this situation. But the French "presence" in the Caribbean does not necessarily mean that these territories must be governed from Paris.

Surinam and the Netherlands Antilles have accepted to be Dutch by choice, not by imposition. These lands will certainly remain "European" for many years to come.

# CARIBBEAN EXPERIENCE

*Kalman H. Silvert*

# The Caribbean and North America

## Frames for the Caribbean Experience

If it is true that only inane generalizations hold equally for the 30-odd Caribbean political units of which this book treats, it is also true that seeing each one as unique is intellectual laziness that can only impede understanding and policy decision. The essays comprising this volume provide the materials for constructing the categorical boxes needed for at least sorting the facts of the many matters that define this unique region of the world. Assembling those categories, however, is not merely a mechanical job. If the chapters supply the materials, they do not indicate how many cubby-holes need to be made, what their diverse sizes should be, or even whether they are to be rectangular, square, or oval. The organization of data, to put it in less facetious terms, is a theoretical matter. The assignment of significance to facts is the task of this concluding section, a job to be undertaken with suitable humility induced by continuing evidence of the fragility of social science constructions and the weakness of most current ideological postulations.

We arrive at this point with many of the bases for ordering our knowledge of the Caribbean firmly settled. Let us, to begin, list some of the generalizations that apply rather more than less to the entire area, and later turn to criteria for dividing the islands into discrete families. In the first instance, a very persuasive case is made by Gordon

KALMAN H. SILVERT, *of The Ford Foundation, has done extensive research and written numerous books and articles on Latin America and the Caribbean (including a chapter in The American Assembly volume on Latin America, 1959). For many years an associate of The American Universities Field Staff, Dr. Silvert is currently professor of political science at New York University, and director of the Ibero-American Language and Area Center there.*

Lewis for weighing the islands' histories in terms of three grand periods: the slaveholding colonial epoch, the post-emancipation or independence period running from the beginning of the last century to the end of World War II, and the contemporary era of national independence or growing domestic autonomy even within a structure of relationship to a metropolitan power. This commonness of background promotes similar social explanations, despite striking cultural differences. At least as important, however, is the second overarching likeness pointed to by all the authors: the intertwining of color and class differences that defines the social structure of each of the islands. The felicitous word, "pigmentocracy," applies in one or another degree everywhere, from mulatto-black Haiti to Latin Dominican Republic.

Yet another constant that appears in all the foregoing analyses is the small size, both physical and demographic, of all the islands. We are accustomed to recognizing the self-reinforcing effects of race and class when they are mixed together, but we have little to go on in discussions of the effect of size of human unit on the quality of human interaction. Small-group specialists in the social sciences sometimes attempt to generalize their findings to nations, but few scholars accept that equation without grave reservations. Indeed, it is even somewhat difficult to disentangle the idea of city-state from that of nation-state. In the Caribbean we are invited to speak of small states and ministates; perhaps the better designations would be town-states, city-states, and small nation-states as descriptive of unit-size, but not necessarily of unit-quality, a matter we shall return to later. In any event, the matter of size invariably introduces a fourth common element—worry concerning the viability of these insular establishments. How most small states are to survive in a big-power world is a question not only of international politics, but of access to markets, of fitting institutional arrangements in which "small" does not necessarily spell "weak," of the proper use of complex modern technology, and of the many other problems which flow from political economies of small scale.

Whatever the problems, however, the Caribbean is not to be classed with the world's *Lumpenproletariat* of underdevelopment. In per capita income terms, most of the islands are on the high side of the intermediately developed, with Puerto Rico falling into the statistical bag of the developed. This common income fact is clustered with other shared economic phenomena: weak economies dependent upon a few exports, spotty concentrations of natural resources, high rates of under- and unemployment, elevated dependence on external sources of capital and technology, and too great market reliance on a few consumers. The demographic facts of Caribbean life reveal generally high population densities, whether in Hispanic, French, British, or Dutch-influenced areas; reasonably acceptable to high literacy rates coupled with low attainments at advanced educational levels; strong migration tides in response to low economic opportunity at home; and those other manifestations of populations mobilized for participant national life, but not blessed with the institutional orders that will permit their full integration into their societies.

Although the list of commonalities is not exhausted, only one more significant constant will be mentioned here—the pervasive and continuing influence of Western culture, no matter the particularities of historical growth, metropolitan power, economic situation, or even class order and nature of institutional structure. The manifestations of the profundity of this identification appear in all the chapters of this book. A stubborn attachment to the verbiage of democracy, even in contemporary Cuban ideology, is a recurrently mentioned symptom of this Westernization. Language, ideal patterns to be emulated, school curricula, ideology, and many other aspects of life-style testify not to what is an ornament, but to what is a primary mover of Caribbean events.

## Modernity and Diversity

The recitation of these common characteristics, and their synthesis into an overall picture, serve at least the negative purpose of telling us what the Caribbean is not. Great droves of peasants living at subsistence are not the fate of the Caribbean; nor is it like some of Africa's new states, damned by tribalism and uncertainly held together by thin veneers of foreign-educated elites. Conflict between church and state is in the past, and battles against colonial overlords do not loom in the future. The meaning of these and other indications of complexity is that the Caribbean's problems are not solvable through simple quantitative changes—more food, fewer people, increased housing, more or less of what is. Rather, the problems are qualitative as well as quantitative—how communities are to be organized; the nature of national identities that are to be forged; the substantive meanings of varied styles of integrating individuals and groups into national and local and supranational communities; the mix of ideologies that can explain and rationalize and stabilize the processes of change. In sum, then, most of the Caribbean islands have developed enough internal strength through institutional complexity and specialization to begin to determine the shapes of their own social fates. This is the positive meaning of their common heritage and their common being today. Within their likenesses, however, they are sufficiently different so that they can neither coexist under universal sociopolitical umbrellas, nor carelessly transfer experience from one to the other.

We need not recapitulate demographic, geographical, or even political administrative ranges of diversity; the contributory chapters have described those differences quite adequately. The body of this book has set up typologies of the Caribbean islands by size, by criteria of economic viability, by political organization, by race and class, by degree of cultural cohesion, by historical relationship to European and American powers, by contemporary international relations, and only inferentially, by what must be of the greatest interest in a concluding chapter—the combination of these factors in terms of general social effectiveness. The attempt to arrive at such a synthesis will demand of us that we combine all the factors mentioned, and speculate concerning the qualitative significance of the quantitative facts we will be putting together.

We must begin by defining what it is that we mean by effectiveness, or viability, not of any kind of society, but of one that pretends to fit and enjoy the modern estate. We need not stretch for esoteric criteria; the following list is suggested, in no particular order of significance:

a. A viable modern society possesses mechanisms for the orderly transfer of political power through time.

b. A viable modern society possesses an urban life style. It is not that such societies necessarily include large cities, but rather that an urbane and worldly quality characterizes social relations. Another way to put it is that the secular city increases freedom of choice in personal relations and consumer habits. "City air makes man free" is a medieval legal dictum still meaningful today and not belied by the fact that some urban situations imprison man. That is, it is possible to live in cities and not be urbane, and possible to be urbane and live in the country. It is the quality of urbanity that is important, not ecological fact.

c. A viable modern society possesses an industrial life style. Again, the reference is not to labor within industrial complexes, but to the consumption of industrial products and to work relationships determined by merit through impersonal market mechanisms. It is not necessary that a particular country have either large cities or a massive industrial complex in order to enjoy a ramified communications system and an open class structure permitting individuals to find their places according to their talents and desires. If this looseness of association between physical plant and human orders were not so, it would be impossible to explain the relative degree of advance of Costa Rica within Caribbean basin countries, or that of Denmark within Europe.

d. A viable modern society organizes itself in a community pattern whose largest unit is the nation-state. The earmarks of national community are that all men are equal before the laws and the community's institutions, no matter the accidents of their birth or their systems of beliefs. What is required in return of the citizen is his recognition of that community as deserving of his ultimate loyalty in the event of international conflict or of such other conflicts as those arising from religious, economic, or ideological beliefs and interests. The national community is the organizing unit for the legitimacy which produces the consent that makes possible governmental effectiveness and the settlement of dispute in such manner as to avoid ultimate showdowns and promote the acceptance of interim, working solutions.

   **e.** A viable modern society possesses an educational institution open to all, and which empowers individuals, without regard to class or color, to participate in the national community and share in the industrial and urban cultures of the modern situation.

   **f.** A viable modern society possesses a system of explanation of its existence—or an ideology, or appropriate set of them—which reinforce fitting human relations, rationalize "national identity," and stabilize the intricate social relations that build flexibility into modern, secular societies.

Every author in this book speaks in one or another way of the difficult search for national identity and national organization in the Caribbean. The above list of criteria is suggested in order to crystallize the elements of the modern national society, and to permit us to ask in which respects given Caribbean societies are near to or distant from national status. The question is being begged as to *why* it is that such desires for national organization are almost universal in the developing world. Perhaps the cause is emulation of the experience of the developed world; perhaps something in the nature of man channels his gregariousness into the largest vessels he can find. Whatever the case, we surely are dealing with a combination of factors, these and others. In any event, we cannot address ourselves to a general discussion of the Caribbean societies without somehow dealing with a political desire that is also a program for overriding social organization.

We have neither the data nor the space rigorously to characterize the Caribbean societies by these criteria. Nevertheless, even a summary exercise in organizing our materials along these lines should reveal developmental gaps and policy problems among our cases. To begin with the thorniest case, Cuba, we find that the Castro government has been strongly pursuing the creation of many aspects of national community, but has made little progress in institutionalizing its political process. Even confirmed *antifidelistas* are usually willing to give his government high marks in such endeavors as education, race relations, medical attention, and the mobilization and integration of lower-class elements into national life. Even Castro himself gives his efforts low marks in lessening personalism, ordering administrative procedures, organizing the mechanics of national economic life, and inculcating a full range of attitudes toward work and social life that will lessen the need for coercion and exhortation. Whatever the pros and cons, within the Hispanic portion of Latin America, Cuba has become one of the most secularized and national of all states, able to survive an amazing array of adversity stemming from internal disarray as well as external opposition. The explanation does not lie merely in the relatively high degree of advance to be seen in pre-Castro Cuba; the failures and successes of the present Cuban government could not have occurred without that regime's inheritance from the past, but they also could not have happened without the personal, ideological, and international power configurations created by the principal actors in Cuba's ten-year drama.

The Dominican Republic, to remain within the Hispanic orbit a bit longer, does not by any means exhibit the same degree of national organization as does Cuba. Ranking low on almost every indicator suggested, its politics are a clear reflection of a population left grossly unprepared to comprise a national citizenry. Generations of authoritarian rule have deprived government of legitimacy and thus of continuity, have contributed to a class structure that impedes social mobility, have supported an economic structure antagonistic to the development of urbane people and industrial organization, and have prevented the growth of indigenous systems of explanation that can provide the dignity of social self-awareness. The potential developmental advantages of an ethnically homogeneous population and of an agriculturally rich island have thus been washed away in a swamp of greedy authoritarianism complicated by international fear and short-sightedness. The Cuban and Dominican cases are very well worth this contraposition, for their divergent histories underscore the autonomy of human action and power as it is practiced even within similar geographical and cultural settings.

If Cuba is to be counted among the most national of Caribbean states, although in twisted form, and if the Dominican Republic is one of the less national, Haiti can be counted as the least national of all. Often called the Mississippi of the Americas, because its vital statistics always put it in last place among those countries belonging to the Organization of American States, Haiti lacks a social recruitment base for a politics of national development. Its leaders may have the education and the will to mould world ideologies to their perceptions of Haitian needs, and even to create original systems of thought, but the ready creation of an articulated and self-aware popular following is probably not possible under present social conditions. Cuba's leaders profited from the ease of their campaign of national mobilization; recent Dominican experience also reveals that a reasonably large percentage of its population is organizable for nation-building ends; by this critically important measure of readiness for modernizing change, Haiti probably falls entirely short, any nationalistic government it may have in the future condemned to mobilize its population through the dangerous exercise of charismatic appeal and force, whether benign or malignant in intent.

Jamaica and Trinidad, the two largest British-influenced independent states, show strikingly differing configurations from Cuba and the Dominican Republic, let alone Haiti. Traditionally economically monocultural, as their Hispanic neighbors, tied to specific international markets for both purchases and sales, lagging in higher educational facilities, and weighed down by even more rigid class systems, Jamaica and Trinidad are similarly in a crisis of national identification within their particular institutional structures. Still able to operate within neo-parliamentary governmental forms, party politics and economic power and color and class have become entangled in a form of pluralism that has thus far permitted constitutional process to overcome political disturbance, and has bought some time for the working out of the processes of equalitarianism that are so important to nation-building through the mitigation of divisiveness. High unemployment rates in these contexts are not only economic facts; they are also descriptive of alienation from the other institutional mainstreams of national life. The ethnic mosaic of Trinidad, the Guyanese ethnic confrontation opportunistically fomented in that country's recent party and ideological history, and the remaining color resentments of Jamaica provide fertile soil for future conflict, especially if such differences continue to be reinforced by class divisions. Still, in these cases confusion of such categories is a good thing, and no one of these countries is paralyzed by caste-like exclusions, although desperate class antagonisms are entirely possible. Great social distances between strata of their populations prevent the emergence of the urban and industrial life-styles within which other diversities can be maintained, and both the quality and quantity of their educational systems are insufficient for the state of readiness of their populations. Their relatively high degrees of attachment to institutionalized political process and to the rule of law are assets that should not be squandered in a narrow drive for economic growth, one of whose ends must be precisely the enrichment of the political structures that already exist.

Frank McDonald's essay in this book makes all the above points, and more. He emphasizes that it is not only the larger states of the Commonwealth Caribbean, but rather all of them which suffer from a lack of economic autonomy that has its direct reflection in the maintenance of systems of social exclusion that prevent national consciousness from becoming effective. Black Power movements in those islands, then, become anti-foreign white and economically collectivist as the means toward social cohesion within each island, and perhaps among them. Color consciousness, thus, is reinforced by apposite class lines, which in turn are an immediate reflection of raw economic circumstance. McDonald emphasizes that drives to dismantle this linkage are common to all the former British islands, whether large or small, whether politically independent or in associated state status. From the viewpoint of the present discussion, the significance of McDonald's analysis lies in his reaffirming that the conditions of effective nationhood are holistic —that all of them are needed, in one or another effective combination. We can also draw another important interim conclusion: nationhood does not depend on formal political sovereignty, but on the appropriate organization of community. A third conclusion that we can also make clear at this point is that population and territorial sizes influence the paths through which nation-building proceeds, but are not determinants of such nationhood. By this stage in our discussion, we are able to affirm that the Caribbean demonstrates that, when it comes to nationalism, Anguillans share the restlessness of their maritime neighbors in the largest Caribbean states, such as Cuba and Jamaica.

These three summary statements—the holistic nature of nationhood, its independence of formal sovereignty, and its variability in terms of size—permit us to situate Puerto Rico, the Virgin Islands, and the Dutch and French islands in their fitting places in this discussion of diversity within sameness. The McDonald treatment of the Commonwealth Caribbean is neatly different from Stephansky's discussion of Puerto Rico; the former emphasizes the consequences of economic dependence, while the latter underscores the significance of political form and meaning within a situation of economic advance. Puerto Rico is an integral part of the complex American mainland economic structure, no longer condemned to producing dessert crops for export and to importing luxury goods for its resident elite. Its educational system is complex, and it has a large floating population able to move back and forth between the island and the major cities of the mainland. The weak fabric in the web of Puerto Rican social development is political in the grand sense: a confusion of cultural identities, a lack of ideological conviction, discomfort with the juridical structure of the state in its relations with the United States, a sneaking suspicion that the Puerto Rican experience is not transferable to neighboring islands because of the special relation with the mainland, and a lack of definition of how much responsibility to accept as a part of the United States and how much as Puerto Rican. Surely problems of class, color, employment, economic development, educational growth, and the role of religion in cultural life all remain important. The point being made here, however, is that economic change and closely allied occupational mobility have tended to lead the parade of Puerto Rican developmental elements; the lagging aspects are primarily political in nature. Conversely, formal solutions to political problems have preceded economic elaboration and some measure of self-determination in the Commonwealth Caribbean. In both places, the strands of national integration are strained by this uneven development.

All the authors of this volume comment on the complexity and diversity of the Caribbean. Even a hasty reduction to speculative generalizations, which is what we have been about so far in this chapter, leaves us with an appreciation of variety and of potential. Only the mean-spirited will see the Caribbean's mixed development in a pessimistic light, for they are the ones who equate complexity with trouble, and go searching always in vain for the one magic button which will bring social contentment into being. But we should learn from worldwide experience that there is no single secret to be found. As the Caribbean islands have been assuming their own political and social identities, and breaking away from the culture-bound nostrums of their respective colonial offices, they have also begun to be the site of the arguments and strategies for development under test elsewhere in Latin America, Asia, and Africa. It is to the Caribbean variants of these recipes for change that we now turn.

## Ideologies of Development

For the purposes of discussing strategies for change, the Caribbean should be thought of within the more general Latin American environment. It is not only that Cuba, the Dominican Republic, Haiti, and sometimes Puerto Rico are normally classified as within Latin America, but rather that the loosening or breaking of colonial ties throughout the area point up analogous situations which make some Latin American experiences increasingly applicable in the Caribbean basin. Like the islands, Latin America is an intermediately developed outpost of Western culture. Also like the islands, political autonomy is threatened by economic fragility and dependence. Employment problems, desires for industrialization, class and race complexities, the "special relation" with the United States, internecine quarrels, and many other problem areas are endemic to Latin America, as they are also for the Caribbean. Ideological disputation concerning the most viable as well as the most desirable paths to development is now virtually the same throughout the Caribbean as it is and has been in Latin America for the entire post-World War II period.

The contributing authors are unanimous in suggesting, implicitly or overtly, one or another reformist approach to Caribbean development, while they all also make varying degrees of reference to revolutionary ideologies. As in the case of national integration, however, the proposals all tend to be lineal; that is, they suggest change should start in one primary institutional area of social life, and that then general progress will follow as summer the springtime. The three major lineal approaches continue the tradition of developmental policy of the industrial states during the past 25 years, and, baldly put, are as follows:

*1. The economic approach.* The classical developmental strategy, consciously attempted in Latin America since the mid-thirties, argues that industrialization is the road to emancipation from one-crop, exploitative relations with the developed world. Industry was to bring in its train educated people, opportunity as well as desire for advancement, the creation of middle-class interests, and political pluralism and democratic process. Instead, some of Latin America's most economically developed countries have found very different ways of life. Argentina has been in political disarray for 40 years, Mexico has become a single-party authoritarianism, Brazil is in the grip of the military, and Uruguay is in an unhappy torpor. Not even economic emancipation has flowed from industrialization, for the new factories have increased the need for foreign exchange for constituent parts and to satisfy increased effective demand. Inflation and industrialization, increased inequality of income distribution and industrialization, and political instability and industrialization have been the correlates—and not the automatic path to social decency initially projected. The reasons for these occurrences have been debated endlessly, of course. Some 12 years ago, it began to be fashionable to declare that the quality of population must make a difference, and the era of social development opened.

2. *The social approach.* The social development argument is that economic advance is a necessary but insufficient condition for development; individuals must also be empowered so that they can escape from their class position, and make themselves able to be more productive workers and more rational consumers. The favored method is education, of course. But social development programs, supported after the establishment of the Inter-American Development Bank by "soft" loans administered through the Social Development Trust Fund, also included assistance for housing, the establishment of cooperatives, and many other devices to erode the gap especially separating lower- from middle-class groups. The Alliance for Progress was designed to combine economic and social developmental approaches, permitting Latin and North Americans to work together in a complex mix of private and public funding, with expenditure patterns sufficiently flexible to fit each particular country. It would be unjust to label this attempt a failure, for it did not have the time, the funds, the ideological decisiveness, or the sure knowledge to work through to completion. If self-sustaining and free societies were to be the fruit of these programs, however, it is obvious that Latin America did not respond; there are more overt governments of force in Latin America now than before the Alliance was launched—a statement that should not be seen as describing cause and effect.

3. *The panacea of political union.* Not since the nineteenth century have political men placed much faith in constitutions and political forms as means of assuring the good public life. This shying away from the political dimension of development has been reinforced by the entrance of international organizations and banking agencies into development assistance; the overt exaction of political conditions for aid smacks of interventionism, an increasingly unpopular concept in international affairs despite the frequency of its real occurrence. Instead, faith in form has been transferred to pressures for regional organiza-

tion. The dream is old in Latin America, dating from independence and the Bolivarian ideal of Gran Colombia. Earlier in this century, Peru's Aprista party pushed for a gigantic Indo-American structure to balance the Latin against the Anglo-Saxon in this hemisphere. Within recent years we have seen the collapse of the Caribbean federation, and the hesitant gropings of such emulations of European experience as the Latin American Free Trade Association, the Central American Customs Union, and most recently the Andean Group. Latin Americans have entered into these economic arrangements with scarcely hidden hopes of eventually being able to arrive at political union. Unhappily, only modest but still somewhat important economic gains have been their lot, and in no case have planned goals for organizational growth been met. The economic sense of these arrangements is clear: they are designed to create larger markets for Latin America's industrial plant, to rationalize production and achieve economies of scale, and to permit a relatively free international flow of investment capital among Latin American countries. There is also a scarcely hidden debility, however, which is that the horizontal expansion of markets across international borders may well have the effect of inhibiting the vertical growth of markets within countries which would permit greater equity of income distribution. In any event, the success of none of these agencies has as yet been sufficiently sustained to permit rigorous judgment of their areas of efficacy.

Counterposed to these reformist schools are revolutionary approaches to development coming from both right and left. Their common element is that they assume that iron control of the state is the independent variable from which will flow other aspects of development. That is, they do not assume that formalistic political arrangements, economic change, or social preparation will lead to desired political change; their view is that the political organization must be seized first, and then employed as the instrumentality for socioeconomic development, which in turn can assist in political evolution. Many variants of these views are under experimentation in Latin America. A few are summarized as follows:

a. *Tutelary military governments*—The present governments of Brazil and Peru are both cases in point, despite the fact that the former is frankly rightist in color, the latter inclined toward a quasi-populist nationalism. They are revolutionary not merely in the sense that they supplant constitutional civil government, and employ novel forms of political torture and repression in the case of the Brazilians, but that they also change the power distribution system. The Brazilian government has supplanted the traditional liberal element in that country's upper class, and has stripped the intelligentisia of its power; the Peruvian administration has broken the power of the landed aristocracy, and is beginning to change the life-chances of rural and urban lower-class persons.

The two governments also vary widely in their approach to economic development. The Brazilian government employs the power of the state to constrain wages, suppress effective trade union organization, and inhibit economic nationalism, thus promoting foreign investment and encouraging local entrepreneurs by guaranteeing high profit margins. The Peruvians are moving toward a state capitalism as rapidly as their techniques and understanding of the politics of the situation permit them to do so. It is this difference in attitude that in turn probably makes the major difference in the amount of repression exercised; indeed, the Peruvians have engaged in only the most minimal exercise of police control of the opposition.

Juan de Onis' article describes the old-fashioned manner in which the Trujillo administration in the Dominican Republic carried out a developmental policy. The first Batista administration in Cuba is also an early form of tutelary military government. The best contemporarily analogous case in Central America is that of Nicaragua.

b. *Falangist and other populist movements of the right*—No mature fascism has ever managed to take office in a Latin American country, but nationalist, corporativist[1] movements have existed since the thirties, and they have been revived in modern form in Argentina and to some extent in Brazil. Peronism, for example, has evolved into a more overtly populist movement than when it was in official power from 1946 to 1955, and is thus logically moving into alliance with certain groups of Argentina's left. More than a simple union of convenience among groups sharing respect for the same violent means, a national Marxism is developing that has already gained significance in Argentina's internal politics, and has some chance of spreading in a Hispanic world accustomed to thinking of institutional organization in hierarchical and corporate terms. The formal organization of the Mexican polity is already quasi-corporate; although that country has its peculiar mix of authoritarianism and democracy, it is not a fascism in any classical sense of that word. The Caribbean has been little influenced by these currents that are perennial in other Latin American countries, and there is little reason to think that the former British, Dutch, and French areas are susceptible to this kind of ideology.

c. *Nationalist socialism*—To a social scientist or anyone interested in the sociology of knowledge, Cuba is one of the most interesting cases of guided social change to be found anywhere in the world. For the moment, leave aside the grisly facts of Cold War, the inflamed language on all sides, and the dryness of statistical numbers games. Castro and his associates are attempting to create an absolutely equalitarian, national community based on a theory of value that has nothing to do with economic criteria, and everything to do directly with the affective meaning of man's activities in his community. Only Maoist China approaches the degree of radical innovation being pursued by Cuba's leadership, who

---

[1] The corporate state, in its classic Mediterranean sense, would organize political representation on the basis of an individual's occupational and class positions. Corporate theory posits the creation of a series of hierarchically organized institutional "pillars," such as the church, the military, the industrial sector, the agricultural sector, and so on. The leaders of each "pillar" then form an oligarchical ruling "committee."

unabashedly speak of the creation of a new man—new in his sense of good and bad, in his world view, in his approach to work and labor, and in his identification with community. Obviously, we cannot know whether Utopia will become Havana. But the very radicalness of the present Cuban vision has served to limit its attractiveness to mass groups in other countries: the price in cultural change seems impossibly high, the concatenation of leadership elements and followership dedication and North American *laissez passer* too accidental to permit easy replication. Thus it is entirely understandable that the Cuban case has been self-isolating in the Caribbean, as well as isolated.

Our earlier attempts at typology-building may demonstrate their usefulness again at this point. Haiti, the Dominican Republic, and such states as Jamaica and Trinidad do not at this time have the available masses to make possible a repetition of the internal dynamics of the Cuban revolution. If elites in alliance with limited numbers of others can make an armed revolt, they would not find it as easy as in Cuba to integrate great groups of lower-class and lower middle-class persons into national institutional structures. Still, all such matters are relative, and long-term predictions in such a matter are feckless. Whatever the future may hold for the Caribbean as a whole, whatever the real degree to which the Cubans approach their ideal state, that country is now unequivocally the most secular and socially national state in the Ibero-American world. Whether it will become even more isolated from its geographical and cultural neighbors, or a more meaningful example, depends rather less on Cuba than on conditions in the surrounding area.

The search for national viability and adequate ideologies is just beginning in most of the Caribbean. The role of the industrial states, and especially of the United States, will continue to be critical in this unfolding odyssey.

INTER-AMERICAN RELATIONS

The concern of the United States for the Caribbean, and its long-standing readiness to act unilaterally in its perceived interests, are well documented throughout this book. From the earliest days of the republic, some political men have seen Mexico, Central America, and the Caribbean as crucial to United States national development; later, some definers of Manifest Destiny included much Caribbean real estate in what was to be the Greater America. It was only much later, however, at the turn of this century, that physical force accompanied political and economic interest into the region. Since that time, in one or another degree all Caribbean governments have had to mix into their political analyses the facts of United States cultural, economic, political, and military behavior.

American intentions are, however, not easy to guess. Often North American attention is directed elsewhere, and Caribbean policy has been conducted by military and diplomatic persons accountable only routinely for their actions, isolated from high policy levels in the absence of crisis situations. In addition, before World War II, American activities in the Caribbean were carried out in a simplistic surety of what was right and good, unencumbered by the ideological and scientific doubts that have crept into foreign political and economic relations in the past thirty years. Most important, however, is that American policy has been and is ambivalent in motivation. For example, President Nixon, according to *The New York Times*, told Yugoslavia's President Tito in October 1970 "that all nations should respect 'the rights of others to choose their own paths' and applauded Marshal Tito for giving heart—by his independence from Moscow—to those who chart their own political course." If that statement were taken literally, then one could confidently state that all North American armed and covert intervention in the political affairs of Caribbean states would be eschewed during President Nixon's tenure. And, indeed, there is a long-standing American tradition favoring self-determination. Still, one can always argue, as did Dean Rusk during the Dominican crisis of 1965, that any leftist revolution favors Communists, that Communists are part of an international network, and therefore that American intervention to counter leftist revolution is necessary in order to preserve self-determination. The fact of the matter seems to be that the United States has acted overtly in countering recent leftist moves in at least three Caribbean states, but has been able or willing only to harass the most important case, Cuba. If American policy has a clearly discernible bias, it also lacks explicitness, evenness of application, and consistency either of criteria or of interpretation of adduced fact. The reasons for this confusion are many.

First, as is notorious, there is a genuine and profound confusion among Americans concerning the proper role of this country in the world. This primary puzzlement is certified by uncertainties concerning the effectiveness of American developmental programs overseas—and more than a little suspicion that aid is often counterproductive, always interventionist, sometimes arrogant, always the product of guesswork, and all too often a preliminary of military commitments to protect what have become vested interests.

Second, the American public has been slow to understand the relation between conventional weapons and the marriage of missiles to thermonuclear explosives; policymakers, too, are confused concerning the optimal mix of military men and equipment necessary to present world conditions. This uncertainty is compounded in an area close to the United States, one which traditionally has been designated as obviously vital to national security, as our "backyard," as the ultimate test of our determination to protect ourselves, and so forth. In the past, when distance was a critical military matter and the United

States was comfortable behind its ocean bastions, no American government could, with domestic impunity, look lightly upon a military threat implanted in the Caribbean. It is not that today's situation is entirely different, but that it is sufficiently changed to demand more subtle judgments than in the past. For example, when President Kennedy took to television to warn the Soviet Union to withdraw its missiles from Cuba, he made a point of saying that we would remain within the bull's-eye of Russian IBMs whether the missiles were in Cuba or not. He was trying to introduce psychological software into what is too often treated as only a question of hardware.

Third, then, is the very complex set of United States attitudes toward Latin America and the Caribbean. There can be no certainty in describing these attitudes, of course, and even less surety in ascribing them to significant sectors of the American population. For example, midwesterners know little of the black population of the West Indies; but observers of the racial scene in the East, as well as in such Canadian cities as Toronto, know of the leadership role carried out by Caribbean migrants, and recognize a cultural difference between American and Caribbean black populations. Again, where Spanish-speaking populations mix, it is well-known that Cubans are much more prepared to assume middle-class roles in American society than Puerto Ricans or Dominicans. Indeed, the motion picture, *Popi,* was built around the theme of the favored reception given to Cubans in New York, and the discrimination practiced against Puerto Ricans.

The cloudy and unevenly distributed perceptions of Caribbeans are hardly cleared up when matters of ideology and national security enter. From the beginning, the Cuban revolution has provoked very sharp reactions in the United States; they do not need repetition here, except for the comment that Cuban events have so deeply affected North American attitudes as to enter into giving tone to American politics. Few ordinary Americans react profoundly when economic interests are threatened in the Caribbean, but certainly their feelings are sharpened when Russian nuclear submarine bases are reported abuilding in Cuba, when warned of threats to the Panama Canal in Guatemala, or when told that Guyana is becoming a Communist outpost on the South American continent. Military actions in the Caribbean, then, cannot solely be responses to real military activities by others; they must also be military aspects of political pressures and appreciations inside the United States. It is in this way that the Cold War must intimately affect United States-Caribbean relations so long as United States-Soviet relations rely so heavily on psychological elements in order to avoid nuclear ones.

Another complex psychological strain is set up by the tension between domestic and international needs in the American polity. If the United States wants to abandon the role of world policeman, does it

also want to lay down its variant of the White Man's Burden? Does it
wish a "special relationship" with Latin America, and a particularly
special one with the Caribbean because of geographical proximity?
Confusion is amplified by the relationship of Britain, France, and the
Netherlands to the Caribbean, with many Americans not knowing
which islands are independent and which in juridical relation to a
European power. Thus, concern with other than Haiti, Puerto Rico,
the Virgin Islands, Cuba, and the Dominican Republic is often seen
as merely juggling the hot chestnuts of others.

This kaleidoscopic set of public attitudes gives government and
pressure groups broad freedom of action in all matters except those
concerning Cuba. Even the latest Dominican invasion, although it
occasioned a wide wave of anti-administration rhetoric and caused the
first open break between Senator Fulbright and President Johnson,
was generally viewed as a spark off the Cold War-Vietnam-Middle East
bonfire. Soon, that incident passed into mythology as a great administration victory, and little mention of it is now made outside circles
of specialists. In the absence of conviction and the presence of confusion, the definition of issues remains securely in the hands of government officials and groups with special interests in the Caribbean—a
leeway not at all conducive to policy continuity, for it promotes reactions on the basis of personalities and transitory perceptions and
explanations, instead of actions bounded by established understandings
and limits.

These relative uncertainties concerning United States intentions and
behavior in the Caribbean are little cushioned by the international
political position of the independent states of the area. Unable to form
their own federation, uncertain concerning the costs and advantages of
membership in the Organization of American States, and increasingly
developing independent foreign policies of their own, they are in no
position to engage either in collective bargaining or in hard horse-
trading on their own. Three recent conferences sponsored by the
University of the West Indies on political and developmental problems
of the area document the difficulty of these island republics in finding
a comfortable niche for themselves, whether with surrounding Latin
American nations, the United States and Canada, or their former
European metropoles.

For their part, the Latin American nations, when they bother to
consider the non-Latin Caribbean, are as ambivalent as the United
States in their attitudes. Long accustomed to thinking of the Organization of American States as Latin America *cum* Anglo-Saxon North,
they are not entirely enthusiastic about an influx of new English-
speaking small states. In addition, to the shame of many of them, let
it also be said that they are not overjoyed at the prospect of com-
mingling with "black" states—even though they are very quiet on this

point, of course. More basic to their doubts, however, is their essential disdain for the OAS as an effective international mechanism. They are more comfortable with their United Nations Economic Commission for Latin America, and with the Inter-American Development Bank, than with an OAS they have for so long seen as merely an arm of United States foreign policy.

Certainly for the near future, then, the United States will remain the single most important international influence on the Caribbean, with effects varying by the degree of internal cohesion of each government, the relationship of each to Europe, and the nature of political events inside each and in the United States. Such influence is obviously dangerous not only to the Caribbean, but to an overextended and uncertain United States. In recognition of the unforeseen effects that always flow from overt intervention, the Kennedy administration after the Bay of Pigs added what was in effect a non-intervention political corollary to its Alliance for Progress then in full process of formation. The policy, expressed in virtually so many words, was that the United States would not intervene in the internal affairs of any Latin American government unless there was an obvious, clear *Cold War* threat to American national security; that is, unless the link between a Latin American state and the Soviet Union was express and military in direct implication. Otherwise, the worst that a Latin American state could risk was the economic, political, and social disfavor of the United States— a cold handshake instead of a warm *abrazo*. Coupled with avowed friendship for constitutionally chosen civilian governments, the policy bid fair to reduce military adventurism in Latin America and to remove American policymakers from necessarily tricky and projective decision-making.

Unfortunately, the Kennedy policy of restraint and attack (the latter element clearly evidenced during the missile crisis) was short-lived, coming to a resounding end in the Johnson administration with the Dominican intervention. Its revival would be a stabilizing force in the Hemisphere, and would give room to the Caribbean states for that internal experimentation through which they will have to pass to attain the internal strength which is their only long-term guarantee of integrity and security—as it is that of the United States, too.

## Conclusions

The Caribbean states cannot give themselves the luxury of fooling themselves with the mythology of the large states. Such countries as the United States and Russia can delude themselves into thinking that their space and resources somehow give them a telluric kick, that coal and iron and frontiers make the man. The Caribbean islands would do better to make the simpler and more accurate presumption that in

social matters there is only one natural resource: human beings themselves. Athens and Florence are more appropriate models for Tobago
and Antigua than are Germany and Sweden; Israel and Denmark are
more fitting prototypes for imitation by the Dominican Republic and
Jamaica than are France and Canada. The lesson that emerges from
barren Athens and desert Israel is that in the last analysis it is the
quality of population that is the ultimate determinant of development.
The Argentines, comfortable in their spacious and rich homeland, can
allow their lush farmlands and fat cattle to make up for the deficiencies
of their political organization. The Caribbean peoples, crowded onto
their beautiful islands, do not have such margin for error.

The reformist, as has been pointed out, finds it difficult to work
directly on the quality of individuals and the nature of social organization: those problems are at the heart of grand politics, and the reformer
seeks other ways to affect such matters. A major unanswered question
both of development theory and international development policy is
how to manage such basic change without courting highly risky and
often counterproductive turmoil. Although this book is not the forum
for such speculation, perhaps its major contribution is to point out,
in chapter after chapter, that the Caribbean offers one of the most
exciting and promising theaters for this kind of development.

Whatever the specific paths that may be chosen, and the ideologies
fashioned to justify and guide further change, the process will be eased
and rationalized by a clear understanding that the Caribbean needs
simultaneous centralization and decentralization. That is, the rationalization of relations among the islands needs to take place together with
the deepening of community identification within each state. Viewed
in this light, federation of any sort, or arrangements like CARIFTA,
are no substitute for the erosion of class and color lines within each
island, the development of overarching national institutions and the
guarantee that all persons will have access to those institutions and
the other hallmarks of the modern estate. Conversely, insular political
cohesion is not a substitute for a rationalization of international economic relations, common diplomatic fronts, the creation of a viable
set of international political relations, and those other devices, practices, and habits of mind that contribute to effectiveness at home and
abroad.

These steps toward the creation of national and international power
in the Caribbean can be eased by the understanding and sophisticated
assistance of the great powers, near and far. Whether they have the
generosity, the will, and the skill to do so remains a moot question.

# Index

# The American Assembly
## COLUMBIA UNIVERSITY

# About the American Assembly

The American Assembly was established by Dwight D. Eisenhower at Columbia University in 1950. It holds nonpartisan meetings and publishes authoritative books to illuminate issues of United States policy.

An affiliate of Columbia, with offices in the Graduate School of Business, the Assembly is a national educational institution incorporated in the State of New York.

The Assembly seeks to provide information, stimulate discussion, and evoke independent conclusions in matters of vital public interest.

## AMERICAN ASSEMBLY SESSIONS

At least two national programs are initiated each year. Authorities are retained to write background papers presenting essential data and defining the main issues in each subject.

About sixty men and women representing a broad range of experience, competence, and American leadership meet for several days to discuss the Assembly topic and consider alternatives for national policy.

All Assemblies follow the same procedure. The background papers are sent to participants in advance of the Assembly. The Assembly meets in small groups for four or five lengthy periods. All groups use the same agenda. At the close of these informal sessions, participants adopt in plenary session a final report of findings and recommendations.

Regional, state, and local Assemblies are held following the national session at Arden House. Assemblies have also been held in England, Switzerland, Malaysia, Canada, the Caribbean, South America, Central America, the Philippines, and Japan. Over one hundred institutions have co-sponsored one or more Assemblies.

## ARDEN HOUSE

Home of The American Assembly and scene of the national sessions is Arden House, which was given to Columbia University in 1950 by W. Averell Harriman. E. Roland Harriman joined his brother in contributing toward adaptation of the property for conference purposes. The buildings surrounding the land, known as the Harriman Campus of Columbia University, are fifty miles north of New York City.

Arden House is a distinguished conference center. It is self-supporting and operates throughout the year for use by organizations with educational objectives.

## AMERICAN ASSEMBLY BOOKS

The background papers for each Assembly program are published in cloth and paperbound editions for use by individuals, libraries, businesses, public agencies, nongovernmental organizations, educational institutions, discussion and service groups. In this way the deliberations of Assembly sessions are continued and extended.

The subjects of Assembly programs to date are:

1951——United States–Western Europe Relationships
1952——Inflation
1953——Economic Security for Americans
1954——The United States' Stake in the United Nations
——The Federal Government Service
1955——United States Agriculture
——The Forty-Eight States
1956——The Representation of the United States Abroad
——The United States and the Far East
1957——International Stability and Progress
——Atoms for Power
1958——The United States and Africa
——United States Monetary Policy
1959——Wages, Prices, Profits, and Productivity
——The United States and Latin America
1960——The Federal Government and Higher Education
——The Secretary of State
——Goals for Americans
1961——Arms Control: Issues for the Public
——Outer Space: Prospects for Man and Society
1962——Automation and Technological Change
——Cultural Affairs and Foreign Relations
1963——The Population Dilemma
——The United States and the Middle East
1964——The United States and Canada
——The Congress and America's Future
1965——The Courts, the Public, and the Law Explosion
——The United States and Japan
1966——State Legislatures in American Politics
——A World of Nuclear Powers?
——The United States and the Philippines
——Challenges to Collective Bargaining
1967——The United States and Eastern Europe
——Ombudsmen for American Government?
1968——Uses of the Seas
——Law in a Changing America
——Overcoming World Hunger